To Erica,
who drove me crazy
To Deven,
who drove me sane

Contents

Preface   xiii

Introducing Self-Psyching   1

Self-Psyching and You   1

Why Self-Psyching Works   2

The Foundations of Self-Psyching   6

Relaxation   6

Behavior modification   6

Traditional wisdom   7

Body therapies   8

What Self-Psyching Is Not   9

How to Use Self-Psyching:
A Step-by-Step Guide   10

Identify your problems   10

Monitor yourself   11

Measure your behavior   12

Choose your techniques   13

Set your goals   14

Schedule your self-psyching efforts   16

Make a trial run   16

Reinforce your successes   17

Breaking the Self-Psyching rules   17

Using the Sources of Further Information   18

Precautions: Roadblocks to successful
Self-Psyching   18

The Promise of Self-Psyching   20

Accepting Criticism and Criticizing Others   21

Alpha Waves   22

Anxiety   22

Assertiveness Training   26

Autogenic Training   35

Autosuggestion   41

Behavior Rehearsal   42

Biofeedback   49

Biorhythms   55

The Blues and The Blahs   63

Boredom   63

Breaking a Date   64

Changing the Sequence of Events   65

Chewing on Things   69

Compulsiveness   70

Conflict Avoidance   72

Covert Sensitization   73

Crying   78

Daydreaming   80

Depression   80

Desensitization   84

Disagreeable Tasks and Encounters   92

Disappointment   94

Disciplining Others   95

Disorganized Thinking   96

Distressing Situations   97

Dreaming   97

Embarrassment   98

Embarrassment of Admitting Ignorance   98

Ending a Relationship   99

Exercise   100

Fantasy   104

Fatigue and Lethargy   113

Fear of Disappointing Others   115

Fear of Expressing Anger   115

Fear of Expressing Opinions   117

Fear of Failure   118

Fear of Recommending   119

Fears and Phobias   119

Feelings of Inadequacy   122

Floods of Unwanted Thoughts   123

Flooding   123

Forgetfulness   128

Frustration   129

Grief   131

Guilt   131

Hair Pulling or Plucking   134

Headaches   135

Helplessness   136

Hoarding   136

Hopelessness   137
Hostility   137
Imagination   139
Inability to Make Requests   139
Incompatible Behavior   140
Indecisiveness   144
Inefficiency   146
Inhibitions   146
Insomnia   146
Interviewing for Jobs   148
Knuckle Cracking   149
Lack of Concentration   150
Lack of Privacy   150
Lack of Self-Confidence   151
Lethargy   151
Loneliness   151
Losing at Sports and Games
Without Anxiety   152
Losing Your Temper   152
Making Friends   154
Managing Time   155
Marital Problems   155
Martial Arts   156
Meditation   157
Meeting New People   173
Minor Emotional Complaints   173
Modeling   174

Nail Biting   182
Negative Practice   182
Nervous Habits   185
Nightmares   187
Obsessions   188
Overeating   189
Overworking   192
Pain   194
Perfectionism   194
Pessimism   194
Picking   194
Prayer   195
Problem Drinking   196
Procrastination   197
Productivity   198
Psychodrama   198
Psychosomatic Complaints and Pains   199
Public Speaking   200
Punctuality   201
Punishments   201
Relaxation   205
The Relaxation Response   213
Rewards   216
Ritual Behavior   222
Role Playing   222
Running and Jogging   223
Sadness   224

Sales Presentation Failures   224
Scratching   225
Self-Consciousness   225
Self-Denial   225
Self-Hypnosis   226
Self-Punishment   228
Sexual Hang-ups   229
Shyness and Inhibitions   230
Sleep   232
Smoking   233
Speaking Up   235
Standing Up for Your Rights   235
Stimulus Control   236
Stress   244
Study Habits   244
Tardiness   245
Teeth Gnashing   246
Tension   247
Test Anxiety   247
Thought-Stopping   247
Transcendental Meditation   254
Work and Study Habits   257
Worrying   257
Worrying About Money   258
Yoga   259

Preface

The writing of this book was largely inspired by my experiences while working for the publishers of the most widely read popular psychology magazine in America, *Psychology Today*. I served as staff writer for their textbook department, member of their book club editorial and reviewing staff, and finally as editor of the division that develops books for the general reader.

The working conditions were casual, the surroundings idyllic. Our offices were situated in several buildings scattered throughout the resort community of Del Mar, California. We were only a block or so from the beach; there was always a fresh, salt smell in the air; flowers bloomed everywhere; and sea birds called to one another outside our windows. In this delightful setting, dozens of professional, highly trained people prepared books and articles to meet the demands of a national audience hungry for the most readable, accessible, and authoritative coverage of the science of human behavior.

Each day I would go through manuscripts submitted by psychologists and psychiatrists, medical doctors, cultists, gurus, eager amateurs, food faddists, former mental patients, and as-yet-undiagnosed crackpots. The stacks of submissions rose daily, filling my shelves and overflowing my desk despite all my efforts to get ahead of the authors' output. There were dozens of books on improving one's sex life and scores on self-assertion, behavior modification, forms of relaxation, and creative drug use. There was even a manuscript on the therapeutic benefits of belly dancing. As I examined unpublished works my firm might want to publish and as I selected and reviewed published books to be offered by the *Psychology Today* Book Club, I detected a pattern that encouraged me to undertake the writing of *Self-Psyching*.

I discovered that many of the best books — those of greatest value to average, intelligent, nonacademic readers — were written by nonacademic authors. Skilled writers with a broad background in their subject, generalists who were open-minded and clearheaded, seemed better able to capture the essence of a topic and present it in an interesting, involving, and informative fashion. Books like Julius Fast's *Body Language* and *Creative Coping*, Gail Sheehy's *Passages*, Adam Smith's *Powers of Mind*, and Michael Korda's *Power and Success* were lucid, incisive, exciting, and *useful*. These authors were neither degreed psychologists nor physicians, yet they were able to provide millions of average people with both solid information and an entertaining reading experience. They were able to summarize and popularize even the most technical and specialized material. Such books made important data available to the largest audience.

I determined that there was a genuine need for a similarly simple and direct discussion of psychological methods for gaining greater control of one's life. And because I had spent my entire career making often difficult and abstract knowledge accessible to readers lacking specialized training, I felt I could write just the sort of book so many people seemed to desire.

Contemplating my own background, I felt that my years of schooling, writing, and editorial work had prepared me to produce an instructive book on human behavior. I had already published *The History of Popular Culture*, describing human pastimes and preoccupations throughout history. And my work on hundreds of books dealing with psychotherapeutic techniques had exposed me to a wealth of material that nonspecialists are seldom able to make use of.

There were, of course, dozens of books on behavior control, coping, dealing with emotional problems, and gaining greater self-awareness. But most of them were written by experts to describe, explain, chronicle, or praise their clinical or experimental findings. Few seemed interested in supplying readers with specific instructions for the regular use, on their own, of the experts' methods for handling problems in living. If readers were to enjoy the benefits of the techniques described in such books, it was expected that they place themselves in the hands of therapists trained in using these methods. Moreover, the tone of the books was almost universally that of insiders talking to outsiders. Jargon, methodological disputes, defense of one treatment modality over another, and similar academic matters made average readers feel that they were witnessing rather than participating in what might be a helpful therapeutic process. And even when expert authors did furnish instructions for using their methods, their guidance usually detailed rigid techniques that gave readers no options. Few books offered straightforward step-by-step presentations that readers could adapt to deal with their unique problems.

My goal was to fashion a new kind of self-help book. Having worked on college and high school textbooks in various fields, I knew that it was possible to communicate even complex concepts and procedures in a digestible style. I had, for instance, in authoring the second edition of a basic textbook entitled The Psychology Primer, presented the fundamentals of psychological thought in some 300 readable pages. And in dealing with so many psychological works, I had learned that in recent decades significant progress had been made in formulating effective self-help techniques. I was convinced that I could write a practical guide to self-directed therapy and behavior change. But it wouldn't be enough to tell readers how such techniques work; I had to give them adequate information on using each method, on their own.

I set myself the task of boiling down the mass of published material into a coherent, easily usable form. I tried to find the solid how-to facts, to isolate effective, proven, tested techniques for gaining greater control over one's life, for coping with common emotional and behavioral difficulties. Whatever the source of the information I collected, my aim was to find techniques that people could actually use by themselves, on themselves, to get concrete results for themselves.

Self-Psyching is a compendium of methods that work. The techniques presented are distillations, variations, combinations of the best therapeutic approaches that you can employ without the guidance of a trained counselor. They are offered in a form that allows them to be used most readily for handling the typical complaints that most often lead people to read self-help books in the first place.

Self-Psyching is an encyclopedia of psychological techniques, a first-aid guide supplying short, easy instructions on how you can make immediate use of methods rooted in the techniques of relaxation, behavioral modification, traditional wisdom or common sense, and body therapy. The contents of the book are arranged alphabetically. There are dozens of articles on common emotional and behavioral problems. Each of these problem articles contains cross references to techniques that can help you solve the problem in question. The alphabetical organization of both problem and technique articles permits you to move quickly and easily from consideration of what's troubling you to learning what you can do about your various problems.

This format gives you direct access to many efficacious techniques. It does not direct you elsewhere for aid but gives you the tools you need to aid yourself here and now — though it does provide suggestions for further reading that will broaden your understanding of any techniques you choose to employ.

If you have ever waded through hundreds of pages of the latest self-help best seller only to discover that a few paragraphs would have covered the entire matter or that there was little practical information in it to use on your own or that you really didn't know what the author's point was — *Self-Psyching* is for you. The author of this book is a person like you, someone who faces the same kinds of personal and social stresses that you face and who has found out how to help himself. *Self-Psyching* is a joint experiment in which you and I join in the search for reasonably effective solutions to commonly experienced problems.

Introducing Self-Psyching

SELF-PSYCHING AND YOU

If you are a ninety pound weakling, after using this book you will still be ninety pounds and a weakling. But you can become a ninety pound weakling better able to deal with your own feelings, cope with the actions of others, and find ways to be the person you want to be. With the step-by-step guidance of this book, you use proven techniques to improve your capacity for coping with the stresses of life and to control your habits and behavior so that you can function more successfully. These techniques do not purport to change your basic nature or to mold you into an ideal that I or other writers have set up for you.

The book supplies the raw materials and the tools for self-improvement, and your willingness to work with what you have can make them work for you. The techniques presented do not offer deep character analysis, do not probe for the underlying causes of your personal or social problems. Each method is designed to provide relatively fast and sure relief from symptoms, to apply psychological first-aid to your emotional and behavioral difficulties. Without exploring your buried motivations, Self-Psyching permits you to feel better about yourself, to act more effectively and confidently in a variety of situations.

Psyching up. Some of the techniques in this book teach you to increase your level of excitement, involvement, commitment, or concern. They can help you overcome fatigue and lethargy, boredom, fears and phobias. Such techniques as Behavior Rehearsal and Assertiveness Training permit you to confront people and situations you might otherwise avoid and to do so with more confidence, desire, and resolution. You can learn to work, play, and compete with higher energy levels and a greater expectation that you will succeed.

Psyching down. Other techniques aim at lowering your level of excitement or agitation. With them you can overcome the anxiety that commonly develops in so many stressful situations. They show you how to control emotions and habits that have been stimulated by your responses to certain events, people, or expectations. Learning to relax even in the face of stress and tension is basic to self-psyching. Moreover, Relaxation and related techniques for learning to psych down enable you to then psych yourself up in the most controlled and appropriate manner that will serve you best.

Achieving balance. *Self-Psyching* encourages you to develop a proper balance between stimulation and relaxation; to find out what feelings, moods, attitudes, and actions most realistically reflect the person you really are. It permits you to gain control of yourself and yet still be yourself.

WHY *SELF-PSYCHING* WORKS
Self-Psyching **works because it puts will power on a scientific basis.** Very few people can break such habits as nail biting, overeating, or heavy smoking through sheer will power. Will power is unlikely to make it possible for you to get along better with your friends and family; to cope with the manipulative behavior of strangers; to overcome minor emotional complaints, fears, or compulsions. But through the systematic application of self-psyching techniques, which work in place of will power, almost all of us can gain greater control over our lives.

Self-psyching techniques help you handle problems you may have thought were beyond your control. The methods are based largely on scientific research and clinical studies that have demonstrated the human potential to monitor and modify our own behavior. Strategies that have worked on people with severe emotional illnesses have been adapted for this book to make it easy for you and other basically healthy people to overcome typically troublesome problems.

In much the same way that the experimenters and clinicians have undertaken their work, *Self-Psyching* involves a direct and structured attack on a wide variety of problems. You learn to use each technique as if you were involved in an experiment — except with this approach you both direct and are the subject of your own research and therapy. You can proceed confidently from step to step with each method, guided by clear, simple, and complete instructions. And as you master one problem you gain an increased ability to tackle other complaints. Eventually, by the regular utilization of various techniques, you build up an impressive self-psyching repertoire which you can readily make use of to improve various aspects of your life.

Self-Psyching won't give you the power you lack. It will give you something better: scientifically proven methods to systematically apply at will. *There's* your will power.

Self-Psyching works because it is a natural process. *Self-Psyching's* methods are based on the natural processes by which we develop our typical patterns of feeling and behavior. For many decades behavioral scientists have been unearthing the buried secrets of human behavior and formulating procedures for gaining conscious control over forces that were long believed to be beyond our ability to regulate. With the discovery that most human behavior is learned came the conclusion that behavior can therefore be unlearned. It is quite possible to modify the troublesome aspects of your behavior by altering the learned, natural response patterns that you have developed to sustain the ways you think, act, and feel. The clearest example of this process is, perhaps, the role of habits in our lives.

A habit is a pattern of consistent behavior that is learned through repetition, usually over a long period. We are all creatures of habit. Habits give our lives consistency and predictability. We rely on them to make many aspects of our lives easy and automatic. Our daily routines might well be difficult and demanding if we had to follow them without relying on our habits.

Think about the way you start a typical day. Every morning you probably wake up at about the same time, roll over, stretch, and stand up in about the same way. Maybe you even say the same words or think the same thoughts as you arise. Perhaps you flip on the radio or TV; maybe you light up a cigarette before getting out of bed. You are likely to follow a fixed series of actions in the bathroom, moving from one activity to the next with an almost machinelike, unswerving progression: You shower and then shave or put on your make-up; you always shave one side of your face first or always make up one eye before the other. And when you dress you almost certainly step into one leg of your pants before the other and consistently button your shirt or blouse from top to bottom or bottom to top.

As an experiment, try altering your morning routine. Shave before showering; put your shoes on before dressing; don't turn on the radio; brush your teeth before washing your face. Two things are likely to happen. First, you may discover that you have missed some steps in your routine: You haven't brushed your teeth, you leave the house without a handkerchief or belt, or you neglect to put on lipstick. Second, because you have disrupted your naturally established habit pattern, each action probably took longer, required more effort, and added to your feeling uncomfortable or stressed.

The ability to modify or extinguish troublesome habits is central to *Self-Psyching*, because habit shapes so much of our lives. Most of the techniques in this book teach you to employ the same natural learning processes through which you acquired your habits. They work quite naturally to reprogram your responses to break various habits.

The source of our problems is not only our heads or our bodies but an intricate meshing of the two aspects of our being. Mind and body constantly exchange signals to produce both good and bad feelings, appropriate or unrewarding behavior. Basic, automatic biochemical processes link the mind and body of each human being, creating a response network through which thoughts and moods affect feelings and actions and how we feel or behave influences our thoughts. Showing a person who may not be hungry a picture of some delicious food can induce the signs of hunger. Likewise, a picture or thought of a member of the opposite sex is a sexual appetite inducer.

Many of the techniques in this book permit you to gain a considerable degree of control over your mind-body system so that you can better cope with both internal and external pressures. Your boss, spouse, children, lover, organizations of which you are a part, society itself, quite naturally operate on this system and may well cause you problems this book could help you handle better. Self-psyching techniques can show you how to apply your natural patterns of adaptability to stress and increase your capacity to learn, unlearn, or relearn critical ways of responding to life's demands.

Self-Psyching works because it provides immediate feedback. Reading a book will make it possible for you to control your behavior and feelings only if it offers methods that bring results — soon. However potent the techniques, if you don't detect rapid improvement in your outlook and actions you will be unlikely to stay with the program offered by the book. *Self-Psyching* has built-in feedback devices to help you maintain your involvement in your self-directed experiment in self-control. Each technique includes guidelines for measuring your success. They set a limit on how much time you should put in before you see results. They advise you how to improve your performance if you don't see sufficient change fast enough and direct you to supplementary or alternative techniques that may be needed to improve your control.

The best feedback, the most encouraging factor in any therapy, is discernible progress. Because of this, *Self-Psyching* teaches you to proceed one small step at a time. Success with any one step builds the confidence you need to try more difficult procedures or attack more resistant problems. This incremental progress reinforces you through almost constant positive feedback as long as you employ the program.

Self-Psyching works because it permits many small victories. Success with any one of the techniques will breed greater confidence in your ability to handle more and more difficult problems. And mastery of any part of a problem encourages you to attack other aspects of that problem. The process of striving for even the smallest victories produces a pleasant momentum: Each minor gain contributes, eventually, to a major triumph over yourself or your circumstances. Just as you don't have to be an Olympic swimmer to keep from drowning, you don't have to master every technique in this book to see solid results, to feel that your life is coming more under your own control.

The instructions for using each technique are organized to permit you to confront portions of your problem one at a time. As you jump over each hurdle you race on to the next. You don't have to solve all your problems or every part of any one problem to feel that you are making progress. You'll notice almost immediate progress as soon as you begin conscientiously using each technique.

Self-Psyching works because it provides techniques of proven utility. The techniques in this book have been drawn from four major areas: Relaxation, Behavior Modification, Traditional Wisdom (or Common Sense), and Body

Therapies. The delineation of these four areas is somewhat arbitrary because some techniques employ elements from several of these approaches and some fall clearly into only one. But it can help you identify the origins of the techniques and assures you that all of the problems dealt with in this book can be — and in experimental, clinical, and ordinary life settings have been — overcome through the systematic application of the principles underlying these fundamental methods.

As you begin learning and using self-psyching methods, you can do so with the confidence that many other people — some of them far more distressed than you probably ever will be — have been helped by these techniques. You can trust the efficacy and utility of this program of self-directed therapy because it has been constructed on a firm foundation of research and treatment.

THE FOUNDATIONS OF *SELF-PSYCHING*

Relaxation. Many common emotional and behavioral problems are little more than manifestations of an inability to cope with day-to-day stresses and tensions. The articles on Relaxation and related techniques provide several sound measures for countering the anxiety caused by stress.

The relaxation methods are based on the concept that it is impossible to be both tense and relaxed at the same time. (The article on Relaxation supplies details on the nature and value of this aspect of self-psyching.) By learning to relax in stressful situations, you will perform better, feel better, and live more joyfully. Relaxation techniques are easy to learn and are readily applicable to a wide variety of common problems.

An ideal way to begin your *Self-Psyching* program is to master at least one relaxation technique. The articles on Relaxation, Autogenic Training, and even Meditation provide ample guidance in this basic approach to self-control. And mastery of one of them is necessary before you can employ a number of the behavior modification techniques.

Behavior modification. The scientific essence of self-psyching is derived largely from the area of psychology known as behaviorism. Behaviorists have been working for decades to develop methods for influencing and controlling human actions and emotions. Researchers and therapists, in laboratories and in clinical settings, have set an admirable record of successes helping even highly disturbed individuals learn to gain control of their behavior and feelings. Of greatest significance to the readers of this book is the fact that behaviorists have recently discovered — in their work with psychotics, retarded people, and patients troubled by relatively minor emotional and behavioral problems — that potent behavior modification techniques can be effectively applied in programs of self-therapy. It has been shown that people can learn to modify and control their own behavior with some of the very methods that heretofore have been applied only under the direction and continual monitoring of trained therapists. A great many of the techniques in this book are based upon these self-modification procedures.

Technique articles on Covert Sensitization, Desensitization, Flooding, Modeling, Negative Practice, Rewards, Stimulus Control, and Thought-Stopping are among those in this book that are based on the work of behavioral scientists and clinicians. The articles on particular problems tell you which techniques are most suitable for your specific difficulties.

For example, Desensitization and Modeling have been enormously successful in helping people overcome common fears and phobias. Negative Practice is surprisingly effective in breaking nervous habits. And Thought-Stopping works quickly and easily on minor, but troublesome, compulsions and obsessions.

Background information on classic experiments and landmark successes with each technique has been included in the articles on major techniques to broaden your knowledge and to encourage you about how potent these methods can be.

Traditional wisdom. Some elements of *Self-Psyching* have been employed for centuries, even millennia. Some aspects of such commonsense approaches have been incorporated into the instructions on using the techniques: keeping things in proper perspective, accepting the inevitable or refusing to accept the intolerable, letting nature take its course, going with the flow of events, learning the necessity and value of compromising, creatively employing humor, distracting yourself, and finding sources of personal inspiration and self-stimulation. In addition, you are expected to bring a measure of common sense to your handling of the problems described. Even though common sense is an uncommon commodity, most people have much of it to draw upon if they are taught to do so in an organized fashion.

As an example of applying traditional wisdom to emotional problems, consider humor and laughter, which are natural antidotes to fear and anxiety. The formal technique of Incompatible Behavior shows you how to make humor work in specific ways and at your bidding. Similarly, the creative use of imagination in the techniques of Fantasy, Covert Sensitization, and Behavior Rehearsal can be a source of inner strength for coping with a wide assortment of problems such as insomnia, facing disagreeable tasks and encounters, and breaking habits.

Traditional wisdom contributes sources of personal inspiration — both concrete and imaginary — to your life. Many of us link physical objects, pictures, words, or songs to some strong, comforting memories. Some people get a lift or rekindle their confidence and excitement by contemplating pictures or quotations that have deep personal connotations. Keeping such sources of inspiration on your wall can pick you up when you are down. Likewise, reading literature that you find especially inspirational or merely carrying around a touchstone or other object whose feel distracts you from the pressure of day-to-day anxieties is one of the simple, traditional means of calming, stimulating, or balancing your emotions. The various methods in the Fantasy article encourage you in systematically exploiting such things to change your mood to better deal with worry, guilt, low-grade depression, and distressing situations.

Certain major techniques, like Meditation, were developed long before the psychological sciences identified their therapeutic capacities. They have probably been in use since prehistoric times. Such methods have an important place in Self-Psyching.

Body therapies. Although most Self-Psyching techniques work on the mind, several deal mainly with the body, which in turn influences thoughts, attitudes, and emotions. Somatic approaches to problems like anxiety may work faster and better than many psychological therapies. Most forms of Relaxation call upon you to work out the tensions in your muscles and change your patterns of breathing to counter tension and stress. Exercise and even controlled Anger can be refreshing and restorative.

Learning to express emotional problems physically — a

process sometimes referred to as visceral learning — is an important part of a number of currently popular therapies in which touching, exercise, and even screaming are employed. Although such techniques require someone else to direct you (perhaps to touch or manipulate your body to free your emotions), this book can help you learn to modify your thoughts, feelings, and behavior by influencing your body. And you do so on your own. *Self-Psyching* draws upon the recognized interaction of mind and body by offering such techniques as Assertiveness Training, Autogenic Training, Biofeedback, Incompatible Behavior, and Negative Practice.

WHAT *SELF-PSYCHING* IS NOT

This is not a book for people with serious mental or emotional problems. If you are psychotic you will not be reading this or any other book with any degree of interest or comprehension anyway. And even if you are severely neurotic, professional assistance is called for and the time you spend reading this or other self-help works will merely keep you from getting on with the serious business of proper psychotherapy. Throughout the book there are cautionary notes advising readers who may have more serious problems than they realize to seek competent aid.

The book is not for strictly or largely physical problems. They, too, require professional intervention. If you have a tic or stutter because of a brain dysfunction, don't read about how to fix it — get a doctor to help you fix it.

Self-Psyching is not a guide to therapeutic techniques; it provides direct access to many efficacious techniques. There are already dozens of books describing the many methods now in use in clinical and group settings. This book doesn't direct you elsewhere for aid after telling you what such techniques can do; it gives you the tools you need to aid yourself here and now.

The book is not intended as a comprehensive survey of every form of therapy that is being used today or has been used in the past. The contents are neither all-inclusive nor exhaustive in their examination of the field. Instead, only those techniques or aspects of techniques that offer the greatest chance of being of genuine and immediate use in a self-directed program have been included. For this reason, therapies such as est, psychoanalysis, rebirth therapy, primal therapy, and all the other approaches that require involvement in a supervised program directed by a leader, therapist, or other expert have been left out of *Self-Psyching*.

Although the problems dealt with are common, the book is neither trivial nor intended to be taken lightly. Its contents are not offered as fuel for cocktail party talk. If you want to read about problems and techniques and talk about what you have read with friends, numerous other books are perfect for that. *Self-Psyching* is to be used, and it is easy to learn how to use it successfully.

HOW TO USE *SELF-PSYCHING*: A STEP-BY-STEP GUIDE

There is a wide range of techniques for you to use. But choosing and correctly employing the ones that will work for your own specific problems require following a systematic procedure. To begin with, overcome the temptation to jump right into the technique articles. You must first get a clear picture of the particular problems you want to subject to self-psyching.

Identify your problems. Think about your feelings and behavior and try to focus on a problem that you can make as specific as possible. Avoid vague, general impressions. Concentrate on what you do or don't do, what you feel or don't feel, what you like or don't like.

For example, it's fine to say that you want to be more assertive, but to make *Self-Psyching* work you must specify what aspects of your life are marked by insufficient assertiveness. Are you unable to speak your mind to people in authority, friends, or close relatives? Are you typically stymied by waiters or salespeople? Pinpoint the situations or individuals that leave you feeling nonassertive or manipulated.

Approach the identification of your problems as if you were a scientist preparing to conduct an experiment. Lay out the precise elements of your behavior and feelings that are influenced and to which you can then apply the techniques in *Self-Psyching*.

You must understand that it isn't enough, for instance, to sum up your problem as general unhappiness or even specific unhappiness with your job. Zero in on the persons or occasions that make you unhappy with your job. Is it your boss? Your inability to talk to your boss? Your fear of speaking up at meetings? Your inability to preserve sufficient privacy while working to get your job done? Is it the anxiety you experience because of your inability to talk to your boss? If you're manifesting signs of anxiety that can be traced to your difficulties in such specific areas as these, you can find appropriate technique articles listed in many problem articles such as Disagreeable Tasks and Encounters and Standing Up for Your Rights.

Isolating the individual problems you wish to attack doesn't require a massive self-evaluation. But you do need to gather some basic information, some baseline data — both to be sure you have pegged your problems correctly and to enable you to measure the effectiveness of the techniques you try. You must know how you were behaving and feeling before you begin using any method if you are to accurately identify your problems and adequately assess the efficacy of each technique you employ.

Monitor yourself. Get a diary or small notebook and begin keeping a log of your everyday behavior. Make notations about what you normally do and where, with whom you interact, and how you think and feel. You can keep an even more portable record on 3 x 5 cards. Mark off sections of each page or card of your diary into hours of the day and categories of observation. Record problem areas that emerge at specific times, in specific places, and are associated with specific individuals or activities. The sample diary page, pictured below, will give you a rough idea of what you're after, though each person will be the best judge of how detailed this personal record need be.

Plan to keep your record for at least a week or two. As soon as you form clear impressions of the sources and specific aspects of your problems, record keeping can give way to problem solving. But you may want to resume your self-monitoring later to see how well a technique is working for you.

You may, of course, already have all the elements of your problem clearly in mind. If so, you need not take the time to monitor your behavior but can proceed directly to the selection of proper techniques mentioned in the articles on each problem you can clearly describe.

The diary-keeping process is a valuable one because it may reveal new aspects of even well-recognized problems. These aspects may suggest self-psyching techniques that you might otherwise fail to consider. You may even discover that the monitoring process alone contributes to increased control and improved outlook. By seeing your supposed problem in

Sample Page From Self-Monitoring Log

	Activity	Place	People Present	Thoughts or Interaction	Feelings
8 a.m.	breakfast	kitchen	spouse	argument over bills	anger, frustration
10 a.m.	paper-work	office	alone	none?	boredom
lunch	eating	cafeteria	2 friends	small talk	pleasant, confident
1 p.m.	meeting	boss & 6 others	board room	giving report	anxiety
3 p.m.	little	office	alone	contemplating poor showing at meeting	worry, guilt
5 p.m.	driving home	car	alone	recapitulating day's activities	depression
dinner	eating	dining room	spouse & kids	strained silence	frustrated
7 p.m.	watching TV & eating	living room	spouse & kids	squabbles	growing despair
9 p.m.	reading	den	alone at start	interrupted continually by kids	anger at nonassertion
11 p.m.	retiring	bedroom	spouse	sexual activity, but unable to get spouse interested or to make sufficient effort to do so	anger, frustration

the context of all your other activities and emotions you may gain a much-needed perspective and decide that the problem is not as bad as you had imagined. Conversely, by revealing such earmarks of your behavior as nervous habits that you were not aware of engaging in as much as your record indicates, you may find additions for your list of target problems.

Some people have found that just keeping a behavior record measurably decreases problems, that they seem to be automatically attending to various minor difficulties that, before monitoring themselves, they had not attempted to cope with at all.

Measure your behavior. You can strengthen the record-keeping process by actually measuring your behavior — that is, by counting the number of times your target behavior manifests itself. Make tally marks in your log or carry a counter of some sort, such as the cheap plastic counters used to keep golf scores. Or, fill a pocket with toothpicks or matches and move them one at a time to another pocket each time you count a target behavior or feeling. (Do be cautious in reaching into your pocket.) Log in the total at the end of the day.

After you start employing a *Self-Psyching* method, such quantification of your problems is a behavior modification technique that also permits you to accurately determine if you are having any success with the technique.

The more specifically you can describe (and even quantify) your problem, the easier it will be to look up your problem in the article of the same name and run down the list of technique articles for dealing with each complaint. Obviously, not every problem experienced by humankind can be included in any one book, and people see the same problem in different terms, so your problem may be described by other wording. However the book refers to your problems, if you are able to divide them into smaller units you are likely to find the weakest link in the chain of actions and feelings that sustain those problems. You can then identify your problem and be guided to the best technique to use.

Choose your techniques. Keep up your record and use the contents to guide you first to the alphabetically arranged problem articles and onward to the technique articles, likewise arranged. With this procedure, the alphabetical organization of the book should give you rapid access to all the information you need to make profitable use of *Self-Psyching*.

There may be some techniques in the book that particularly interest you and that you'll want to read about right away. This is one way to get into the book. And to permit you to proceed efficiently in this fashion, each major technique article opens with a list of the sorts of problems on which it works best. But the most orderly way to choose a technique is to read one or more of the problem articles that relate to you. These problem sections guide you directly to the methods best suited to handling particular problems.

Most problem articles refer you to several techniques. The techniques so listed are ordered roughly according to their suitability for that problem, but not everyone will get the best results with the number one technique listed. The third one may be best for someone. And it may require a combination of techniques to fully master your problem.

Only by trying various techniques on a problem can you determine what your particular situation requires. You should soon discover which ones work best or not at all for you. Desensitization, for example, works for most people who want to deal with fears and phobias, but some find the method too slow and do better with Flooding, which is faster but a bit traumatic for many people.

To fit a particular technique to your unique problems and personality, try several and measure their impact. If one doesn't seem to be working, go over the instructions for using it and see if you've followed all the steps. Each technique recommends a specific trial period before you should see results. If it takes you too long, it may well be that the approach is not for you. You may need to use that method in concert with another or might do better with another technique entirely.

The provision of several techniques for most problems gives you alternates to fall back on if you have little success with any one method or if varying circumstances call for a little bit of this, a little bit of that. Give each technique the fair test that its instructions call for, but feel free to switch to another method if the first simply fails to produce results.

Set your goals. The setting of *Self-Psyching* goals is both part of the procedure for using this book and a therapeutic technique in and of itself. The very process of goal setting gives you a new degree of control over your life. It encourages you to create a part of your future that you can — and probably will — fulfill. Goal setting is a device for ordering your priorities and gaining a sense of direction. It helps counter the sense of helplessness, drifting, purposelessness, and fruitlessness that often typifies depression.

The instructions for each major self-psyching technique include a reference to this general discussion of goal setting. The more you use the book the easier it will become to employ this aspect of the process of self-control. Try to make your goals conform to the following overall principles:

1. *Make your goals specific.* Avoid long-term, general goals like happiness, success, a good marriage. You may indeed achieve such broad and distant goals — and *Self-Psyching* may help you reach them — but you want to progress toward these goals step-by-step, specific goal by specific goal.

If you suffer from anxiety, make it your goal to remove

anxiety in specific situations, one situation at a time. As you handle each anxiety-provoking situation, your total burden of anxiety will diminish and you will feel better, be happier.

If you specify the clear and precise steps you can take to overcome tardiness or procrastination, become a better decision maker, learn to speak up more comfortably before groups, success and increased self-confidence are in store for you. And if you use techniques that help you avoid arguments with your spouse over trivial issues, your marriage in general should improve.

Self-Psyching is geared to dealing with sharply defined problems and clearly delineated goals. The better you are at specifying what you want to achieve with this self-control program, the more likely you are to succeed with the techniques.

2. *Make your goals reasonable.* It makes no sense to set goals you have neither the time, money, nor ability to pursue. A trip to Europe is an admirable goal; saving ten dollars a week to accumulate enough for the trip is reasonable. Losing thirty pounds is an unrealistic weight-loss goal and your failure to do so in a relatively short time will probably discourage you from going on. But the more reasonable goal of losing a pound or two a week will show results right away, and in a month you will be well on your way to achieving your desired weight.

3. *Modify your goals as circumstances change.* Be flexible about what you hope to achieve. If you set a goal too high, don't be afraid to back off and lower your mark. If you find you are getting results faster than you expected, set higher goals. Nothing in the *Self-Psyching* approach is carved in stone. You are the controlling factor and your needs, successes, and setbacks must regulate how you proceed.

4. *Make a self-psyching contract.* In your efforts to establish and meet your goals you might prepare a contract covering what you hope to achieve in dealing with each problem. As you begin to tackle a problem, make a list of the precise goals you want to reach. By putting them in writing, by making a contract with yourself, you will specify what you are trying to achieve and encourage yourself to stick to your self-control program more conscientiously. The contract adds an element of formality that such a self-directed form of therapy may require.

As you make use of *Self-Psyching*, you will compile several contracts. Check and revise them periodically to monitor your progress and to determine if you should modify your efforts. Your behavior log is a convenient place to set down each contract.

Schedule your self-psyching efforts. Identification of your problems will give you important clues to the best times and places to employ particular techniques. Obviously, just before bedtime is the time to practice most methods for dealing with insomnia. And if coping with a particular person is a problem, you'll have to devote at least part of your self-psyching efforts to occasions when you encounter that person. Each technique article specifies when and where it is best to practice.

The duration of your practice sessions will vary with the techniques chosen and with the nature of each problem. Some methods, like Meditation, call for daily practice; others need only periodic implementation. Follow the instructions in the technique articles as closely as possible for maximum benefit. And feel free to take more or less time with any one practice session or an entire program of using a technique. Let how the technique works for you be your guide.

Make a trial run. Test the self-psyching approach with some problem, say, breaking a nervous habit like nail biting. Start your self-monitoring log and count the frequency of nail biting episodes, indicating when, where, and under what circumstances you bite your nails. Read the problem articles on Nail Biting and Nervous Habits and then consult the technique articles on Stimulus Control, Rewards, Changing the Sequence of Events, Negative Practice, Incompatible Behavior, Covert Sensitization, Relaxation, Meditation, Thought-Stopping, and Self-Hypnosis. You will not, of course, have to try to use all of these techniques right away. Read through them quickly and then try them one at a time to achieve maximum impact.

Follow all the instructions for any one technique fully and conscientiously. After you have used the method for the suggested time, resume your self-monitoring to measure your success. Your behavior log and your own informal observations should tell you if you are overcoming your problem.

Such a trial run — with nail biting or any other problem you'd like to attack right away — will allow you to test both yourself and the approach used in this book. Give both a fair chance. Stick with a technique for the indicated length of time; recheck the instructions on the method if you fail to see good results in that period; try the technique again; then use alternative methods if the first doesn't pass the test. One or more of the techniques should work for you. If not, you may have a problem of sufficient seriousness to call for professional therapy.

Reinforce your successes. As you master any element of a technique, as you succeed in overcoming any small part of a problem, and finally, when you feel you have a problem really licked, reward yourself. All aspects of self-psyching will be easier and more effective if you reinforce your successes as soon as possible after they are achieved.

It may be helpful to make a list of what you consider adequate, yet reasonable, rewards. Start with what pleases you: buying an article of clothing, eating out, taking in a movie or play, engaging in a favorite hobby or sport. Try to reward yourself immediately after attaining one of your specified goals. If this is impossible or inconvenient, give yourself tokens that you can accumulate toward earning the full reward. A token can be as simple as some small counter you've previously assigned an arbitrary value. And the process of awarding yourself tokens is in itself reinforcing. When you've amassed enough tokens, you can take your actual reward. Read the article on Rewards for a complete discussion of self-reinforcement. It includes tips on such procedures as establishing realistic values for tokens.

An essential element of reinforcement is your taking some sort of reward or reinforcement every time and as soon as possible after you have scored a behavioral victory or emotional breakthrough, no matter how small. If you reward each measurable success you will reinforce your new behavior and encourage yourself to continue working toward even greater successes.

Breaking the *Self-Psyching* rules. Don't follow any of the guidelines, instructions, or "rules" in this book mindlessly. In the beginning, as you are familiarizing yourself with the use of this book, as you are learning to make the techniques work, you would do well to stick by the instructions. But once you know what you are doing and are getting good results, modify or vary the approach you take to best suit your particular problems, goals, and personal style.

Using the Sources of Further Information. At the end of most technique articles and some of the major problem articles, citations are given to published works you might want to consult to expand and deepen your knowledge of those methods or problems. These bibliographic references, called Sources of Further Information, have been chosen to give you access to books and articles that are both authoritative and readable. You need not read these works in order to make self-psyching work for you, but their contents may satisfy your curiosity about many aspects of the techniques and problems with which you will be dealing. Both classic studies and the latest materials have been suggested to make available detailed information for which there was neither space nor any pressing need in the presentation of the self-psyching program. Use of these sources can add to your enjoyment and appreciation of *Self-Psyching*.

Precautions: Roadblocks to Successful Self-Psyching. You must take certain precautions to prevent unnecessary failure along the road to self-psyching. First, read through an entire technique article before you attempt to make use of the method. The articles are like recipes: It is pointless to start to make brownies when there is no chocolate in the house and you haven't read far enough into the recipe to learn you'll need it. It is similarly wasteful and frustrating to start working with a technique that may require time you can't spend or efforts you're unwilling to make.

Second, don't try too many techniques at once, undertaking several behavior change programs at the same time. As you begin to learn self-psyching, tackle one technique at a time to bring down only one problem. Later, as your self-control skills increase, building upon one another, you'll be able to handle several problems concurrently. But at the start, move slowly and cautiously.

Third, avoid overexpectations. Don't set your goals too high and don't expect miracles. If your goals are too general, you may never reach them. If you have a smoking habit you've been fighting for twenty years, you can't expect to stub it out in a few weeks. Moderation will reap you significant rewards. You'll make a promising start by cutting your smoking from two packs a day to a pack and a half. Progress by surmountable stages and celebrate even minor successes.

Fourth, be prepared to cope with the reactions of other people. Some people will support your self-psyching efforts; others will deride or even interfere with your endeavor.

Avoid those who you decide are making it hard for you to maintain your desired behavior. If you are working on weight control, you would be wise to spend less time with people who eat often or who always seem to be offering you doughnuts or candy. And if you are working on Assertiveness Training, you will quickly discover which people undermine your progress toward greater self-assertion and which ones may misinterpret your new behavior as aggressiveness or bad manners.

There is no hard-and-fast rule about who may or may not hinder your self-psyching. Your own perceptions are your best guide. Keep in mind this is a self-initiated program for your own purposes. You are not out to please or manipulate others. So please yourself by avoiding or seeking the responses of other people as you see fit.

Fifth, be prepared to see what psychologists call defense mechanisms: You may find yourself resisting even positive changes. Change is frightening and it is a human trait to get cold feet — emotionally speaking — on the path to change. People tend to be as afraid of success as they are of failure, especially when success may mean the loss of some habit, compulsion, or other pattern of behavior that has been gratifying in its familiarity, if in no other way.

Beware of rationalizations that argue for your giving up the program: You don't really want to change, people like you better as you are, you can cope with some problem (you know you can't), the techniques don't really work (you haven't given them a fair test). It is impossible to effectively monitor your behavior and emotions to determine what problems need attention if you repress how you feel and hide from yourself how you honestly act. For example, if in recording your behavior you repress — lie about — the degree of anxiety you experience in dealing with certain people or situations, you cannot know how great your problem may be.

Old habits die hard. But their death frees you from practices detrimental to your well-being. Don't mask or distort the seriousness of your problems by rationalization, repression, and other defense mechanisms. Honest self-appraisal can rip away that mask and put your feelings and action into sharp focus.

Sixth, don't be put off by any seemingly difficult instructions in the technique articles. When practiced systematically, all the steps of each method are well within the capacities of all but the most severely disturbed individuals.

Seventh, understand that *Self-Psyching* outlines programs

for symptom relief, behavior control, and coping. It is not a course in self-actualization, training in altered states of consciousness, or personality transformation. Although some of the techniques, like Meditation and Biofeedback, can also alter consciousness, for the purposes of this book, that is not their goal. Here they are intended primarily to alter *behavior*. Many people deeply involved in organized consciousness alteration or self-actualization may still benefit from *Self-Psyching*. You can be a self-actualized person, be able to modify your consciousness at will, and still be a nail biter and not find it within your power to ask for a raise.

Most people will be able to use the techniques in this book to good effect. But some people's life choices and personalities may generate difficulties over which most of these techniques have little influence. Because *Self-Psyching* doesn't offer personality change or the cure for deeply rooted emotional illnesses, readers with problems that adamantly resist the influence of these techniques are encouraged to seek the aid of professional therapists trained in dealing with profound mental disorders and character weaknesses.

THE PROMISE OF *SELF-PSYCHING*

Your ultimate goal in using this book is freedom. And freedom is a goal that you can achieve by gaining the power to understand and cope with your own feelings and actions instead of submitting them to the control of others or of your own self-limiting reactions or unrewarding conditioning. *Self-Psyching* can teach you to control your responses to various people and situations rather than having those responses manipulated by actions and emotions over which you are not expected to have any control. Without changing yourself or others, you can change the way you behave and feel.

The techniques in this book can teach you to begin to live your life as you want to live it — not by making yourself into a new person but by learning to function fully and freely as the real you, *as the person you want to and can be.*

Accepting Criticism and Criticizing Others

Many people cannot accept criticism gracefully. When it comes to criticizing others, many are surprisingly inept as well. Coping with or dealing out criticism begins with distinguishing between that which is constructive and that which is destructive — manipulative or even spiteful — criticism.

Constructive criticism from trustworthy sources should be welcomed. When someone who genuinely cares about you and your feelings points out a deficiency and gives you advice on how to improve yourself, consider that person's views as helpful and worthwhile. Chances are that those closest to you will give you an honest appraisal. Even highly critical comments from people who like you can be accepted because you know that their aim is to help you make more of yourself, encourage you, enable you to advance and build up your confidence.

Destructive, manipulative, or spiteful criticism is easy to spot because it tends to put you down, embarrass you, diminish your self-esteem. It often comes from people who have never shown that they care much for you. They may dislike you and customarily compete with you. They tend to criticize you in front of others, knowing it will make you feel worse.

Destructive criticism may be handled in a number of ways: You can laugh it off, check it out with your "real" friends, or critically analyze it yourself. Even unfriendly criticism might reveal problems that merit your attention. A positive response to this criticism may be to your benefit.

Assertiveness Training can show you how to deal with unhelpful manipulative criticism and even make it easier for you to accept constructive, though particularly distressing, criticism. Modeling offers guidance in changing your attitude toward being criticized. And Desensitization and Behavior Rehearsal can help you prepare for situations in which you expect to be criticized.

If you are called upon to criticize others you should, of course, try to do so in a friendly, constructive manner. But you may find it difficult to handle such tasks and feel uncomfortable once you bring yourself to voice criticism. The article on Disagreeable Tasks and Encounters discusses useful ways for approaching this problem.

See also:
  Disagreeable Tasks and Encounters
  Disciplining Others

Techniques to try:
  Assertiveness Training
  Modeling
  Desensitization
  Behavior Rehearsal

TECHNIQUE

Alpha Waves

See:
  Biofeedback

PROBLEM

Anxiety

Over millions of years of evolution, our survival as a species has depended on the very biochemical responses to stress that today produce the debilitating and destructive symptoms of the common complaint we call anxiety.

Before civilization, when people were continually exposed to the threats and dangers of their natural environment, they had to rely on their bodies to make instant, appropriate responses to every sort of demand. Large predators, attacks from other humans, and the challenges of an inhospitable world — familiar fears and the dark unknown — all required people to choose instantly between fighting and fleeing. Survival did not permit the luxury of thoughtful contemplation before such critical decisions were made. The process had to be virtually automatic, and, fortunately, our ancestors (at least those who survived) had the capacity to marshal the internal resources needed to cope with life-and-death demands and to do so without the intervention or guidance of their minds. We, like all animals, retain this crucial capacity — but the creation of civilization has removed most humans from that natural environment in which this ability was adaptive and protective.

The problem is that our bodies continue to function as if we still lived on the African savanna or in Ice Age caves. Any threat or challenge, perceived or imagined danger can trigger the physiological responses that aided our ancestors but cause us distress and discomfort.

The automatic stress reaction was useful and adaptive in prehistoric times because it encouraged virtually instantaneous response to real threats. The cry "Leopard on the ledge; everybody run!" produced immediate action that saved lives. Each individual's internal, biochemical changes in response to such threats provided the energy and incentive to prompt movement toward safety. But today, although many threats, challenges, and stresses may be real, most often they assail us in circumstances that don't permit clear, physical reactions.

When you get a memo stating, "Sales figures are down," when you learn that it will take four days and three hundred dollars to get your car working again, when the school calls with the news that your child will have to be held back for a year, when your firm is purchased by a conglomerate and you will have to move to a city a thousand miles away or lose your job, you feel the stress and your body readies itself for fighting or fleeing — but whom do you fight and where can you flee? Unlike your prehistoric forebears, you must stay and cope with stress; you must deal with the anxiety that arises from the automatic stress reaction that in the modern world has few obvious outlets.

Just what is this natural, necessary, and often inescapable physical process that produces anxiety? Changes in our blood chemistry, our heart and circulatory system, our nerves, skin, and digestive system take place automatically as we reflexively prepare to deal with threat. This is all very well if we face a genuine threat. Walking down a dark city street and hearing the rapidly approaching footsteps of a possible assailant requires the same state of readiness for fight or flight that encountering a leopard on a cave ledge demanded of our forebears.

But the problem is further complicated when this powerful and complex process is initiated when we are merely going through such routine behavior as driving a car, working at a desk, or dialing the telephone. What does it mean when we experience dramatic internal changes when no threat is apparent — when we are simply trying to get to sleep, make a report at a business meeting, or take a test? It means that we are likely to suffer some or all of the distressing symptoms of anxiety and thus be prevented from performing well or even functioning normally.

The reality of our evolutionary heritage is that anxiety can be triggered by stress generated by our own thoughts and feelings as well as by outside agencies. Our bodies cannot tell the difference between real and paper tigers. In either case great demands are placed on our bodies, but when there is nothing palpable to fight or flee from, there is no chance for natural relief through action and effort. We become bows that are drawn but not released, explosions contained within ourselves.

World-renowned biochemist and endocrinologist Hans Selye, the foremost authority on stress, believes that stress is part of life and that if we were incapable of responding to stress we could not survive: "Complete freedom from stress is death." It is rather like the old joke about bad breath being better than no breath at all. Anxiety is a price we pay for being human and alive. But although all of us are subject to stress, not everyone is plagued by anxiety, and most of us can learn to lessen the ill effects of this pervasive problem.

Anxiety is manifested in many ways, not all of them obvious. Awareness of the signs of anxiety is the first step toward learning to cope with it. There may be a general feeling of being unwell; things seem out of balance, all wrong. Muscles may tighten up, fists and jaws clench, the neck feels stiff, the brow wrinkles. Anxious persons typically rub their necks or try to pinch out the tension they feel across the bridge of the nose. Sweating may become noticeable and the palms of the hands are apt to get clammy. At the same time the mouth can go dry, and chills or feelings of uncomfortable warmth (or both, alternatively) are possible. As the body prepares itself to face danger, breathing speeds up and the heart pumps faster and stronger. Painful sensations (especially backache or simply "hurting all over") signal internal transformations. Those who are anxious can be troubled by diarrhea, frequent or copious urination, or the feeling that they must urinate. And because the anxiety process is preparing the body for action, hunger is suppressed and the ability to sleep or get to sleep diminishes. However, fear of anxiety may produce depression and a generally off-balance reaction to life that may be manifested in overeating or sleeping too much.

Even if the preceding physical symptoms of anxiety are not acute, some other early signs may appear. Appearance, behavior, and manner of speech and thought may subtly alter. The skin tone can change. Movements can become uncharacteristically awkward, leading to missteps and fumbling. The anxious may grimace, twitch, or experience tics, muscle spasms, or a fidgety feeling. It may be difficult to speak without hesitation or slips of the tongue. Normal intellectual activity can seem unusually difficult: The anxiety process does not encourage contemplation or concentration but immediate expenditure of energy without much mental activity. Comedian Don Knotts, on the old Steve Allen TV show, created a character who personified the anxious, tense, uptight individual. He fairly rattled with tension and the image he projected is a reasonably accurate picture of a person suffering from anxiety.

People plagued continually by anxiety can become aggressive; have little tolerance for frustration; be prone to panic attacks; overuse alcohol, cigarettes, or drugs. They have an increased tendency toward heart disease, hypertension, certain forms of arthritis, dermatoses, asthma, and ulcers.

Anxiety is clearly no small matter. And dealing with it means making a concerted effort to identify the situations, people, or occasions that trigger any of the symptoms of anxiety. Finding that you tend to suffer from anxiety, you can learn to employ any of a number of the potent techniques described in this book.

The articles on Desensitization, Relaxation, Meditation, Stimulus Control, Autogenic Training, Fantasy, and Self-Hypnosis will give you a good start in combating anxiety's effects or preventing it from getting out of hand. They can help you alter your responses to stress and modify the circumstances that provoke anxiety.

Whatever technique you try, approach it with the attitude that anxiety is a disruptive influence in your life and one worth counteracting. Others have successfully employed these techniques, so can you. And the fact that anxiety is a natural, built-in process should not deter you. Pain is natural, bleeding is natural, rain is natural. But this doesn't mean that you shouldn't do anything to lessen pain, stop bleeding, or keep from getting soaked.

You need not remove anxiety from existence to master it. And when you do achieve even a small degree of control over anxiety, you will have gained a significant measure of control over the quality of your own life.

Techniques to try:
Desensitization
Relaxation
Meditation
Stimulus Control
Autogenic Training
Fantasy
Self-Hypnosis

Other techniques that may be helpful:
The Relaxation Response
Transcendental Meditation
Assertiveness Training
Behavior Rehearsal

TECHNIQUE

Assertiveness Training

Particularly useful in dealing with such problems as Standing Up for Your Rights, Shyness and Inhibitions, Disagreeable Tasks and Encounters.

May contribute to coping with Anxiety, Fears and Phobias, Sexual Hang-ups, Procrastination, Work and Study Habits.

Supplementary or alternative techniques: Behavior Rehearsal, Desensitization, Modeling.

WHAT ASSERTIVENESS TRAINING IS

Assertiveness is an affirmation of your self, the reasonable and correct posture taken by normal people who justly believe that their feelings and opinions matter. Assertiveness

Training teaches you to express both outrage and satisfaction, to register displeasure and affection. The assertive person believes in freedom of action and expression, within reason, for everyone. Assertiveness Training doesn't promote lack of consideration and won't turn you into an aggressive monster; it will keep you from being manipulated by others.

Assertiveness Training also serves to counter stress. It activates a natural psychological reflex that inhibits anxiety, in much the same way that relaxation does, by blocking anxiety-provoking stimuli with newly conditioned responses.

HISTORICAL DEVELOPMENT

The theory of assertiveness goes back to Pavlov's conditioned-reflex experiments with dogs. The names most closely associated with the development of modern theory are Andrew Salter, Joseph Wolpe, and Arnold Lazarus. They demonstrated that assertiveness can unlock inhibited feelings and help one overcome anxiety in a manner similar to the way relaxation counters stress: It is all but impossible to feel inhibited or anxious at the same time you are asserting yourself.

BASIC ELEMENTS OF ASSERTIVENESS TRAINING

Identifying the problem (see Introduction)
Setting goals (see Introduction)
Organizing your assertiveness practice
Learning Andrew Salter's six basic disciplines
Practicing
Checking your progress (see Introduction)
Employing the technique with other problems

HOW TO USE ASSERTIVENESS TRAINING

Identify the problem. You should consider Assertiveness Training if you have trouble with encounters with bosses, spouses, sales clerks, waiters, even total strangers — especially if your encounters make you feel tense, anxious, or spineless. If being shy or withdrawn is reducing your enjoyment of life, if an inability to stand up for your rights results in your being manipulated by others, if a gnawing fear of hurting or displeasing others prevents you from being yourself, Assertiveness Training is in order. The technique will increase your self-confidence in facing any encounter where your rights, opinions, or needs may be placed in direct opposition to those of other people.

To decide what problem to attack first, examine your unmodified behavior and attitudes to see how nonassertive you really are. There are signs of lack of assertion that you can look for: saying yes to demands or requests you feel you should deny; accepting products, services, or explanations you actually find unacceptable; holding in your feelings (positive or negative); or otherwise giving way to the actions or attitudes of other people. Guided by the instructions in the Introduction, keep a daily log of such signs as concrete evidence of specific instances of nonassertion.

Use your daily log to compile a checklist of nonassertive impulses detected over the next week or two. If you accept a bad bottle of wine or poorly prepared dish from a waiter, put that on your list. Note any time you let people crowd in front of you in lines. Indicate each time you agree with a statement you really believe is wrong. Pay close attention to each time you say no, especially to bosses or other authority figures, when yes is the honest, appropriate response. And add a notation to any entry recording an encounter during which you feel tense and ill-at-ease while failing to be assertive.

Once you have compiled your log of nonassertive impulses and identified the most troublesome of them, you can proceed to the active diminution of each in turn.

Take on one problem at a time. And as you master each, you should notice that the remainder of your problems are diminishing appreciably, without concerted effort on your part: even a little success with one or two problems can make you a generally more assertive person.

Set goals. You should have two sets of goals: general, long-term desires about the overall nature of your behavior and short-term targets to serve as steps toward your greater goals. For instance, you may want to reduce anxiety and become a more self-confident person. These are long-term, inclusive goals. But to reach them you must attain several lesser goals, each of which will increase your confidence in being assertive and reduce the total load of your anxiety. Such shorter-term goals might include: dealing comfortably with your boss, your mother-in-law, pushy sales clerks. Perhaps the first goal you may want to achieve is telling a coworker, who seems to start every work day by killing time with small talk in your office, that you have things to do and need to be alone.

Working one step at a time is basic to this approach, as it is to so many self-psyching techniques. But each step taken moves you closer to your goals at an ever-accelerating pace.

Organize your assertiveness practice. Arrange to practice assertiveness in a highly organized way contrived to breed success with a minimum of risk. This means making a list of possible practice behaviors derived from your nonassertiveness checklist, ranked from the least demanding to the most difficult and threatening.

Try to make your list of practice behaviors long and complete. Give yourself plenty of room to maneuver. And what goes into the list is a personal matter, dependent upon the sorts of people and situations that trouble you regularly. This practice list will include many short-term assertiveness goals and some long-term objectives. Numerous ideas for the list should be provided by your nonassertiveness checklist. A sample list might look like the following:

1. Ask a friend to give you a ride home from work.
2. Ask a friend to go out of his or her way to run an errand for you.
3. Deny a friend's request to spend time doing something you'd rather not do.
4. Refuse an invitation for a lunch date you know will take so long that it will cut into your working time.
5. Refuse to take on work for a colleague, especially if you typically do so.
6. Send back a dish that is unsatisfactorily prepared or which you didn't order.
7. Demand that improperly done repairs on your car be done over without charge.
8. Speak up when someone cuts in front of you in line.
9. Tell your spouse you don't feel like going to your in-laws for the regular Friday night supper and bridge.
10. Express your feelings about your boss's decision or a company policy, even if trying to do so usually makes you anxious.
11. Take every opportunity possible to show you are a self-confident person whose feelings must be taken into account.

The trick is to try the easiest things first, moving gradually to riskier encounters. In the beginning avoid situations likely to end in defeat and failure. Don't begin by walking into a waterfront bar and demanding that the members of a motor-cycle gang respect your rights.

You don't want to make the leap directly from asking the paperboy to try to get the paper on the porch instead of in the bushes to rushing into your boss's office to disagree argumentatively with some order. Trying tough tests too soon or moving too swiftly from easy to hard trials can be totally demoralizing.

Learn Andrew Salter's six basic disciplines. Salter, one of the founders of Assertiveness Training, developed his Conditioned Reflex Therapy a generation ago. He observed that society inhibits our emotions and conditions most people to repress how they actually feel. He noted that children are born without inhibitions and begin life by freely and fully expressing their needs and wants. But socialization starts to stifle their natural assertive responses almost immediately. Salter's therapy was designed to restore this original, healthy expressiveness by reconditioning people's responses to overcome inhibitions and denial of feelings.

At the heart of Salter's method are six "disciplines" that anyone trying to become more assertive should learn. The six disciplines are interrelated, so the consistent use of any one makes it easier to employ the others. When you first learn and begin to use Salter's disciplines, there is the danger of feeling that they will turn you into a self-centered boor, a thoughtless egomaniac. It calls for a studied, exaggerated practice at first, to break down nonassertive conditioning. After a while, however, you will become more spontaneous and outgoing. As you make assertiveness practice a regular and modulated part of your normal behavior, you'll be able to use the disciplines with less effort and without seeming to demand the new respect that others should soon be granting you.

Learn Salter's six disciplines and incorporate them into your program of Assertiveness Training:

1. *Feeling-talk.* This is the conscious, deliberate expression of what you actually feel at any given moment. If you like or dislike something, say so immediately. And say so in unambiguous, expansive terms. Don't say, "Maybe we should have stayed home tonight." Say,

"That movie (dinner party, meeting) was a crashing bore, a big waste of time (money, effort)." Likewise, don't withhold your praise. If you like what someone has done, how they look, what they have said — say so. "You look smashing tonight," "You really played that shot perfectly," or "I can always depend on you" are statements that make you feel as good as the person you praise.

Don't withhold praise of yourself. Say aloud, "I knew I could do that," or "I couldn't miss; my game is right on today." The regular use of self-praise builds your confidence, validates your true worth. Resist the temptation to be self-effacing. And don't extend feeling-talk to self-criticism, which can undermine your efforts to condition new self-confident responses.

Employ feeling-talk to express relief, determination, anguish, surprise, impatience, complaint, anticipation, discomfort, or any truly felt emotion. Holding emotions in is what you are trying to overcome, so lose no opportunity to let them out through feeling-talk.

2. *Facial-talk.* Let your face show how you feel. Frown if you are unhappy; scowl if you are angry; grin, even laugh, when you are pleased. Don't overdo it, but don't be so reserved that your face masks your real feelings. There is a connection between your outward, physical appearance, expressions, and postures and your internal emotions. If you make yourself display your true feelings, your emotions will be liberated. You will feel better because you will be feeling and acting more naturally.

3. *Contradiction and attack.* If you agree with what others have said or done, use feeling-talk to express your agreement. But if you disagree, immediately register your dissent — openly and energetically. Let your emotions guide you. Simply say what you feel. By contradicting and attacking the statements you "feel" are wrong, you condition yourself in self-expression and thus you build confidence in your own reactions while affirming your right to have your own opinions.

Because we are all conditioned to keep quiet unless we have factual justification for refuting what others say, this can be hard, at first. Keep at it, despite any initial discomfort, and soon you will recondition yourself to express your feelings without self-doubt or embarrassment.

4. *Use of I.* Go out of your way to introduce the word *I* into your conversation. Be quite deliberate and energetic about it. This flies in the face of all you may have learned about being reserved and modest, but it is fundamental to this therapeutic technique. It is especially important to attach this personal pronoun to statements of affirmation, demand, respect, intent, or emotion. Say, "I want," "I need," "I know," "I care," "I feel" at every opportunity. Assert your individuality by identifying yourself. The use of *I* reminds you to be yourself, calls attention to the fact that you have needs and desires. It teaches your behavioral reflexes to tap your emotions and guard you autonomy.

5. *Agreement with praise.* Be honest about your response to praise. We all love to be told how good we look, how well we have performed, how accomplished we are. Most of us say nothing in response, having been brought up not to blow our own horns even when someone else has done so already. Pride is a sin and modesty a virtue, but for purposes of Assertiveness Training it is worthwhile to intensify good feelings produced by praise through your agreement with it. If someone says, "My, you look thin and fit," don't say, "Oh, I still have a long way to go to hit my best weight." Say something like, "Sure, I've been sticking to my diet, exercise every day, and have never felt better in my life." Practicing self-praise will build your confidence by concentrating your attention on the positive comments of others — comments that in the past you may have failed to notice.

6. *Improvisation.* Be spontaneous. You want to release your emotions, not lock them into new patterns. So be ready to react immediately and unself-consciously to all stimuli. In the past you may have made all sorts of plans, but when actually faced with problems you responded unsatisfactorily, perhaps frozen into inaction by your inability to implement a decision. Make no plans; just be ready to react honestly and openly, externalizing your emotions, expressing your feelings.

Salter's six Conditioned Reflex Therapy disciplines should be considered basic tools to be used in attacking the various elements of nonassertiveness you have already listed. Throughout your assertiveness practice, keep all six in mind and try to bring as many as possible into play. In the beginning, make it a point to use each one often, every day. Soon their use will become second nature and you will become correspondingly more assertive.

Practice. By practicing assertiveness, you will soon prove to yourself that certain acts or situations need not automatically lead to anxiety and defeat. And by trying things you might never have done before because you've been afraid of offending people, you will see that others probably won't get angry. Even if they do, you can take the heat.

Starting with your easy goals, practice as many of the items on your list as you can fit into your schedule. Don't let a day go by without trying to master a few. And when in your nonpractice hours you experience put-downs because you lack assertiveness, counter the negative effects by practicing something on your list you know you can handle. You will refocus your attention on rights and needs, and the successful demonstration of your budding assertiveness will condition you to respect yourself and should increase other people's respect for you.

You will know that your practice is going well by seeing that you are moving up on your list from easier to tougher encounters. And you will know you have graduated from practice to true assertiveness when you tend to forget about the list and simply plunge into encounters that once might have left you trembling, if you could face them at all.

Assertiveness Training is not just a matter of learning tricks or techniques; you actually learn to be assertive by asserting yourself. As you become sufficiently assertive to handle tougher and tougher situations, there is a snowballing effect. You get more assertive, so you assert yourself more, becoming yet more assertive. In the end, protecting your rights will come naturally.

Practice assertiveness until you feel that you're not letting others rob you of your rights. Don't aim for a day during which you will get your way in every encounter; that isn't the point. Assertiveness Training is *not* intimidation training. You needn't make others feel bad or small in order to feel better yourself. The training is defensive, not offensive — in both senses of the word!

Check your progress. Throughout your practice, as soon as you find that you are comfortably assertive in a particular situation you are ready to attack some more difficult problem. Do so.

Employ the technique with other problems. The progress from easier to tougher encounters is built into the training program. One success will encourage you to attempt dealing with a more demanding problem. And, of course, continually update your list to include additional areas of nonassertiveness as your ability to handle even the toughest problems increases.

PRECAUTIONS

Most people find that only a few weeks of putting Assertiveness Training to work brings marked results. But if after a month or so you have not made headway it may be that, because of ingrained guilt, distaste for assertiveness, or fear of counteraggression, you may first require exercise with Desensitization to rid you of anxiety. Once you have sufficiently laid your fears to rest, you can come back to Assertiveness Training with greater hope of success.

If your problems resist self-psyching, you might want to seek help from a trained psychologist at a center specializing in assertiveness problems. Such places may be found by inquiring of your local medical society or association of psychological clinicians.

By becoming more assertive you are likely to discover unexpected sources of inner confidence and strength of will. Assertiveness Training is a sort of phone booth into which Clark Kent steps and out of which Superman may fly. Test yourself with the method and try your wings.

Sources of further information:
Alberti, Robert E., and Emmons, Michael L. *Your Perfect Right – A Guide to Assertive Behavior.* 2nd ed. San Luis Obispo, Calif.: Impact, 1974.
Bach, George R., and Goldberg, Herb. *Creative Aggression: The Art of Assertive Living.* New York: Avon, 1974.
Fensterheim, Herbert, and Fensterheim, Jean. *Don't Say Yes When You Want To Say No.* New York: Dell, 1975.
Salter, Andrew. *Conditioned Reflex Therapy: The Direct Approach to the Reconstruction of Personality.* New York: Capricorn, 1961.
Smith, Manuel J. *When I Say No, I Feel Guilty.* New York: Bantam, 1975.

Autogenic Training

A form of relaxation particularly useful in dealing with such problems as Anxiety, Stress, Tension, Migraine Headaches, some Tension Headaches, Psychosomatic Complaints, Insomnia, Disagreeable Tasks and Encounters.

Supplementary or alternative techniques: Relaxation, Meditation, The Relaxation Response, Biofeedback, Desensitization, Self-Hypnosis.

WHAT AUTOGENIC TRAINING IS

"Autogenic" means self-regulated, and Autogenic Training (AT) is a program of exercises that train you to attain a marked degree of physical and emotional relaxation. With it you learn to lower your level of consciousness, producing discernible changes in circulation, muscle tension, respiration, and alpha waves (See Biofeedback article).

HISTORICAL DEVELOPMENT

The method is most closely identified with the research of Johannes Schultz, a neurologist and psychiatrist, and his collaborator W. Luthe.

Their studies into the therapeutic applications of autohypnosis are the foundation of Autogenic Training. Although related to self-hypnosis, the technique may be seen as a kind of biofeedback that doesn't require the use of supportive devices, and recent experimentation with biofeedback machines has confirmed the efficacy of AT. AT has resulted in measurable muscle relaxation, slowed heart rate, and altered blood flow, which changes the temperature of the body's extremities. These, and related physiological changes, are incompatible with states of tension, stress, and anxiety. Physiological changes are the basis for AT's success at relieving, reducing, or preventing the ill effects of tension and anxiety and for combating tension and vascular headaches.

The technique was designed to be taught by therapists or instructors, but it can be learned and practiced on your own.

BASIC ELEMENTS OF AUTOGENIC TRAINING
Identifying your problem (see Introduction)
Choosing the proper time and place
Learning the technique
Practicing AT regularly and continually

HOW TO USE AUTOGENIC TRAINING

Identify your problem. The logical targets of AT are any problems involving anxiety, tension, or stress. If you are troubled by such commonly experienced complaints, AT is an effective and readily applied relaxation technique worth learning.

Choose the proper time and place. Once you master the elements of AT, you will probably be able to practice it at almost any time, even in stressful and distracting situations. But when first learning the method, choose a quiet place where you will not be disturbed for a half hour or so, where you can lie down, and where the lights can be dimmed. Pick a time of day when you can devote at least thirty minutes to practice. Many people find the evening best, especially when dealing with insomnia.

Learn the technique.
Attain a peaceful state of mind and body: Begin your practice session in a horizontal position, on a bed or the floor. (Once you've mastered the technique you can sit or even stand while using AT.) Be sure your clothing is loose and comfortable. Close your eyes.

Begin by reciting to yourself a phrase like, "I feel calm" or "I am at peace." Repeat the phrase in your mind over and over again, concentrating — without straining — on the words and relating them to the growing sense of peacefulness you will feel in your body and your spirits. This self-hypnosis works, if you concentrate, if you believe it will work, if you want it to work, if you *just let it work.*

A passive attitude is the key: Focus on what is happening to your body and allow it to happen without willing, forcing, or anticipating results. Listen to the command phrases in the mind but instead of trying to do anything to follow the commands to relax, merely observe the results. See if you feel less tense; let your mind explore your body to detect diminished stress. And when you give yourself the AT command that your hand should feel heavy or warm, concentrate on the process while it's taking place instead of trying to make the process work — *feel* the heaviness and warmth, don't strive to produce the feelings.

With passive attention, or passive volition, you become an observer of phenomena that your mind initiates but that you do not try to control. This is what makes AT work. You train yourself to start internal changes and you then observe and feel these changes without forcing them to take place. And the method works better as you gain the ability to let go more, as you surrender to the process and permit your body to manifest the signs of increased relaxation. At first this approach may seem difficult and contradictory, but it gets very easy once you learn to give most of your attention to the tranquil and passive inspection of the way your body feels as you use AT.

Get a sense of heaviness in one hand: When you start to feel that your mind and body are calm and peaceful, begin to concentrate on your right hand (or left hand if you are left-handed). Say to yourself, "My hand is getting heavy." Repeat the suggestion and concentrate on how your hand feels — it will begin to feel heavier and heavier. Muscle activity in the hand will decrease and tension will be replaced by discernible relaxation.

Feel warmth in that hand: To the heaviness you have begun to feel, add awareness of growing warmth. Say to yourself, "My hand is getting warmer." It will respond if — without trying to force it — you merely sense the temperature of your hand and concentrate on its growing warmth. Your nervous system will respond to your passive attention to the feelings in your hand by increasing circulation to the extremities.

In laboratory experiments, some people were able to raise their hand temperature as much as ten degrees. The mechanism that permits this increased circulation to the hands also involves the blood vessels of the head. So learning this part of AT can permit you to combat migraines, which are caused by dilation of cranial arteries. As soon as you feel a migraine coming on, perhaps when you experience the disturbance of vision that is a first sign of its onset, tell yourself that your hand is getting warmer. Concentrate on this until you feel the warming. As the blood vessels in the hand dilate, the distention of arteries in your head will be correspondingly reduced and the migraine should be halted.

Allow the heaviness and warmth to spread through your body: Having learned to let your hand get heavy and warm, you can now permit those feelings to flow throughout your body. Concentrate on how your hand feels, then let your attention move over your body. Passively observe the sensations in your other hand, your arms, your feet and legs, your trunk and back. Repeat to yourself phrases related to the various parts of your body. You may feel the heaviness come on so that you have a sense of sinking into the bed or floor. However, some people have a floating sensation first, followed by heaviness. An overall warm and heavy feeling may not occur in your initial practice sessions. But give yourself time and the feeling will come.

Breathe regularly: Throughout your practice of AT, try to breathe normally. Don't gulp air or inhale deeply. Everything, including your breathing, should be peaceful, normal, regular. Don't force or speed up your breathing.

Concentrate on the feelings in your abdomen: Only practice this step after several days of practicing the earlier steps. Tell yourself, "My abdomen is pleasantly warm." As you learned to do with your hand, let the nice warm feeling grow deep in your abdomen, your solar plexus. This warmth should give you a keen sense of well-being at the same time that it permits you to see if the central portion of your body is tense. Feel the tension, but counter it by letting your abdomen grow warm and calm. The tension should recede. At first this may take several minutes, but as you become adept at AT, you may be able almost instantaneously to respond to the thought that you feel soothing warmth in your abdomen. This part of AT is thought to work because it affects your central nervous system, bringing repose.

Let your forehead feel cool: The above steps in AT might be followed with a cue like, "My forehead feels cool (not cold)." This can cue relaxation in your face and brow, which may initiate a calm, peaceful feeling. This step should not be attempted unless you've gained quick and sure control over the earlier steps, because its improper practice can bring tension and even cause migraines.

End your practice – the return: After you run through all the steps of AT you will be relaxed, but do not simply jump up and get on with your business. As a transition to normal activity stretch your arms, flex the muscles to tighten them and thus end the relaxation state you've put them in. Then breathe deeply a few times and open your eyes. You're done for this session.

This completes the training of the various sections and systems of your body, leaving your circulatory, respiratory, muscular, and nervous systems free of tension because you have allowed them to unwind, rest, gain relief from the strains your normally strenuous demands make on them. During AT, you feel better because you passively allow your body to take a rest. You don't add tension by striving to relax. By autosuggestion you change the demands and let the body seek its own best level of tension, which is very little tension at all. The result is stress-free moments that carry over into your nonautogenic, fully conscious, highly demanding daily routines.

Practice AT regularly and continually. Because you get better at AT the more you practice, make it part of your daily routine. Run through the full program at least once a day — twice if you can. If you cannot find enough time, at least do the first few steps to get the sense of heaviness and warmth in your hand. This can be done at any time and in most places and in itself provides significant relaxation.

As you get better at AT, it will become quite easy to cue the responses you want and feel almost instantly more relaxed, even in the face of stress. But this almost automatic response will probably be achieved only after several weeks of regular practice without long stretches between practice sessions.

One of the most convenient ways to regularize your practice of AT is to run through the method before bed. It will loosen you up, clear your mind, make it easier to get to sleep. And should you wake up during the night, an AT session can give you the sense of calm you need to get back to sleep.

Another way to insure that you get regular practice is to make it one of your normal responses to potentially distressing everyday demands. Before difficult encounters, do a short version of the program, perhaps just cuing your hand to feel warm and heavy. AT can prepare you for various business, personal, and professional confrontations that are normally characterized by stress and anxiety. If such situations are common in your life, using AT to prepare for them will give you regular practice. And when you are really good at AT,·you should be able to sneak in some practice *during* tough encounters.

There are readily available occasions for practicing and the practice is cumulative in its effects, snowballing until you can remain relaxed in most situations.

Carry on your regular and continual practice until you see real results — clear-cut responses like the feelings of warmth, heaviness, and relaxation. This should begin almost at once. But it may take several weeks before AT gives you appreciable voluntary control over the symptoms of anxiety. Don't give up on AT until you've put in six to eight weeks of regular practice. And because it is so easy to use, if it does work for you you'll probably never stop using it.

PRECAUTIONS

Most people have few problems with AT. Of course, like all self-psyching or guided therapeutic techniques, there are some people for whom the method simply won't work. Such people push, force, try to will the results that AT can produce only if you *let go, let* the process work, and merely watch it working.

Don't try to *make* your body respond to the cues given during AT practice. Relax and quietly observe that your hand is getting heavier and warmer. Those feelings will appear and get stronger — if you allow them to. You must get outside yourself and observe what is happening to you as if some external agency were causing what you feel. Your subjective sensations will give you feedback you can learn to rely on to confirm that the changes you seek are occurring.

It may help to visualize your body's internal changes — to see as well as sense the blood flowing into your hand as you tell it to warm up, to picture your hand (or whole body) pressing down from the growing heaviness.

The trick is to achieve passivity, to attain the low-level trance that the AT phrases and tranquil self-observation can bring. In that state of reduced concentration your mind stops racing, your internal systems stop functioning at peak levels needed when you are fully conscious and facing the world's demands, and your body is released from tension and refreshed. It grows warmer because of modified circulation and feels heavier because the muscles are no longer straining unnecessarily.

Some precautions with AT must be taken if you have hypochondriacal tendencies. Because AT involves focusing on the body's sensations — something hypochondriacs do too much of already — practicing the technique may make one feel worse, not better. If you are such a person, you may notice all sorts of new pains and discomforts that you had missed in more fully conscious, pre-AT days. Discontinue your practice of the method if such results appear and persist for several days.

If you wish to employ AT for migraine or tension headaches, be on the safe side and consult your physician first. Headaches can signal the presence of physiological disorders requiring treatment by a doctor.

Finally, if you are planning to use AT as your main relaxation technique to support your efforts with other methods like Desensitization, first be sure to take several weeks to practice AT sufficiently to get quick and noticeable relaxation.

Sources of further information:
Luthe, W. *Autogenic Therapy, Research and Theory*. New York: Grune and Stratton, 1970.

Rosa, Karl R. *You and AT: Autogenic Training — The Revolutionary Way to Relaxation and Inner Peace*. New York: Saturday Review Press/E. P. Dutton, 1976.

Schultz, J. H., and Luthe, W. *Autogenic Therapy, Autogenic Methods*, Vol. 1. *Autogenic Therapy, Application in Psychotherapy*, Vol. 3. New York: Grune and Stratton, 1969.

TECHNIQUE

Autosuggestion

See:
Self-Hypnosis

Behavior Rehearsal

Particularly useful in dealing with such problems as Disagreeable Tasks and Encounters, Shyness and Inhibitions, Standing Up for Your Rights, and Conflict Avoidance.

May also reduce Anxiety associated with various coping problems and assist you in overcoming Fear of Failure, Procrastination, and Fear of Expressing Anger.

Supplementary or alternative techniques: Desensitization, Modeling, and Assertiveness Training.

WHAT BEHAVIOR REHEARSAL IS

This is a technique for increasing your ability to handle problems by practicing — ahead of time, in a controlled situation, and in detail — what you would like to say and do under pressure of an actual encounter. Practice teaches you to order your thoughts and master your emotions to a degree usually unattainable in the face of the stress and the spontaneous rapid movement of events in real life. Behavior Rehearsal is a dress rehearsal to help you learn your lines and plan your actions. You know ahead of time how you want to cope with the people and situations that have inhibited or manipulated you in the past. By retraining your emotional reflexes you gain confidence and the ability to handle problem situations effectively and with composure.

HISTORICAL DEVELOPMENT

The origins of Behavior Rehearsal lie in the work of Jacob L. Moreno, founder of psychodrama. Beginning with his "Theater of Spontaneity" in Vienna in the early 1920s, Moreno worked out a therapy he hoped would increase the effectiveness of psychoanalytical treatment. Within a formal stage setting, patients were the central figures in dramas and trained assistants — serving as "auxiliary egos" — played the parts of significant persons in the patients' lives.

These dramatized episodes provided both patients and therapist with greater insight into the causes of problems. Pent-up emotions were released in the highly structured, safe environment of the controlled stage setting as troublesome attitudes and patterns of behavior were identified. Moreno and his followers found psychodrama a tension-reducing technique: Patients learned to respond more openly to their own feelings and to those of others.

Joseph Wolpe and other behaviorists drew upon Moreno's work to develop Behavior Rehearsal. Unlike Moreno's method, all the stage trappings, assistants, and the many formal techniques of self-dramatization were not called for in Wolpe's approach. The therapist and patient were the only actors and the therapist's office the only stage. The main elements preserved were role-playing and the central notion of rehearsal.

By rehearsing stressful encounters, with patients playing themselves and the therapist taking the roles of various individuals who make patients anxious, the patients can practice more proper, more relaxed responses. Starting with relatively unstressful situations and working up to the most distressing ones, patients can learn what it is about their behavior that is causing them trouble. The therapist may offer advice about what to say, how to say it, how to stand, how to move, when to raise certain issues, when to remain silent.

Therapists sometimes play the part of the patient. This role-reversal permits patients to see their strengths and weaknesses from the perspective of other people. It enables them to get outside themselves, in effect to talk to themselves, and be far more objective about what elements of their behavior need modification. And by using modeling techniques, therapists can provide examples of effective means for confronting situations patients find distressing. Therapists can point to the successful behavior of others or act out how they would handle target problems. Both role-reversal and modeling give patients greater confidence and provide material on which to draw in rehearsing for actual encounters.

Behavior modification therapists have been using rehearsal for many years, helping wives and husbands who cannot communicate without bickering, workers who cannot deal effectively with their bosses or colleagues, individuals who are too shy to make rewarding social and professional contacts. Persons from all walks of life and with all sorts of problems have been helped.

Wolpe himself treated a woman who could not bring herself to ask anyone for any sort of favor because she was so fearful that she might inconvenience them and thus earn their displeasure. During therapy Wolpe played the role of a colleague who lived near her and had the patient rehearse asking him for a ride home from the office. Starting with a request that he go only one block out of his way, the patient worked her way up to greater distances and greater inconvenience. At the start, merely contemplating the request to take the colleague just one block out of his way caused the patient great anxiety. But after only two sessions, in which the scene was rehearsed several times, the woman could ask Wolpe (acting as the colleague) for the ride with no anxiety at all. Other sessions helped her get rid of any tension associated with requests involving greater inconvenience.

This case demonstrates how Behavior Rehearsal can reduce anxiety and enhance a person's ability to act with freedom and assurance. And the case shows that most of the benefits of role-playing and rehearsal can be obtained before a person has to face a stressful real-life situation. Of course, it is in actual encounters that the effectiveness of rehearsal is tested, but by the time of the test most persons who have used the technique are able to deal comfortably with situations that formerly plagued them.

The psychological principle at work comes from learning theory, which holds that all behavior, even unproductive behavior that brings unhappiness and distress, is learned. Behavior Rehearsal makes it possible to modify behavior, to recondition responses — to learn — in ways that will make future encounters more fulfilling because they are less anxiety-provoking and under greater control.

The rehearsal method outlined in this article is not as formal as either classic psychodrama or Wolpe's behavioral therapy. It does not call for a therapist's involvement. You can use the technique without outside assistance. But, of course, if it is convenient and proves to intensify the technique's effects, feel free to call upon a friend or relative to assist in the process by playing roles and rehearsing with you.

BASIC ELEMENTS OF BEHAVIOR REHEARSAL

Recording your behavior prior to employing the technique (see Introduction)

Identifying the problem (see Introduction)

Creating a scenario (with increasingly difficult variations)

Performing the scenario (with or without the aid of another person)

Measuring your response

Testing yourself in the real world

Recording your behavior to verify that changes have taken place (see Introduction)

Repeating the technique with other problems

HOW TO USE BEHAVIOR REHEARSAL

Record your behavior prior to employing the technique. Following the instructions on Monitoring Yourself and Measuring Behavior in the Introduction, carefully note the circumstances surrounding the situations that cause you difficulties.

Identify the problem. From prior knowledge and from your record keeping you should be able to narrow down the factors at work until you can isolate specific targets for attention. Pinpoint recurrent patterns involving those situations, individuals, or actions that most often create problems. (You may find it necessary to progress to your target problem by first creating scenarios about less threatening encounters.)

Create a scenario. Write down or dramatize in your own mind what will take place when you attempt to master a situation, handle a task, or face a person you consider a cause of your problem. It is best to prepare a written scenario that will force your concentration and make the scene as concrete as possible short of the real event. Write down details about the physical environment in which the scene will be played out. From your previous experience and intimate knowledge of the problem write down the arrangement of the furniture, the color of the walls, even the smell of the place. Set the time of the encounter, what you will be wearing, anything that will capture the mood you expect. Every detail counts, as it may contribute to your defining and solving the problem.

List the cast of characters. In many cases only one other person will be involved.

Write out the dialogue. Put down the actual words that you believe will be said by you and the other person. Pay particular attention to saying or doing those things that are causing the anxiety in the first place.

Create some variations on the basic scenario, some involving less pressure and difficulty, some far more. Rank them in a hierarchy so that you can go back to an easier version if you find you cannot overcome the anxiety generated in your basic version. Then work your way up by stages to the toughest possible variation.

Perform the scenario. This is where you get into the part you will play in real life before you actually take it upon yourself to handle the rigors of the real encounter. Duplicate as nearly as possible what you will do and say in order to simulate what you will feel — at a time when you can control those feelings. If you expect to feel angry, express anger: Yell, curse, run your heart rate up. In performing the scenario you are doing more than merely reviewing past experiences or thinking about what may happen. You must discharge emotions that have remained within you and contributed to keeping you from fully expressing yourself in the past.

You must be prepared in your performance of the scenario to take both your role and that of the other person and to speak naturally and spontaneously, drawing upon your knowledge of yourself, that person, and your relationship. Speak aloud. Act, gesture, and react as you believe you would if the real scene were being enacted.

Move the play in directions more to your liking rather than going along with what events or other people initiate. You must practice — perform, rehearse — the scenario repeatedly until you have it down pat and have determined that the technique is working.

Remember that it is your choice whether or not to work alone, taking both parts, or with a helpful friend to play a part and offer suggestions. Your success working alone at first may indicate that you can handle the entire enterprise on your own. Using a tape recorder to capture and play back your practice sessions may be the best way for you to see what you are doing right and wrong.

In any event, be sure your practice performances include periods during which you reverse roles, speaking the words you think the other person will say (or having your friend play you so that you can hear and respond to words you might say) and seeing yourself from the other side.

Be sure to perform the scenario over and over again until you no longer dread facing the scene in real life. This could take one or two weeks or longer.

Measure your response. You have rehearsed enough when you no longer feel anxious or unhappy either about the target encounter or about any of its possible outcomes. Examine your feelings when considering your problem. Do you experience anxiety at the prospect of a real-life test? You will know you have responded favorably to Behavior Rehearsal when, after several sessions of a half hour or so, extending anywhere from a few days to two or more weeks, the problem doesn't really seem so great after all. This means you're ready for a dress rehearsal.

Test yourself in the real world. If it is practical to do so, go to the actual place of the encounter and try out your performance, alone or with your role-playing friend. Run through the scenario a few times. You should then be able to take on the real person or situation at your convenience.

Upon facing the thing or person you once dreaded, you'll be overwhelmingly surprised to find that you are calm, self-possessed, and quite unlike what you were before. You have retrained your emotional reflexes to serve you, not undo you.

Record your behavior to verify that changes have taken place. Before going back to your records of your behavior before using the technique, keep another week or two of notations on the behavior you have been dealing with. Pay careful attention to anxiety levels, ability to function without undue hesitation, guilt, and fear.

Compare these notations with your earlier ones. The technique has been successful in the specific area you attacked if you are functioning better and feeling more pleased with yourself. If you see no real sign of change, give it another chance, using a less-demanding scenario and then working your way up to the more complete problem that is resisting your efforts at change. If you still have no indications of improvement, employ a more sweeping self-modification program using Desensitization, Assertiveness Training, and some of the other techniques cross-referenced in the articles dealing with your problems.

Repeat the technique with other problems. If Behavior Rehearsal works on one problem, say, coping with people who invade your privacy, try it with related problems such as ending a relationship, overcoming your inhibitions with your boss, or learning to approach work without procrastinating. You should soon have a long list of tasks, people, and situations you have learned to handle better. Your skill with the technique should increase with use. And the length of time it takes you to record behavior, isolate problems, create scenarios, and perform them will be reduced to a matter of days. As you build your behavior record you will become so aware of what problems still require attention that you will be creating and performing scenarios almost immediately on discovering a problem.

PRECAUTIONS

Do not be put off by the idea of talking to yourself. In this instance, talking to yourself, far from being a sign of mental illness, is a demonstration of enhanced self-control. You decide what is to be said, and you speak the lines in a controlled manner, rehearsing and changing them until you are satisfied you have them right. Yet if you are uncomfortable with the prospect of self-dialogue, find a friend to rehearse with, making sure you take turns playing each role.

There is some possibility that Behavior Rehearsal will undermine your motivation: By planning and performing your scenario you could settle for going only so far and fail to take the process to the final step of the actual encounter. But because the practice of the scenario can make you less anxious — and anxiety is usually at the heart of your problem — the problem is largely solved at that point. So you should have few reservations about going on to actually face the person, task, or situation you've dreaded.

These are minor problems. In general, Behavior Rehearsal is a viable technique for gaining greater control over your life. You learn to experience and adjust to events before they happen. You learn how to react to stressful situations ahead of time, to master emotions that otherwise might overwhelm you in the heat of real-life encounters. Ultimately, you learn to alter your responses to the people, things, and events in your life.

Sources of further information:
Kelly, G. A. *The Psychology of Personal Constructs.* New York: Norton, 1955.

Lazarus, A. A. "Behaviour rehearsal vs. non-directive therapy vs. advice in effecting behaviour change." *Behaviour Research and Therapy*, 1966, *4*, 209-212.

Moreno, J. L. *Psychodrama*. Vol. 1. New York: Beacon, 1946.

Wolpe, J., and Lazarus, A. A. *Behavior Therapy Techniques: A Guide to the Treatment of Neuroses*. New York: Pergamon, 1966.

TECHNIQUE

Biofeedback

Particularly useful in dealing with both general Anxiety and that which is associated with specific tasks or situations.

May also help in handling Tension Headaches, Insomnia, Psychosomatic Complaints and Pains, Lack of Concentration. Could contribute to improved work and study habits and an increased sense of well-being and greater self-awareness.

Supplementary or alternative techniques: Autogenic Training, Meditation, The Relaxation Response, Relaxation.

WHAT BIOFEEDBACK IS

Biofeedback involves measuring and regulating the ways in which our bodies are functioning. We use the process every day, automatically. Our senses allow us to compensate our movements and posture to stay erect while walking or running. Feedback from our muscles can tell us the difference between the force needed to stroke a loved one's cheek and the power required to open a jar lid. There is nothing new or strange about Biofeedback.

Biofeedback has a role in self-psyching because it permits the voluntary control of this automatic process. It enables an individual to monitor and influence the internal forces and natural responses to external events that can produce anxiety and tension.

HISTORICAL DEVELOPMENT

The emergence of scientific Biofeedback is a phenomenon of the last two decades. It is associated less with the automatic processes touched on above than with deliberate efforts to regulate involuntary bodily functions like heartbeat. For centuries Western society believed one could not consciously influence one's own heartbeat, brain waves, blood pressure, and the like. When Yogis demonstrated such abilities fraud was usually suspected. Scientific research has recently provided evidence of the validity of what the Eastern holy men had been doing all along without machines or scientific verification (see Meditation). We now know that regulation of supposedly autonomic functions is indeed possible. The Yogis have done it by long training of their senses and their awareness; Westerners use machines that tell them what is going on inside their own bodies.

The most important breakthrough in biofeedback research came with studies using an EEG (an electroencephalograph), which measures brain wave activity. It was discovered that the person being monitored could learn to modify brain wave patterns by concentrating on altering the tone or TV screen image that indicated what his brain wave activity was. The control of brain waves is central to Biofeedback because of the intimate connection between our moods and emotions and the form of brain waves we generate at any given moment.

For example, the generation of brain waves known as alpha waves is said to be conducive to physical and mental well-being. When human brain wave activity registers between 8 and 13 cycles per second on an EEG, the person is said to be in the alpha state. This condition is of interest in self-psyching because when a person is generating alpha waves — rather than one of the slower or faster wave patterns — important psychological and physiological benefits may be realized. And if voluntary control of this otherwise naturally occurring state can be achieved, a valuable self-regulation tool is at hand.

Researchers have convincing evidence that the alpha state of relaxed, tranquil, passive consciousness can improve concentration and increase a wide range of mental and physical capacities. Psychosomatic illnesses may go into remission, learning powers and creativity may increase, memory capacity and sharpness may be augmented. But, most important for self-psyching, alpha wave generation increases general well-being and resistance to anxiety.

Accomplished meditators seem to readily generate alpha waves (as well as the slower theta waves — 4 to 7 cycles per second — that reflect a deeper state of restfulness conducive to euphoria, daydreaming, or even going into a trance).

Thus, the ability to regulate the brain waves one produces represents the power to modify one's feelings and moods.

Joseph Kamiya, Barbara Brown, Neal Miller, Joseph Hart, Thomas Mulholland, and a few others are pioneers in modern Biofeedback research and training. Their work made it possible for others to begin using the process in therapy, self-discovery programs, and even quasi-religions.

Brain wave devices were soon supplemented in early research by related machinery for measuring heart action (EKG), muscle tension (EMG), the activity of the digestive system, and other bodily processes. Some success was registered with each of these devices.

The most enthusiastic proponents tell you there are few limits on the potential applications of the process. They cite its value in producing deep rest and relaxation (through the generation of alpha waves or by pinpointing tense muscles that can then be relaxed), in lessening the chances of heart trouble and numerous other ailments, in increasing self-awareness and expanding consciousness. Some enthusiasts speak of improvements in sexual responses and even Biofeedback as birth control (through awareness of hormonal balances). Although some of these claims have been challenged, there is no doubt that anxiety can be reduced or prevented, general levels of vigor elevated, learning and work capacities augmented. And the control initially learned with Biofeedback machines has been found to eventually become reflexive, operating automatically even without the use of the device.

Medical applications of Biofeedback include prevention and treatment of severe headaches, tics, insomnia, and diarrhea.

Biofeedback is unquestionably a valuable adjunct to existing physical and psychological therapies. But is it for you? The answer depends on what you want it to do for you. If all you want is the instant high of alpha wave generation, tripping out with a Biofeedback machine is an expensive and complicated approach. The method will serve you better if you approach it as a means for gaining greater control over your mind and body so that you can feel better and live better.

BASIC ELEMENTS OF BIOFEEDBACK

Identifying the problem and setting goals (see Introduction)
Obtaining a machine
Scheduling your sessions
Using Biofeedback and measuring your progress

HOW TO USE BIOFEEDBACK

Identify the problem and set goals. As part of the self-psyching technique, focus your efforts on specific, limited problems. With this in mind, you may choose to attack anxiety associated with particular situations. Similarly, you can handle sharply defined problems — insomnia, tension headaches, nervousness, inability to concentrate, and poor work or study habits — one at a time and measure your progress.

There is also a more general use for Biofeedback. You may find that with the regular generation of alpha waves you will obtain the benefits of deep relaxation, making it easier for you to progress with other self-psyching programs. So the use of this technique might be considered an adjunct to your efforts in other areas. But first you must try Biofeedback on specific problems to gain skill and to see measurable results.

Obtain a machine. The most commonly used and most readily available Biofeedback devices are those that detect brain waves — particularly alpha waves. Such a device is the one you are most likely to obtain and use for most self-psyching problems, though EMG devices work best on headaches caused by tight facial muscles. The quality and dependability of your machine will influence the degree of success you can expect with this method, so you must take great care in its selection as well as in its use.

Not all Biofeedback machines are equally effective or trustworthy. You can spend hundreds of dollars on an alpha wave device that is as likely to register the pulses of your fluorescent lighting as the actions of your brain. Before buying a machine seek the advice of experts working in the field — psychologists or psychiatrists in your community. An improperly functioning machine, especially combined with careless or unskillful operation, poses some real threats: You could find you have trained yourself to generate dangerous or debilitating brain waves rather than the right amount of anxiety-reducing and awareness-expanding alphas. Again, the guidance of experts is called for if you are to get the right machine, one you know will work. And be sure your machine has clear instructions for correct use.

A muscle tension feedback machine (EMG) may be of value to sufferers of tension headaches, teeth gnashers, seriously tense individuals who have a hard time relaxing any other way. Before laying out the money for such a device, however, consult a physician to rule out any underlying organic problems.

You don't have to buy a machine to test your basic ability with Biofeedback. Autogenic Training (see article), which exploits the process without mechanical devices and may be learned easily by most people, is a suggested first step for anyone contemplating the purchase and regular use of a feedback device.

If you do buy a machine, treat it with respect. Whatever you do, don't turn it into a party game to amuse your friends.

Schedule your sessions. The use of a Biofeedback machine should be regulated by time limits set either by the machine's manufacturers or, more importantly, by the nature and response of the problem on which you use the machine. You would do well to limit Biofeedback sessions to about thirty minutes a couple of times a day, if your goal is merely the alleviation of stress and anxiety. Several such sessions should give you the ability to control the feedback signals and begin noticing improvement in the way you feel, and eventually you shouldn't need the machine — even in stressful situations.

If you have a particular target problem like anxiety provoked by specific encounters or tasks, your practice should be engaged in as close as is conveniently possible to the time you face the usually stressful situation. For instance, if you have to give a speech, you should try to find time to use Biofeedback shortly before facing your audience. Likewise, it may prove useful to use your feedback device as soon as possible after an anxiety-provoking encounter, thereby reversing your body's fight-or-flight response toward greater relaxation and calm balance.

Use Biofeedback and measure your progress. Because Biofeedback's main purpose is anxiety reduction, its efficacy is best tested with some anxiety-producing task or situation in your life. For example, you may be one of the many people who are not merely annoyed and frustrated by managing the family budget but are made intensely anxious and pushed to the limits of your composure as you try to make ends meet. Because of the anxiety aroused by the task you probably procrastinate. Use of Biofeedback can relax you sufficiently so that you become more willing to balance the checkbook, sit down with the family to discuss expenditures, and work out a budget for the coming month. If you schedule your budgeting chores to regularly follow a Biofeedback session, the effectiveness of the technique should be reflected in the greater ease with which you tackle your family fiscal matters. You may find it was not your bank balance that bothered you, but having to go through the process of getting ready to prepare to face the task of discovering that balance. Biofeedback teaches you to recondition your anxiety reflexes so that you needn't suffer stress in the face of ordinary, though often distasteful, chores.

In evaluating your progress you can look for some definite signs that indicate whether or not Biofeedback is working for you.

1. Are you getting feedback? Is your machine registering alpha waves, decreased muscle tension, or whatever it is designed to measure?
2. Are you gaining the ability to control the feedback you get and to do so more easily and more quickly with passing time? With each session on your machine you should detect a greater degree of control over the feedback signals you are using. This control will, almost automatically, encourage you to strive for yet greater control.
3. Are you feeling better, experiencing less anxiety, having less difficulty with whatever problem you are working on?

When you discover you are less anxious, more in control — and especially when you find you are feeling the same level of control without the machine or any formal effort to achieve Biofeedback signals — you will know the technique has helped you train your mind and body to deal with the world more successfully.

PRECAUTIONS

What the proliferation of research and practice in Biofeedback means for most of us is that a method now exists for gaining an unprecedented degree of control over mind and body. The method is full of promise — and not a little menace.

The technical imperfections of some machines pose serious threats. For example, if you use a machine that picks up environmental signals or misreads your own signals, you could train yourself to produce brain waves other than the alphas you desire. This would not only mean that the machine wasn't working for you — it would be working against you! And the commercial exploitation of Biofeedback makes it difficult to separate the legitimate, trustworthy mechanisms being marketed from those that are little more than the offerings of con artists. Your defense is either the advice of professionals in the medical or academic community or initial involvement with Biofeedback through supervised programs specifically designed for beginners.

Sources of further information:

Beatty, Jackson, and Legewie, Heiner, Eds. *Biofeedback and Behavior*. New York: Plenum Press, 1977.

Brown, Barbara. *New Mind, New Body*. New York: Bantam, 1975.

Brown, Barbara. *Stress and the Art of Biofeedback*. New York: Harper & Row, 1976.

Jonas, Gerald. *Visceral Learning: Towards a Science of Self-Control*. New York: Pocket Books, 1974.

Karlins, Marvin, and Andrews, Lewis M. *Biofeedback—Turning on the Power of Your Mind*. Philadelphia: J. B. Lippincott, 1972.

TECHNIQUE

Biorhythms

Particularly useful in identifying the best and worst times for attempting to handle Disagreeable Tasks and Encounters, Distressing Situations.

Can help you become less vulnerable to Minor Emotional Complaints, Fatigue and Lethargy, Procrastination, low-grade Depression.

Supplementary or alternative technique: Desensitization.

WHAT BIORHYTHMS ARE

How many times have you said, "This just isn't my day" or, "I'm having one of those days"? Most of us make such statements quite often, perhaps even regularly. Some days nothing seems to go right: Tasks are not completed, wallets are left at home, appointments are forgotten — discomfort and irritability spiral upward as one's already wretched feelings worsen or the mishaps and missteps of the passing hours accumulate.

Biorhythm theory recognizes that such days do exist. They are not the imaginary constructions of individuals who try to explain away their problems by blaming some cosmic calendar. Bad and good days are influenced by biological cycles that begin at birth, and it is possible to chart in advance good and bad days for intellectual, physical, and emotional activities.

Biorhythm is scientific and, though a young science, the body of evidence supporting its theory is growing.

HISTORICAL DEVELOPMENT

The idea that human life is affected or even regulated by cycles, patterns, or rhythms is ancient. The Bible speaks of "a time to every purpose." Renaissance writers were fascinated with the notion that there was "a tide in the affairs of men," that some individuals were in phase with their times and so would prosper whereas others had been born at the wrong time and, despite their otherwise admirable qualities, were doomed to failure and disappointment. But only the development of empirical, quantitative science could provide any sort of hard evidence for the theory that internal clocks and calendars are at work within each of us.

Not until the early decades of this century were the specific factors underlying Biorhythm theory identified and measured. Medical and public health researchers studying recurrent illnesses found that it wasn't so much that certain ailments came and went with measurable frequency but rather that the victims seemed to have periods of greater or lesser resistance and recuperative powers. Related studies identified a cyclical pattern in people's ability to concentrate, reason, and learn. Out of this early work came current Biorhythm theory.

Organizations all over the world have begun to take the existence of human cycles into account when dealing with many serious matters touching people's work, health, and welfare. Hospitals in Europe, Japan, and the United States have begun to schedule surgery and therapy programs to take advantage of people's most suitable physical, emotional, and intellectual conditions as indicated by their Biorhythm charts. Public employees in Japan are given days off or different tasks if their charts indicate they are prone to accidents or errors on certain target days. The results have been the marked reduction of accidents in public transport, and of errors in such jobs as keypunching, indicating that some people on certain days should not be doing their regular jobs or should do them only with full awareness that errors and accidents are likely.

Biorhythm theory does not contend that people are *controlled* by their cycles. These fixed internal cycles should not be thought of as your destiny but as your condition on a given day. Individual personality; your health; environmental influences; the actions of others; apathy and ambition; and many additional factors can modify, negate, or intensify the impact of any biorhythmically determined period. Yet these cycles do seem to have an influence on our lives and are worth knowing about — for self-knowledge and increased self-control.

BASIC ELEMENTS OF BIORHYTHMS

Knowing your cycles
Charting your cycles
Making your cycles work for you

HOW TO USE BIORHYTHMS

Know your cycles. There are three Biorhythm cycles: the physical, which is twenty-three days long; the emotional, psychological, or sensitivity rhythm, twenty-eight days long; and the intellectual or mental cycle of thirty-three days. It is necessary to know the nature of each cycle, the interrelations of the three cycles, and in which portion of each cycle any given day falls. All this is possible, even easy, to compute.

Each cycle is supposed to have begun on the day you were born and each has repeated itself continually since. Because the cycles are different lengths, it is obvious that after the first twenty-three days of your life the three started getting out of phase with one another so that your physical, emotional, and mental highs and lows were unlikely to match very often. But because each cycle follows an invariable pattern of its own and because you can chart the flow of each from your birth to any subsequent date, you can find out where the highs, lows, and crossing points are for today, your wedding day, next Thursday. Thus you are able to prepare yourself for the possible difficulties or benefits you may encounter.

Each Biorhythm cycle has a start, a high period, a midpoint at the same level as the start, and a low period. It takes half the full cycle (11½ days for the physical cycle, 14 days for the emotional, and 16½ days for the mental) to move gradually up and then down through a high period to the cycle's midpoint. During the high periods of the respective cycles, you are able to lay out abundant stores of vigor, have an increased capacity to cope with your emotions, and can think and plan with greater assurance. From the midpoint to the start of the next cycle, the movement is steadily down and then back up and takes half a full cycle. This is a low period characterized by recovery and recuperation. This is when you bank your fires and recharge your physical, emotional, and intellectual batteries for the expenditures to be made during the next high period.

Your goal, of course, is to make the most of your highs and try not to tax yourself when you are in your lows. But the process is complicated by the facts that one rhythm may be in high while another is in low and that the most important factor isn't the highs and lows but the switch points — the starting day of a cycle and the midpoint day. These so-called *critical days* are ones in which your system is changing over from high to low or low to high. On such days you may be in a sort of limbo and trying to behave normally, to function adequately, can be difficult. The critical switch point days are the ones that give us so much trouble.

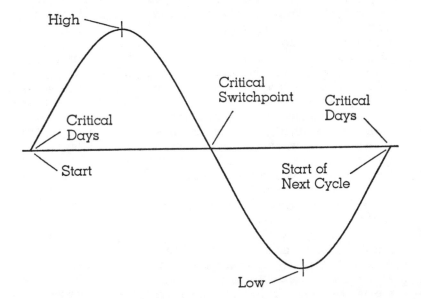

The Biorhythm Cycle

Chart your cycles. There are several ways to proceed. The simplest is to send your birth date to a service that will use a computer to prepare your chart. This usually costs in the area of fifteen dollars. (The names of such services are available in the books mentioned at the end of this article, in the classified ads in the back of popular magazines, and perhaps in your phone directory.)

Almost as easy as having someone else prepare your chart is using a pocket calculator designed to handle biorhythm calculations. Now available wherever calculators are sold and costing around thirty dollars, such a calculator can also be used for ordinary computation purposes.

The best way to chart your cycles — one you can put to use immediately without spending a dime or sending away for anything — involves paper, pencil, and simple arithmetic. Try it now!

Start with your birth date. Figure the number of days from then to your last birthday — 365 days per year, plus one day for each leap year that has passed since your birth — and add the number of days from your birthday to today. The total, say, 13,529, is now divided by 23, 28, and 33. The results will be the number of each of the cycles you have passed through since birth, with some days left over. Those left-over days are the key, because they tell you what day of each of your current cycles you are in.

If your computations tell you that you are in the sixth day of your current physical cycle, the fourteenth day of your emotional cycle, and the twenty-seventh day of your mental cycle, you can figure what sort of day you should be prepared for. Day six of your physical cycle means you are in a high, charged period permitting you to expend full energies. But the fourteenth day of your emotional cycle is the switch point between high and low. So the day may find you very moody, prone to errors, especially in judgment, likely to grate on others and feel them grate on you. Finally, the twenty-seventh day of your intellectual cycle places you in a mental low and you may find it hard to stick with mentally demanding tasks. Your creativity and spark may be dim for a few more days until you move into a new period of heightened intellectual activity and potential at the start of the next thirty-three day cycle.

Having learned to chart your cycles, you need not do all the computations for each day that interests you. You can sit down with a calendar and, in one session, mark — in three colors of ink or pencil — the important points of each cycle: the two critical days at the start and midpoint of each cycle; the high point of each cycle, which is halfway between the start and the midpoint; the low point, which is halfway between the midpoint and the start of the next cycle.

In addition to having a calendar, you may want to chart your cycles graphically, beginning with the starting point of each of your current cycles. Using graph paper with one square for each day of the month — for as many months as you wish to cover — draw a curving line upward from the starting day of each cycle to the middle of the high period, then down to the switch point at the same level as the start day. Then continue the line in a curve down to the middle of the low period, then up again to the start of the next cycle. The line for each cycle should look like two half-circles: The left one will go up and down and, where it ends, the right will go down and up, with the flat base of each being a center line running straight from start day, through midpoint critical day, to next start day. Graph each cycle in a different color. The graph will show in an instant the interactions of the three cycles, and when you fill in dates for each day, you will know your biorhythmic condition for any date you have charted. (See the diagram of a Biorhythm cycle above.)

Make your cycles work for you. Using your calendar or your graph with all three cycles, you can prepare yourself for impending critical days as well as ready yourself to exploit high points.

Say you see that you will have an especially tricky day two weeks from now, a day your chart tells you will be at a double switch point with, perhaps, your physical cycle crossing from high to low and your emotional rhythm moving from low to high. You are not likely to be at your best on this day; you might be emotionally vulnerable and prone to physical clumsiness and lack of stamina. Plan your schedule accordingly, avoiding major activities involving interpersonal relations or physically demanding tasks. For example, don't plan a big party for that night or an important meeting for that day.

Of course, if you find that such a bad day will coincide with plans already made, use your knowledge to prepare for what you may be up against. You can try to take things very slowly, not put yourself out on a limb physically or emotionally. For example, if you have to make a speech on such a critical day, prepare and practice your talk way in advance, get plenty of sleep, and try to undertake the task relaxed and ready for whatever happens — mistakes, criticism, or success.

Similarly, you can regulate your approach to impending good days such as those experienced when your chart shows a combined intellectual and physical high. With your powers peaking, you can take on additional responsibilities, tackle otherwise difficult or distasteful tasks, and know your energy reserves should be adequate. But even here you must be cautious not to exhaust yourself in the sheer exuberance of exploiting such highs. Knowing such peaks are approaching can also warn you to avoid running over other people's feelings by asking too much of those who may not be as "up" as you are.

Learn to identify your best and worst days — partly from using your chart and partly from monitoring your own feelings and behavior on the days your chart indicates are special — and try to make regular use of that knowledge. For instance, try to set deadlines for projects to coincide with your peak periods and try to avoid having to begin projects during emotionally low cycles. Similarly, when your emotional switch point is reached, your vulnerability to minor emotional complaints and low-grade depression will make it foolhardy to press a romance, hit the boss for a raise, or hazard public speaking.

Your success using Biorhythms depends on your willingness to learn what the chart of your cycles means in the light of your experience. Judge the technique by what Biorhythms contribute to your own life.

PRECAUTIONS

The only way to test Biorhythm theory to your complete satisfaction is to try it on yourself. You are your own laboratory and you need not take the word of others — even experts — when your own experience can quickly confirm or invalidate the theory. If your cycles have no bearing or impact on your feelings, energy levels, accident proneness, creativity, and so on, your personality and personal situation may compensate for the cycles' effects. Many people, most notably athletes in the heat of important competition, have been found to perform beautifully despite biorhythmic warning signs.

In testing Biorhythms, be sure to chart your cycles correctly, identify the most critical days, monitor your behavior and feelings on those days to see if the theory holds, and see if your efforts to compensate for impending good or bad days has the desired effect.

Biorhythms are not the only biological clocks ticking away within each of us. Don't forget that daily cycles also affect our lives. If you are a night person you know it; if you are a morning person quick to face the day while your mate is slow to get out of bed, you also know how important diurnal cycles can be in personal relationships. But don't let the characteristics of these daily cycles confuse you while charting and monitoring your monthly cycles. Look for the long-term, averaged-out conditions, not the way you feel at the lowest or highest point of each day.

Don't let Biorhythms psyche you out. Just because you find that a bad day will coincide with an unavoidable task or commitment, don't give up on your chances of success. Being forewarned gives you the chance to prepare and compensate for not being naturally at your best. Biorhythms don't control; they *suggest*. They don't *make* you do anything; they don't predetermine. They indicate possibilities and potentials. Your willful action, taking your cycles into account, is usually what determines the course of your life.

The knowledge of when your down days or critical switch points are should make your depressions less deep, your blues not so blue. You should begin to approach unpleasant tasks and situations with more confidence (and if you don't see signs of improvement in this area, supplement or replace your reliance on Biorhythms with Desensitization). You may begin to see that the apparently violent shifts of attitude among your friends may be because of nothing more than their internal cycles and not because of anything you may have said or done. Friendships, even marriages, can be strengthened through use of Biorhythm data.

Who is to deny that cycles play a role in human life? After all, every adult female has to accommodate herself to hormonal cycles that affect her physical and emotional state. Biorhythms too may be a human heritage. If so, it would be wise to take an interest in them and make the most of what they teach.

Sources of further information:
Luce, Gay Gaer. *Body Time: Physiological Rhythms and Social Stress.* New York: Bantam Books, 1971.

O'Neil, Barbara. *Biorhythms – How To Live With Your Life Cycles*. Pasadena, Calif.: Ward Ritchie Press, 1975.
Thommen, George S. *Is This Your Day?* Rev. ed. New York: Crown, 1973.

PROBLEM

The Blues and The Blahs

See:
Minor Emotional Complaints

PROBLEM

Boredom

Few of us are immune to the dull ache of boredom. Repetitious tasks can be boring; inescapably dull and uninteresting activities are boring; unavoidable humdrum business and social obligations with uninteresting people are boring. Much of life is monotonous and therefore boring. The lack of excitement and variety in our lives can become acutely painful, as when sitting at our desks at 2 P.M. we contemplate the prospect of three more hours with nothing really interesting to divert us. The result is weariness, listlessness, and a lack of mental and physical stimulation that make our lives seem dreary and distasteful. Untreated, boredom can develop into serious lethargy, palpable fatigue, and even depression. Life is too short to put up with something as avoidable as boredom.

Assertiveness Training can help you handle boring people by escaping them or getting them to leave you alone. The creative use of Fantasy can help you counter your boredom with thoughts as fascinating as your powers of imagination permit. And Incompatible Behavior and Exercise can provide novel stimulation to break response patterns that produce boredom. Try these techniques the next time you are cornered by a bore, caught in traffic or on a long line at the supermarket, or just find yourself with nothing to occupy your mind.

See also:
Fatigue and Lethargy
Depression

Techniques to try:
Assertiveness Training
Fantasy
Incompatible Behavior
Exercise

PROBLEM

Breaking a Date

This can be a major problem for some people. Some of us magnify the potential consequences of breaking appointments. We are afraid of what others will think of us or do to us if we disappoint them. The problem is often rooted in an inability to say no to others. We take what seems to be the path of least resistance by accepting every date or appointment, even though our schedules are full or the date is not one we want to make. We may actually obligate ourselves when we have something else we'd rather be doing. Not wanting to hurt someone's feelings by turning them down in the first place, we accept a responsibility we may later be unable to meet. Then, trapped by the original commitment, we don't want to call off the promise that we shouldn't have made.

This vicious cycle can be broken by learning some simple techniques that show you how to put things in their proper perspective.

Assertiveness Training can help identify and respond to your real desires. It will give you the ability to break dates when necessary and keep you from making appointments you don't want to keep. And Behavior Rehearsal can enable you to prepare for turning down engagements or breaking those you shouldn't have made.

See also:
Disagreeable Tasks and Encounters
Fear of Disappointing Others
Indecisiveness

Techniques to try:
Assertiveness Training
Behavior Rehearsal

Changing the Sequence of Events

Especially useful in breaking undesirable habits and in establishing good habits.

May also play a role in dealing with Compulsiveness, Indecisiveness, Fears and Phobias, Shyness and Inhibitions, Marital Problems, Anxiety, and Disagreeable Tasks and Encounters.

Supplementary or alternative techniques: Rewards, Stimulus Control, Desensitization, Relaxation.

WHAT CHANGING THE SEQUENCE OF EVENTS IS

This method takes advantage of the fact that most human behavior is patterned, that actions are carried out sequentially, and that it is possible to modify behavior by disrupting the normal sequence.

HISTORICAL DEVELOPMENT

Scientific work on influencing the sequence of events has usually centered on encouraging the performance of one behavior by linking it to others. Called *chaining*, this approach permits therapists to reinforce one action, then another, in a series that leads to the regular performance of some target behavior. The accomplishment of one link in the chain becomes the stimulus for the performance of the next.

Throughout the 1960s, behaviorists refined this technique as part of their clinical work with institutionalized people who had speech disorders, with autistic and otherwise emotionally disturbed children, with those who had poor study habits, and with both normal children and psychotics in need of effective toilet training. Their approach was a variation of programmed instruction in which patients were taught to move from actions they could already perform to some degree to other, more difficult behaviors. The numerous successes therapists achieved even with profoundly handicapped individuals offer encouraging evidence of the utility of this method for people with average problems.

The chaining approach can be illustrated by some non-therapeutic situations. You can't perform any complicated task unless certain steps are completed in a certain order. You can't build a house roof first. You can't even write a letter until you have learned to read, purchased the paper and pencil, and set aside the needed time. And the entire educational system operates on the chaining approach. You must take one course as a prerequisite to another, studying algebra before calculus, elementary Latin before reading the Latin classics.

For self-psyching, this approach is turned inside out. We unlink the chain of actions that produce problem behavior to undermine that behavior.

BASIC ELEMENTS OF CHANGING THE SEQUENCE OF EVENTS

Identifying problems and setting goals (see Introduction)
Breaking the chain of events
Adding pauses to the sequence of events
Scrambling the order of actions
Observing factors promoting change

HOW TO USE CHANGING THE SEQUENCE OF EVENTS

Identify problems and set goals. Monitor your behavior for several days to a few weeks to determine exactly what steps are involved in a target behavior. Pinpoint the elements of a total behavior by watching and recording what actions you perform leading up to or as part of some habit or undesirable form of conduct. You may find, for instance, that your nail biting commonly follows encounters with certain people, that your inability to make decisions is related to a series of distracting actions, that anxiety is typically precipitated by having to face specific tasks or situations.

Write down as many of the elements in the chain of events as you can identify that lead to or form part of your problem. A typical behavior chain promoting indecisiveness, for instance, might include the following: You have a decision to make; instead of facing the problem and considering what to do first, you light up a cigarette (or get a cup of coffee or otherwise distract yourself); you call someone (or go to someone's office), ostensibly to discuss the issue that requires the decision, but you let yourself be drawn into conversation on entirely different matters; you make a decision — not the one you started with, but on a separate matter such as whether or not to go to lunch before tackling your problem; you go to lunch or go home, putting off the decision; when next you try facing the problem, you start all over with a chain of activities having little or nothing to do with decision making.

Having identified the components of your problem, set at least these two goals: Try the various means to disrupt the chain of events entangling you in the problem and decide which approaches work best for you.

Break the chain of events. Say your problem is poor work or study habits, the inability to get down to work or to stay with a task long enough to show solid results. Your analysis of the problem should have revealed the chain of distracting or disabling actions that led up to your poor performance. Break this chain. If you always find yourself sharpening pencils, making phone calls, paying bills, or merely musing instead of working, attack each link in the chain by consciously excluding it from your normal pattern of behavior. Never use the phone while working — unplug it if necessary. Stop sharpening pencils — use a mechanical pencil.

Do anything other than the activities that have been part of your behavioral chain. You might make lists of things you must do, review similar tasks you have handled, read something that will aid you in your work or studies. Even if such novel activities initially keep you from working, they can serve to break the chain and give you new freedom to alter your behavior for the better. It is preferable to pursue some behavior that is not part of your chain than to surrender to the fixed pattern of behavior that keeps you from accomplishing anything anyway. And these replacement activities, because they are new and under your conscious control, are unlikely to become distractions you can't overcome.

Add pauses to the sequence of events. Instead of actually breaking the chain of events, it may be enough just to add pauses to the typical sequence. This can be especially helpful if your problem involves anxiety that distracts you. If you become anxious before having to speak before a group, that anxiety probably grows through stages. It may begin the night before, as you contemplate the prospect, increase on the day of the event, as you prepare for your speech or report, and culminate in the period just before your performance. Don't let the growing anxiety increase unchecked. As soon as you feel anxiety coming on, pause. Employ each pause to use a Relaxation technique, think about something other than your problem, or do anything else that will alter the pattern of fearful concern that undermines your resolve and effectiveness.

A pause of several minutes after each stage can disrupt the chain and alter your customary behavior sufficiently to short-circuit anxiety. The pauses should be conscious efforts at occupying your mind with some nonanxiety-provoking thought. Relaxation or pleasurable memories can do the trick. Just thinking about something pleasant you have done, of a lovely spot you have visited, of a success you have achieved, or of a person you enjoy being with can fill these pauses with anxiety-resistant responses because relaxation and pleasurable distraction are incompatible with reflexive anxiety.

Practice using pauses over a long enough period of time and you can probably break a particular chain of events and feelings. But if you have an especially resistant problem such as major anxiety attacks, techniques like Desensitization may be called for. And even when dealing with less resistant problems, a Rewards Program and Stimulus Control are useful supplementary techniques.

Scramble the order of actions. Once you know what links constitute the chain of actions binding you into some pattern of behavior, it may be enough merely to rearrange the elements, to scramble the order of actions. Number the links and regularly practice performing action four before action one, for example. This approach may be unsettling at first, but it has proven effective with such problems as nervous habits and compulsiveness.

For example, if you compulsively check to see if you've locked your doors after bathing and getting ready to go to sleep, try taking a bath and preparing for bed only *after* you've made certain all locks are secure. Use the approach and see what happens.

Observe factors promoting change. It is seldom necessary to employ all the steps. As you practice this technique, see which elements work best for you. Make more concerted use of the most effective ones and abandon others. Give yourself a couple of weeks with the method, or at least enough time to discover which ways of breaking your behavioral chains produce positive results.

PRECAUTIONS

There is nothing in this technique that can harm you or seriously hinder your self-psyching progress. At worst, you may be uncomfortable with the disruptions in your normal functioning that the method requires. But you must be aware that although this approach does work for many people, it is not a potent, sure-fire treatment. Knowing its limitations, try it by itself or with other self-psyching methods and judge for yourself if it has a place in your behavior-change program.

Sources of further information:
Mahoney, M. J. *Self-Control: Power to the Person.* Monterey, Calif.: Brooks/Cole, 1974.
Ulrich, R.; Stachnik, T.; and Mabry, J., Eds. *Control of Human Behavior.* Glenview, Ill.: Scott Foresman, 1966.

PROBLEM

Chewing on Things

The habit of unconsciously putting things into your mouth is obviously a problem if the objects you chew on — pencils, pens, eyeglasses — may damage you in some way. Of course, you don't want to poison yourself or swallow something. But there are other typically more troublesome aspects of this habit: The act of chewing, or the evidence left on you or the things you chew, can cause you embarrassment and make you feel that you have insufficient self-control.

Covert Sensitization is a fairly drastic, yet highly effective, technique for breaking this habit, which is used as an example in the article on that method.

See also:
Nervous Habits

Technique to try:
Covert Sensitization

Compulsiveness

Compulsive people suffer from uncontrollable impulses to perform certain acts over and over again. Such people may feel threatened by both the outside world and their own emotions. As a defense against feelings of anxiety, guilt, or inadequacy, they develop stereotyped patterns of behavior that release tension and provide a measure of increased confidence and security. But the price is a rigid, over-organized life spent supporting their compulsions.

Severe compulsions, like the urge to steal (kleptomania), require long-term professional treatment. More common, less serious compulsions may sufficiently interfere with normal functioning that it is worth employing self-psyching to deal with them. For example, someone who always uses the same mailbox is not sick but may feel terribly uncomfortable when forced to trust correspondence to a "strange" mailbox. A minor compulsion, yes, but the person still feels compelled to use only that one mailbox or risk emotional discomfort. Before the problem gets worse and the person permits compulsiveness to take over, he or she should come to grips with the compulsion.

The first step is to identify your compulsions. You *can* live more openly and flexibly without them and need not feel anxious or insecure when these elements of your behavior are altered. In fact, you will alter them yourself.

You will know if you are a compulsive gambler, shopper, smoker, or eater and should be aware that the aid of an expert therapist may be called for. But lesser compulsions, those that may respond to self-psyching, have subtler symptoms. Do you repeat certain actions regularly and unreasonably — checking locked doors again and again though you know they are locked? Could many of the things you say and do each day be considered parts of a ritual rather than a routine, these parts having no real purpose or meaning except that they are fixed in your behavior? Is it very hard for you to throw things away; do you stock up on things you may not really be able to use?

Do you demand impossible consistency from yourself and others? Do you have an inordinate concern with punctuality, cleanliness, or orderliness? Have you an almost mystical faith in certain actions, like believing that you won't have a good day unless you catch your bus at precisely the same time or have a certain parking space every day? If you become anxious over minor changes in your schedule, over the cleanliness or orderliness of your home or office, you probably have a compulsiveness problem.

Most compulsions are not problems in themselves. They create problems because the compulsive person gets very upset when things don't go as planned. It hurts you to be compulsive because it bothers you when you or others cannot live up to the standards your compulsions set. But you can never achieve such perfection because you and others aren't perfect and because compulsions are repetitive patterns linked to recurring behavior. Houses always get dirty; you must go off to work each day; and for compulsive people these recurrences reinforce and justify their compulsions.It is a vicious circle you would do well to break.

Because many compulsions are largely defenses against anxiety, Desensitization can be an effective means for ridding yourself of compulsions. Convert Sensitization has been of self-psyching utility because by facing, in your imagination, the worst possibilities that could arise from giving up your compulsions you can see that the results are not catastrophic. Thought-Stopping, highly effective for obsessions and used by professionals to treat compulsive-neurotics, is worth considering.

You may want to try Flooding, but do so with the understanding that this fairly traumatic approach, if it does not succeed, can make the problem worse and harder to solve. And it may be that your compulsions mask inhibitions, that you follow compulsive routines to hold in your true feelings, so Assertiveness Training could play a role in helping you be less compulsive. Modeling could show you that it is possible to function successfully without being a slave to your compulsions. You might consider the Rewards and Punishments techniques, Stimulus Control, and Changing the Sequence of Events to modify the behavioral settings that inspire and sustain your compulsiveness.

See also:
Obsessions

Techniques to try:
Desensitization
Covert Sensitization
Thought-Stopping

Supplementary techniques to consider:
Flooding
Assertiveness Training
Modeling
Rewards
Punishments
Stimulus Control
Changing the Sequence of Events

Sources of further information:
Cammer, Leonard. *Freedom from Compulsion*. New York: Pocket Books, 1977.
Cautela, J. R. "Treatment of compulsive behavior by covert sensitization." *Psychological Record*, 1966, *16*, 33-41.

PROBLEM

Conflict Avoidance

Even the most nonviolent people, those who have never been engaged in a physical fight, may find themselves in verbal and emotional conflict with others — especially with those closest to them. Conflict seems to be a natural by-product of interaction. As we try to live peacefully together, differences of opinion, of attitude, temperament, perception, or just the state of being too close for too long can cause misunderstandings and arguments.

There are means for minimizing the impact of such confrontations. In the article on Stimulus Control there is a detailed example involving marital conflict. The employment of Rewards and Punishment can supplement Stimulus Control.

Knowing that certain situations typically trigger conflict, you can employ Behavior Rehearsal to prepare yourself, to help you avoid experiencing the worst emotional strains of such confrontations. And if conflict seems to be the result of your overreactions to situations in which you are frustrated by having to repress your genuine feelings, Assertiveness Training could teach you to express yourself more freely and thus avoid explosive emotional release that increases conflict.

See also:
Fear of Expressing Anger
Frustration

Techniques to try:
   Stimulus Control
   Rewards
   Punishments
   Behavior Rehearsal
   Assertiveness Training

Covert Sensitization

Particularly useful in dealing with such problems as Smoking, Drinking, Overeating, and other habits that involve Compulsiveness.

Supplementary or alternative techniques: Stimulus Control, Rewards, Desensitization, Flooding.

Should be employed in conjunction with a Relaxation technique.

WHAT COVERT SENSITIZATION IS

This technique relies on the enormous power of the human imagination. You link images of a pleasurable behavior — but one you wish to change — with very distasteful images. This undermines the pleasure that has kept your habit going and builds new reflexes antagonistic to that habit.

Covert means that the process is learned through imagining both the behavior you wish to change (rather than actually engaging in it) and the negative associations. *Sensitization* refers to your progressive ability to come up with negative images whenever you engage in or attempt to engage in the behavior you are trying to change.

Your imagination influences your actions even if you have not consciously undertaken a program of Covert Sensitization. Before you act or decide not to act, you often think about the consequences and evaluate the outcome of an action, perhaps visualizing the implications of your behavior. Covert Sensitization teaches you to focus your natural powers of imagination on a particular problem and to pair pleasurable habit patterns with distasteful consequences, which will remove the pleasure that has been sustaining the habit.

HISTORICAL DEVELOPMENT

Joseph R. Cautela, who gave the technique its name, has done some of the most important basic research in the area. In experimental and well-controlled settings, he demonstrated that the technique could be used to treat overeating, problem drinking, stealing among juveniles, and some sexual problems (especially those faced by homosexuals trying to become heterosexuals).

Cautela reported teaching a heavy drinker to associate consumption of alcohol with nausea, vomiting, and the embarrassment of getting messily sick in a bar. The patient learned relaxation techniques to prepare for the procedure and was told that his drinking was a pleasurable habit that could only be broken by removing the pleasure. Cautela then taught the man to imagine a typical scene in which he drank — at a favorite bar — and to picture himself getting violently sick even before he had a chance to drink anything. With vivid detail, the patient was encouraged to visualize himself vomiting into the drink that had been placed in front of him, all over his clothes, even onto the bartender. This image of choking and sputtering uncontrollably on the presentation of his favorite beverage was intensified by thoughts of other people in the bar watching him and obviously disapproving.

Then the patient was given an out. He was instructed to imagine himself running away from the disgusting scene and feeling better as he got farther away from the drink that triggered the whole thing. His thoughts of the fresh air, of getting home and cleaning himself up, relaxed him and brought him great pleasure.

The man was taught to practice such imaginings on his own — daily, and whenever he was tempted to take a drink. The target problem was his *desire* for alcohol, not the beverage itself. And that desire could be more effectively diminished through the systematic use of his imagination than by merely eliciting guilt feelings about real-life scenes in which he had done some of the same revolting things he learned to re-create in imagination. When the real things happened he was drunk, his senses sealed off from the hurt and embarrassment. But in the process of Covert Sensitization he was stone-cold sober and the reality of himself drunk had an impact on his mind and conscience and pride. More, the association of bad results with the good-old drinking habit became reflexive: He was conditioned to avoid drinking — the pleasure had gone out of it.

Although Covert Sensitization was developed for use with a trained therapist, it involves a good deal of self-training and practice and might be worth trying as a self-psyching technique.

BASIC ELEMENTS OF COVERT SENSITIZATION

Identifying your problem and setting goals
Relaxing
Imagining a typical scene in which you engage in your target behavior
Picturing all the negative results and feelings your target behavior could produce
Mentally portraying your successful efforts to overcome the negative effects of your target behavior
Concentrating on the good feelings associated with freedom from your target behavior and its bad consequences
Repeating the technique with other problems

HOW TO USE COVERT SENSITIZATION

Identify your problem and set goals. Decide which problem to attack first, understanding that using the method calls for practice at least twice a day, and perhaps far more often if you are trying to deal with a frequently engaged-in behavior. The total time it takes for the technique to work varies from person to person, but you should observe some signs of change within two to three weeks. Set a goal of attacking one problem at a time for at least that long.

Relax. Say you want to break the habit of unconsciously chewing on things like pencils and pens. First, use a relaxation technique that works best for you. Covert Sensitization requires that your mind be cleared of distractions and your body prepared to cope with the internal pounding it may receive from the impulses sent by your imagination.

Imagine a typical scene in which you engage in your target behavior. In a relaxed state, picture the most common situation in which you normally chew on things: at work, during meetings, while reading, on a date, whatever. You should be able to conjure up an image of yourself engaging in or about to engage in this habit.

Picture all the negative consequences your target behavior could produce. Establish in your mind a clear picture of yourself getting more and more nauseated as, for example, you chew away on the tip of a pen. Amplify your discomfort by thinking about what your habit is doing to you: It stains your lips with ink, it gives other people the impression that you're immature and lack self-control, it makes you look foolish. This should make you feel miserable.

Focus on your self-disgust — on the nausea, dizziness, and discomfort your habit has inspired. Mentally examine yourself to see that your palms are getting sweaty, your stomach is churning, and you are ready to vomit. Build up a firm mental image of yourself vomiting as you try to continue chewing on that pen. Think about friends, family, or colleagues watching you get sick, scolding, scorning, or just embarrassed for you.

Mentally portray your successful efforts to overcome the negative effects of your target behavior. Counter the sickening images with thoughts of actively overcoming what has happened to you. Think about throwing away the pen, about getting out into the clean, fresh air. Picture yourself breathing deeply and feeling better with every breath you take. Think about how a nice cool shower would feel, about changing your clothes to remove the evidence of what happened to you while you were chewing on the pen.

Clear your mind of all the bad thoughts you put there in association with your habit and replace them with pleasant thoughts and images related to freedom from unconsciously and uncontrollably putting things into your mouth.

Concentrate on the good feelings associated with freedom from your target behavior and its bad consequences. Mentally fabricate a new scene in which you feel fine because you are not chewing on something and don't want to. Take a mental inventory of yourself: See how your lips are free of any traces of incriminating ink stains, how proud and self-confident you feel. The future looks great and you feel free, in control, your own person. Practice this program of positive imagining at the conclusion of each session of negative fantasy.

The entire routine should take about ten to twenty minutes, including the initial time it takes you to get relaxed. Run through the whole procedure at least twice a day and try to employ it any time you feel an irresistible impulse to engage in your target behavior.

Be sure to take your negative images all the way to their worst conclusion (vomiting, whatever) before you reverse the scene and start feeling better. It is the vividness of the negative parts of the scene, coupled with the target behavior, that makes the technique effective in breaking the habit.

Repeat the technique with other problems. Once you have had some success with one problem, you should find it much easier to employ the technique on other target behaviors. If you start with a relatively minor problem, like an annoying but fairly harmless compulsion, you may find it easier than plunging right in to attack something as formidable as overeating, problem drinking, or smoking.

PRECAUTIONS

Some problems may be encountered with this powerful method. You may find that your image making produces real rather than imagined nausea. The training could also condition you to get ill every time you encounter or even think about the object of your sensitization. You may feel this is a small price to pay for breaking a bad habit. If not, and you wish to reduce the chances of uncontrollable nausea, be sure to prepare yourself for each practice session by becoming fully relaxed.

You should be working on your impulses, not on the objects of the impulses: Try to construct scenarios to focus on the settings and circumstances surrounding your target behavior, your habits, and your urges. Don't concentrate on the objects — cigarettes or candy or liquor — alone.

Covert Sensitization can help change habits like smoking and overeating, but techniques such as Stimulus Control and Rewards may be needed to assure lasting effects. Much depends on the nature of your habit and your response to each technique. (See articles on your specific complaints for further guidance.)

And if your habit is more than a learned reflex, if it is also an established response to situations generating anxiety, you should concurrently undertake practice in Desensitization. It can be a valuable auxiliary technique because it can help you become relaxed and desensitized somewhat first, so that you will be better able to face the distress of the sensitization exercises.

Finally, you yourself have to judge whether Covert Sensitization is bringing you more discomfort than you think it is worth.

Sources of further information:

Cautela, J. R. "Covert sensitization," *Psychological Reports*, 1967, *20*, 459-468.

Janda, L. H., and Rimm, D. C. "Covert sensitization in the treatment of obesity," *Journal of Abnormal Psychology*, 1972, *80*, 37-42.

Rimm, D. C., and Masters, J. C. *Behavior Therapy: Techniques and Empirical Findings*. New York: Academic Press, 1974.

PROBLEM

Crying

Crying can be a great emotional release for us. Grief and great joy often bring on tears, though it is rare to see adult males — especially in America — cry in public. The recourse to tears, however, is far too often a manipulative device, an immature, inappropriate learned response to stress.

People who cry or respond to life crises with similar excesses of emotion usually do so to escape responsibility, deflect criticism, or simply get their own way in social interactions. They often succeed, but at great cost to themselves. They undermine the respect others may have for them by appearing weak and out of control — even if crying is their form of control over others. Their self-esteem and capacity for performing well and coping effectively with life disintegrate; a readiness to cry in tough situations prepares them for failure and loss even before they confront a task or problem.

If you find that you cry or get overemotional in inappropriate settings, you may want to try some self-psyching techniques. Behavior Rehearsal can show you how to face stressful encounters more calmly. Modeling can prompt you to behave as those whom you respect would — without crying uncontrollably whenever you get into a tough spot. Through Stimulus Control you can manipulate the emotional and environmental cues that in the past have led you to manipulate other people by crying. And Relaxation and Meditation can make you a more tranquil person, less likely to break down in the heat of normal confrontations.

Whatever you may have gained from using crying as a typical response to stressful encounters, the price you've been paying is probably great enough to warrant eliminating that response from your behavioral repertoire.

See also:
Disagreeable Tasks and Encounters
Accepting Criticism and Criticizing Others
Losing Your Temper

Techniques to try:
Behavior Rehearsal
Modeling
Stimulus Control
Relaxation
Meditation

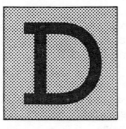

Daydreaming

See:
Fantasy

Depression

When the pressures, burdens, responsibilities, worries, pains, injuries, and other stresses of life become intolerable, depression may be your natural reaction. Depression is an understandable response to physical and emotional stresses and shocks. A serious illness or operation, the loss of a loved one, a professional or personal failure can trigger depression; and several stressful factors acting in concert may have the power to generate an incapacitating depression in you. Some people go through life untouched by more than minor depression; depression strikes others so severely that they require hospitalization.

Depression has many debilitating symptoms and no person is likely to exhibit all of them. One such group of symptoms shows up in your emotional state. The ailment may be characterized by passivity. It seems nothing really matters very much and nothing you do can change the course of events or the direction your life is taking. A sense of futility may engulf you until you seem to run down, your life processes going into low gear: You may become lethargic, fatigued, sleepy but unable to sleep. At first you may overeat in a reflexive effort to stave off the depression, but eventually you may find that you are eating very little and losing weight rapidly. One certain sign of depression is a lack of interest in what is going on around you. You can't get excited about much of anything, even activities that usually spark your interest. Your feelings for people you love may flatten out so much that you feel guilty about not caring enough about them. And guilt may tinge much of your thinking because your growing depression is undermining your effectiveness at whatever you do.

Depression takes its toll on your physical as well as emotional state. Your functioning is bound to suffer while you are depressed. Depressed people are unable to concentrate well or for long. They stop expending energy in normal pursuits and turn inward as they turn off to the world. One of the most distressing signs of depression is a loss of sexual appetite and a failure in sexual performance, often sending depressed people to physicians for help. But some people can't even bring themselves to see a doctor because indecisiveness is another side effect of depression.

As depression takes hold, you may find that you begin to stay away from people and become irritable and touchy when they attempt to make contact with you. Reduced attention to your appearance may contribute to the withdrawal reaction: You may stop shaving regularly, stop using make-up, let your clothes get dirty and disheveled. Your body may tell others how depressed you are: You may slouch, stare off into space, and become uncoordinated and clumsy, bumping into or tripping over objects.

Minor depression, if uninterrupted or continually recurrent, may intensify as major depression. Among symptoms are a noticeable increase in anxiety, with its attendant physical and emotional symptoms (see article on Anxiety), and morbid thoughts, including a preoccupation with death and even contemplation of suicide.

Self-psyching has little to offer people with acute or chronic depression. Such individuals need the help of medical professionals. But the symptoms of the minor depression that the majority of people experience may be alleviated by using self-psyching.

The self-psyching techniques suggested below give you a chance to slow down and reverse the progress of depression before it accelerates beyond your control. To regain your confidence that you can control your life, to overcome your pessimism and negative thinking you must prove to yourself that what you do and think matters in the shaping of your destiny. And it does.

There are some very simple and effective steps you can take that don't involve any systematic techniques at all. First, you can ask for and accept help. Ask those you love and trust to help you with the stresses and pressures you've been crushed by. If bills are the problem try to get a raise, ask your spouse to go to work, get a loan, or ask for an extension on your payments. None of these things need solve your financial problems immediately, but by demonstrating to yourself that actions you initiate can begin to solve such difficulties as paying bills you are actively striving to relieve your depression problem.

Helping others is another simple antidote to depression. Instead of surrendering to depression, try aiding others — perhaps working a few hours a week in a convalescent home or VA hospital. Your time will be better spent and you'll be helping yourself as well.

The responsibility of caring for a pet takes many people out of themselves and counters their depression. These people, especially the elderly who have been left alone by the death of a spouse, derive purpose and optimism from the attentions they give to their pet. The time and interest expended on a cat or dog undermines the development of depression.

Systematic self-psyching techniques can supplement your unstructured efforts. The article on Desensitization will give you guidance in establishing a hierarchy of tasks to tackle one at a time. Set yourself simple tasks and do them each day; then do other, more difficult things. Use the suggestions in that article to set up a routine that will permit you to experience a series of successes — however minor — that will prove to you that you can cope with various aspects of your life. Staying active will prevent the worst symptoms of depression from taking hold and active attempts to do even small tasks that you can succeed at will build your positive outlook.

Use Assertiveness Training to gain greater control of your life. Experiments in mental hospitals have shown that even acute depression is often reversible if the depressed person can be excited and even angered. Therapy through harassment brings the person out of the withdrawal and self-banishment of depression. For instance, patients are told to sand a piece of wood and then are told that they've done it wrong. When they do it over, as directed, they are again scolded for not following instructions. As soon as the depressed patients get angry enough to protest the unfairness of such activities, they are told that they can stop and do what they want. Almost universally, such patients are less depressed. By practicing Assertiveness you can feel more energetic and effective, and you will bolster your own depressed self-confidence.

Incompatible Behavior in conjunction with a Rewards program can help you reverse the progress of depression. To prevent depression from gaining a hold on your emotions, make it a practice to laugh, sing, dance, get out of the house, do some job, complete some task. Even if you are already depressed you can still try — and probably succeed. Incompatible Behavior will give you the means; rewards will supply the incentives. Use Incompatible Behavior and Rewards to stir you to act upon all the things you aren't doing or have trouble doing because of depression. With each success your depression should diminish.

The regular practice of Relaxation or Meditation could immunize you against some elements of depression. Both of these techniques reduce your susceptibility to stress and anxiety, helping you keep the level of psychological pressure in your life low enough to prevent the onset of mild depression.

Fight your depression with activity. Try to get out and get busy. Exercise regularly. Some form of physical activity will do wonders in relaxing depression's hold on your mind and body.

Self-Hypnosis can relieve you from mild depression, too. In a mild trance state you can give yourself posthypnotic suggestions to follow up. By acting on what you suggest to yourself you prevent yourself from sinking deeper into depression through inactivity.

Of course, depression is very often self-limiting; it may disappear on its own after a few weeks or months. But even mild depression can disrupt your life and is thus worth trying to combat. When such drastic measures as antidepressive chemotherapy, electroshock, and hospitalization are required, it is far too late to attempt to slow down and reverse the effects of depression. Though self-psyching may be unable to cure acute depression and may not make significant enough alterations in your life style to prevent mild depression from getting out of hand, the techniques suggested could help you moderate your reactions to depression, increase your capacity for coping, and reveal your most resistant symptoms that you should bring to the attention of your physician or a trained therapist.

See also:
Anxiety

Techniques to try:
Desensitization
Assertiveness Training
Incompatible Behavior
Rewards
Relaxation
Meditation
Exercise
Self-Hypnosis

Sources of further information:
Cammer, Leonard. *Up from Depression.* New York: Pocket Books, 1976.
Flach, Frederic F. *The Secret Strength of Depression.* New York: Bantam, 1974.
Kline, Nathan S. *From Sad to Glad: Kline on Depression.* New York: G. P. Putnam's Sons, 1974.
Seligman, Martin E. P. *Helplessness: On Depression, Development, and Death.* San Francisco: W. H. Freeman, 1975.

TECHNIQUE

Desensitization

Particularly useful in dealing with such problems as Anxiety, Fears and Phobias, Disagreeable Tasks and Encounters, Shyness and Inhibitions.

May also be of help with Sexual Hang-ups, Compulsiveness, Marital Conflicts, Work and Study Habits, Procrastination, Psychosomatic Complaints and Pains, Obsessions, Nightmares, Smoking, Overeating, and Problem Drinking.

Must be used in conjunction with a Relaxation technique.

WHAT DESENSITIZATION IS

Certain situations and stimuli can produce fear, anxiety, or other distressing or incapacitating feelings. But there are basic emotions, needs, and actions that naturally inhibit such feelings. Desensitization is a technique that teaches you to marshal such inhibiting forces and thereby weaken the harmful feelings and prevent them from emerging in situations or under circumstances that triggered them in the past.

For example, anxiety seems to be inhibited by relaxation, sexual stimulation, anger, and some biological drives like hunger. Thus if you learn to face anxiety-provoking situations in a relaxed state, your response to such situations ultimately will become relaxation rather than anxiety. This is because desensitization involves a physiological process known as *reciprocal inhibition*, which enables you to recondition your emotional responses in order to counter feelings that typically trouble you.

HISTORICAL DEVELOPMENT

Desensitization has become a mainstay of professional behavior modification therapy. An extraordinary amount of research has been done on the technique. Experiments and clinical findings have been published. The work of Mary Cover Jones, in the 1920s, especially her classic "case of the boy Peter," inspired much of the subsequent research that is the foundation of current practice.

Peter's overwhelming fear of furry animals was overcome by having him eat in the presence of such an animal. At each meal the animal was brought closer to him. His hunger inhibited his dread of furry animals, which weren't thrust upon him so abruptly that his fear could overcome his desire for food. Within two months furry animals no longer frightened him at all. The principle behind the theory is that fear is learned and can therefore be unlearned.

Today Desensitization is most closely associated with Joseph Wolpe, who refined the method in numerous studies of the effectiveness of reciprocal inhibition in combating problem behavior and distressing feelings. He established the procedures for using relaxation to gradually confront and overcome anxieties, calling his approach Systematic Desensitization. The technique described in this book is based on Wolpe's method.

BASIC ELEMENTS OF DESENSITIZATION

Identifying and isolating the problem (see Introduction)
Setting goals (see Introduction)
Breaking down the problem into separate segments
Establishing a hierarchy of the aspects of the problem
Attacking in your imagination each part of the problem
Applying the technique in real-life situations
Employing a variation on the basic technique

Monitoring your behavior and feelings (see Introduction)
Repeating the entire technique with completely different
problems

HOW TO USE DESENSITIZATION

Most of us use a form of Desensitization without even knowing
it. Any time you eat or take a drink in response to anxiety, you
are trying to desensitize your negative feelings by indulging
in activities that provoke good feelings. It is hard to be anxious when you are eating, absorbed in a hobby, movie, TV
program, or act of love. So in a sense Desensitization is a
scientific and systematic application of a natural process.

A mother is using Desensitization when she gets her child
used to the water by carrying him in her sheltering arms into
deeper and deeper water. Fear is desensitized by gradual
familiarization with the fear object (water) in the presence of
an inhibiting force (trust in the parent). Formal Desensitization is not much different.

Identify and isolate the problem. Follow the guidelines in
the Introduction to pinpoint a difficulty you wish to overcome;
as always be as specific as possible. Decide just what situation or task you want to deal with, what behavior you hope to
modify.

Set goals. Review the passage in the Introduction dealing
with setting goals and establish what you wish to achieve
with this method.

Give yourself enough time to learn the technique and to
give it a chance to work for you. In as little as five or six days
you could witness real change in the way you feel and
behave in some situation that previously restricted you and
made you unhappy. If you are more deeply troubled, several
weeks may be required. Any more than a month or so could
indicate your need for professional therapy.

Break down the problem into separate segments. Begin by
using index cards to record major aspects of the problem.
Write down — one aspect per card — all the things that cause
anxiety or other distress. Be specific!

For example, many people have problems dealing with
dating situations — accepting dates, making dates, being
comfortable on a date. While the following example is from

the point of view of a young woman, such problems, of course, can afflict men and older persons.

Establish a hierarchy. Organize the cards listing the aspects of the problem in order of difficulty. Arrange them in a pile from the aspect that bothers you least to the one that frightens you the most. The pile is the hierarchy to be used in Desensitization and might look like this:

1. Thoughts about being in a situation where I might be asked for a date
2. Talking to a group of old friends, one or more of whom might ask for a date
3. Receiving a phone call from an old friend under circumstances that might involve being asked for a date
4. Being in a group including strangers, one or more of whom might ask for a date
5. Being asked for a date by an old friend, even someone I've dated before
6. Being asked for a date by a stranger I've just met
7. Accepting an invitation from an old friend
8. Accepting an invitation from a new acquaintance
9. Being set up for a blind date
10. Getting ready for a date with an old friend
11. Getting ready for a blind date
12. Having to make social conversation during a date with an old friend
13. Having to make social conversation with a blind date
14. Responding to the physical advances of an old friend
15. Responding to the advances of someone on a first date
16. Feeling uncontrollable attraction for a date
17. Becoming sexually intimate with a date
18. Falling in love with someone I've dated and discovering my feelings are not reciprocated

This sample hierarchy is not meant to be rigid. No two people will have precisely the same list for identical situations. One person's most threatening aspect may be another person's least threatening one. The above list is intended to give you an idea of how a hierarchy is generated.

If you break down your problem into segments, writing each down simply and clearly, you will be able to organize the hierarchy more easily and be able to attack each part of your problem systematically and effectively. Whatever your problem and whatever the character and content of your hierarchy, the Desensitization process has the advantage of being highly specific, targeting just those things you feel will challenge you most as you confront a task or situation. The method permits you to concentrate on one aspect of your problem at a time, and you use the hierarchy to eventually master the entire problem without anxiety.

Hierarchies can be established for a wide range of problems. As another example, take the problem of not being able to face the task of disciplining or firing a subordinate. Here's a possible hierarchy:

1. Just thinking about talking to the subordinate who must be disciplined
2. Talking to a group of people, including the subordinate, about matters of discipline
3. Talking to a subordinate about discipline in general
4. Talking to him about the problem in general — for example, mentioning the company has been having a problem with employee absenteeism
5. Discussing his behavior in general terms in an informal setting — say, at lunch
6. Having a formal interview stating specific complaints
7. Taking disciplinary action against the person
8. Being contradicted by the disciplined person in private
9. Having him become abusive or even threatening in private
10. Being verbally attacked by him in front of others
11. Having to fire him
12. Being physically assaulted by the disciplined or discharged subordinate

Armed with a hierarchy delineating the components of your problem, you are ready to apply the Desensitization process to each component in turn.

Attack, in your imagination, each aspect of your problem.
The first step is to use a relaxation technique. (See the article on Relaxation for guidance in learning such a technique.) Desensitization requires that you be able to achieve a relatively deep relaxation during the self-psyching sessions. It is this relaxation that permits you to face progressively more anxiety-provoking situations; it is the parent that carries you safely into the ever-deeper water of your fears. And your

degree of relaxation during the sessions allows you to measure your progress with Desensitization by signaling whether or not your relaxation is holding as you face successively more anxiety-provoking aspects of your problem.

Use your relaxation technique to put yourself in a relaxed, comfortable, confident mood. Be sure your body is free of tension and your mind emptied of distracting and distressing thoughts. Then take the first card from the stack comprising your hierarchy and contemplate the scene as you think it will be played out.

Make it as vivid as you can. Imagine what will be said, what you and the other people present might be wearing, what the surroundings will be like, how you will feel. At the first twinge of anxiety about the scene — at the first sign that your relaxed state is crumbling: say, nervousness, sweating, dryness in the mouth, jaws clenching — stop imagining what it will be like. Block out the image and restore your composure by employing your relaxation technique: Go through the entire relaxation routine if you must.

When you are again relaxed, re-create the same scene in your mind. Continue until you can think about the scene without any anxiety. Then go to the next card.

Practice the above procedure, using your relaxation method, until you have mastered each card's contents in turn, until you are able to face — in your imagination — the possibility of your worst fears being realized. When no scene produces anxiety, when you no longer have to call upon your relaxation technique to stave off bad feelings, you have unlearned your negative responses to the entire problem. You should now be able to run through your entire hierarchy without using relaxation, because the anxiety should automatically be countered by your new conditioning. You have desensitized yourself to face the real problem, person, or situation without feeling anxious or inhibited.

As you get better at your relaxation method, it will take less and less time to get relaxed during Desensitization sessions and it will take fewer and fewer repetitions of scene setting before you can diminish your list of problem components.

Work slowly, taking thirty minutes or more per session, and perhaps dealing with only one or two scenes per day. But keep at it.

Apply the technique in real-life situations. It is possible to practice Desensitization using real-life, rather than imagined, settings. This *in vivo* Desensitization requires more experience with the general method: You must actually attempt to confront each aspect of your problem as detailed in your hierarchy.

Decide well in advance what you will try to achieve. After planning your approach, identifying what you will deal with, you do your relaxation routine and launch into the feared scene. You call in that subordinate or go ask the boss for a raise. You meet your blind date fully relaxed and ready for whatever may happen.

Be sure to start with the least anxiety-provoking component of your problem. See how things go, analyze your performance afterward, then try the next hardest step until you work your way up to the final and most difficult confrontation. You may find that you'll need to employ an abbreviated form of your relaxation technique even during the confrontation, and if you can do so it will make things easier. But because events often move too swiftly for you to try relaxing or even breaking off the encounter, it would be a good idea to have tried Desensitization in your imagination first, before actually undertaking the *in vivo* approach.

Whether the basic method, the *in vivo* form, or a combination of the two will be best is a matter for you to decide. Consider how much control you will have over the components of your problem in a real-life situation and think about what will happen if things get out of hand. Your own knowledge and feelings should guide you.

Employ a variation on the basic technique. Variations on the basic method may also prove useful:

1. Instead of clearing your mind of an image as soon as it provokes anxiety, it may work better for you to maintain the image and "relax it away." That is, keep the scene in mind and employ relaxation until the anxiety diminishes. Then go on to the next card and repeat the process until you have relaxed away the anxiety inspired by each component in your hierarchy.
2. Construct a multiple hierarchy including problems from various areas of your life rather than a single-theme hierarchy. You might list anything that customarily causes anxiety. This method does not depend so much on the particular scene imagined, but rather on training yourself to respond to anxiety with inhibiting relaxation that reduces bad feelings. Multiple hierarchies provide

a rich source of anxiety-provoking scenes. They help you change your reflexive responses by increasing your opportunities to learn to relax in the face of whatever negative emotions are prompted. By bombarding you with anxiety-provoking stimuli, this approach duplicates the less-controlled character of real-life situations to a greater degree than the basic Desensitization technique. But try the basic first. Use this variation only after you have become highly skilled at using relaxation to face anxiety-provoking scenes in a single-theme hierarchy.

Monitor your behavior and feelings. Using the instructions in the Introduction, compare the way you feel and act after using Desensitization on a problem with your prior experiences. If you have met your goals, go on to the next step.

Repeat the technique with completely different problems. Try Desensitization on other problems, following all the steps outlined above. Because Desensitization accustoms you to breaking problems up into manageable parts, it can be valuable in dealing with all sorts of tasks and difficulties. For example, it can play a role in learning to overcome procrastination and to improve work and study habits. With Desensitization, you make it a practice to take things one at a time, to see the smaller and more solvable problems hidden in larger and seemingly unsolvable problems. And this approach steadily builds your confidence because your success with one part of a problem inspires you to go on to the next part.

PRECAUTIONS

Failure during an early stage discourages some people from attempting to make further progress. The trick is to proceed gradually. Whatever your problem is and whether you use only the basic method, *in vivo* practice, or some variation or combination of approaches, you can expect solid and rather dramatic results if you take things one step at a time. Just don't move too quickly, try to take steps that are too big for you, or start at a stage too high to cope with for your mastery of the technique. As with many of the self-psyching techniques in this book, don't give up if you have some difficulty seeing immediate results.

Each conquest of some aspect of your problem—no matter

how small — each triumph over anxiety will give you greater confidence to go on until you have control over the entire problem, over all parts of your hierarchy. As a result, you will vastly increase your trust in your ability to modify your own behavior and govern your emotions — with this and other self-psyching techniques.

Sources of further information:

Fensterheim, Herbert. *Help Without Psychoanalysis*. New York: Stein & Day, 1971.

Paul, G. L. *Insight vs. Desensitization in Psychotherapy: An Experiment in Anxiety Reduction*. Palo Alto, Calif.: Stanford University Press, 1966.

Smith, Manuel J. *Kicking the Fear Habit*. New York: The Dial Press, 1977.

Wolpe, Joseph. *The Practice of Behavior Therapy*. 2nd ed. New York: Pergamon Press, 1973.

Wolpe, Joseph. *Psychotherapy by Reciprocal Inhibition*. Palo Alto, Calif.: Stanford University Press, 1958.

PROBLEM

Disagreeable Tasks and Encounters

All of us, at various times, face tasks or encounters we would rather not, or believe we cannot, undertake. A typical example is the supervisor who is virtually incapacitated by the thought of having to discipline or fire a subordinate — even an incompetent one. Large organizations get around this problem by creating impersonal and automatic procedures that, once triggered by rule breakers or shirkers, make the firing of another human being a clerical matter with little or no emotional content. Other firms leave such work to persons hired for their ability to handle the dirty jobs that must get done. But, for the majority of us, no institution or person can or will take care of the tasks our nature and sensibilities tell us will be disagreeable. We have to face them on our own.

Some people permit a difficult or disagreeable aspect of a task or situation to overwhelm them entirely. An individual might quit school because one term paper or examination was too tough to complete; someone else might quit a job because of an unwillingness or inability to deal with one offensive coworker; and many people typically stay away from parties because one of the guests might be a former spouse or lover. Such people reduce the potential joy and achievement in their lives by concentrating on the distasteful, or seemingly distasteful, facets of situations that may well include other, quite pleasant elements.

There are tasks and encounters that may not, in themselves, be difficult, but our fertile imaginations can make it hard to cope with them. Too often we believe situations will be far worse than they turn out to be. We amplify our uncertainties and insecurities until we are paralyzed with anxiety. Imagining the worst, we are frozen into inaction, unable to undertake a task or even make the decision not to undertake it.

There are many effective techniques that we can use to enable us to handle tasks and encounters we dread, techniques rooted in the valid psychological theory that all of us are products of social and personal programming that can inhibit action or cause distress. The techniques can make you more aware of the actual factors at work in stressful situations. Some are based on clinical and experimental studies on both animals and humans, even highly disturbed, institutionalized humans. Some teach you to reprogram your responses to gain greater control over your feelings and behavior in anxiety-provoking situations.

You may habitually avoid tasks and encounters you expect to be disagreeable. If it is in your interest to face such situations, Stimulus Control, Rewards, Punishments, and Changing the Sequence of Events can teach you to alter your behavior and give you new incentives for tackling problems that are to your benefit to handle.

If anxiety characterizes your response to certain tasks and encounters, Desensitization is indicated as a way to prepare yourself in stages for stressful situations. Behavior Rehearsal, too, can prepare you in advance for situations that usually generate anxiety, while Flooding can wipe out your basic aversion to specific undertakings.

Assertiveness Training can help you overcome the guilt you may feel about avoiding certain situations; it can teach you to express your fears and desires freely, to speak up when you have been unfairly placed in an uncomfortable situation. And with it you may learn that if you examine more closely the tasks and encounters you now consider wholly bad, their positive facets may come to light.

If the task or encounter you dread is one for which you can

control the timing — breaking off a relationship, asking for a date, a raise, a loan, a favor — you might try charting your Biorhythms, a procedure for learning the best and worst times for attempting various types of projects. And Modeling could contribute something by bolstering your confidence through the positive examples of those individuals who successfully cope with all sorts of difficult situations.

Whatever the nature of the task or encounter you find distressing, some of these techniques should help you face it with confidence, with the firm expectation of completing it satisfactorily and without anxiety.

Techniques to try:
Stimulus Control
Rewards
Punishments
Changing the Sequence of Events
Desensitization
Behavior Rehearsal
Flooding
Assertiveness Training
Biorhythms
Modeling

PROBLEM

Disappointment

Disappointment about failing at some task, at hearing that you haven't been accepted by a college or country club, that you have been turned down for a loan, that there are no more tickets for a show you wanted to see, or that someone can't keep a date with you shouldn't be incapacitating. But such news can cause stress and anxiety, even low-grade depression, and there are self-psyching techniques to furnish emotional first aid.

Employing a Relaxation technique should relieve anxiety and tension. Incompatible Behavior will enable you to replace reflexive sadness with a more cheerful, upbeat attitude. And Exercise or any body therapy that is tension releasing will help you work out the stresses your body may develop and discharge the frustrations you may feel at not being able to do anything about the disappointing news you have received. And, if you have faith in the healing powers of grace, Prayer can be a comfort.

It is unreasonable to expect that your every desire will be fulfilled or that you can accomplish everything you try, but it is unnecessary to let disappointment make you unduly tense, sad, or anxious or to keep you from trying to get the most out of life.

Techniques to try:
Relaxation
Incompatible Behavior
Exercise
Prayer

PROBLEM

Disciplining Others

Many people find it hard to criticize, correct, or discipline others. Even many business executives are made exceedingly uncomfortable by the task of bringing other people's shortcomings to their attention. Sure, drill sergeants and NFL coaches seem to enjoy pointing out the failures of those in their charge; they are chosen, in part, for their ability to be openly critical and are paid to be stern disciplinarians. But what about the rest of us?

Do you take special pains to avoid confrontations with those it is your job to supervise? Do you delegate the task to an associate? Do you leave it to your husband or wife? Do you arrange your life so that you don't have the time to undertake such activities? Or do you start to criticize or correct someone and end up saying that everything is really all right?

Your reluctance may arise, in part, from your fear of how the other person will respond to your discipline. Like most people, you probably don't want others to dislike you, and criticizing people can make them angry and resentful. Consequently, disciplining situations understandably generate anxiety in you. But Desensitization and Behavior Rehearsal work well to reduce that anxiety, to make it easier for you to undertake the task of disciplining others with a minimum of self-consciousness and guilt.

Assertiveness Training can teach you to be frank and factual about someone's shortcomings without becoming inconsiderate and cruel. Discipline and criticism can be constructive, helpful, and kind. And if it is part of your duties to discipline others you can learn to handle the task without disregarding either the truth or your own feelings.

The technique of Changing the Sequence of Events is a good supplementary method by which you can disrupt the normal pattern of activities that culminates in your anxiety about facing a situation in which you must discipline someone.

See also:
Disagreeable Tasks and Encounters
Accepting Criticism and Criticizing Others

Techniques to try:
Desensitization
Behavior Rehearsal
Assertiveness Training
Changing the Sequence of Events

PROBLEM

Disorganized Thinking

Your ability to think in a straight line, to make effective plans and organize your activities can be undermined by obsessive worry, forgetfulness, preoccupation with thoughts over which you have little control, and generally disorganized thinking. In your efforts to master a problem you may find that your mind distracts you from your purpose by raising side issues and by promoting feelings that cause you to sidestep the difficulty at hand.

For example, as you study for an examination you may be unable to concentrate on the book you are reading because you can't stop going over in your mind the possible outcome of the test. In your worry over what grade you may get, you keep yourself from studying and thereby increase your chances of getting a bad mark. If you are trying to plan your speech and actions for a business meeting or some personal encounter, you may be distracted from preparing an effective presentation because you can't seem to think about anything but what others might say or feel before, during, and after. In such instances you need to focus on the problem at hand, not on the possible repercussions or implications of your plans and actions.

Thought-Stopping is specifically intended to handle disorganized thinking; it can keep your mind from wandering fruitlessly into areas beyond that which requires your full attention. Behavior Rehearsal can make it easier for you to make and remember sound plans and to face the emotional fallout of your plans. And Relaxation and Meditation will teach you to get your emotions on an even keel, to slow your racing mind at times when you need to organize your thoughts and actions.

See also:
Floods of Unwanted Thoughts
Obsessions

Techniques to try:
Thought-Stopping
Behavior Rehearsal
Relaxation
Meditation

P R O B L E M

Distressing Situations

See:
Disagreeable Tasks and Encounters

T E C H N I Q U E

Dreaming

See:
Fantasy

Embarrassment

See:
Shyness and Inhibitions
Disagreeable Tasks and Encounters

Embarrassment of Admitting Ignorance

Some of our sharpest memories of school days are of those awful moments when the teacher threw out a question we couldn't answer. While a few students would wave their arms wildly, hoping to be called on, many of us tried to slide out of sight under our desks lest we reveal our stupidity or lack of preparation. The *Peanuts* cartoon strip has immortalized such embarrassing moments, down to that moment of reckoning when the teacher has extracted a wrong answer and the rest of the kids assault the uninformed victim with their cruel laughter.

From early childhood on, we are faced with a troublesome contradiction that conditions many of us to fear admitting our ignorance and to avoid the experience of being proved wrong. Although we are taught that learning is largely a matter of asking questions, the deprecating responses of our peers, parents, and teachers to our state of not knowing lead to our reflexive avoidance of situations that reveal ignorance. This natural reluctance to risk embarrassment can inhibit our social development and diminish our self-confidence and self-esteem.

A sign of maturity in us is our ability to say: "I don't know,"

"I don't understand," "Please explain it to me." Pretending to have knowledge we lack and fearing to vocalize our ignorance are self-destructive patterns that deprive us of knowledge and prompt us to avoid potentially rewarding encounters in an effort to stave off the anxiety that we have come to associate with revealing what we don't know. These destructive behavior patterns are usually so deeply ingrained that we need more than an act of will to change them. We must recondition ourselves with psychological techniques designed to help us unlearn such ways of acting and learn new, more productive behavior.

Techniques of Assertiveness Training have been particularly successful in teaching people to admit their ignorance and to feel right and good while doing so. Rapid and marked results can be obtained in a relatively short time and the solution of this problem can bring surprisingly significant changes in one's day-to-day interactions. Desensitization works for firmly entrenched fears of admitting ignorance or facing embarrassment.

Techniques to try:
Assertiveness Training
Desensitization

PROBLEM

Ending a Relationship

The termination of a relationship can make you feel happy, relieved, renewed. Having broken off an affair, a romance, a partnership, you no longer must be bound to the past, you are ready to start a new phase of your life, your options cease to be limited by the needs and demands of the person to whom you have been tied. But most people are also likely to experience a great deal of unhappiness, regret, and perhaps guilt. The techniques recommended here are intended to make it possible to end a relationship with a minimum of negative feelings.

Any long-standing relationship involves your personal commitment to another human being. You have invested time, energy, and emotion and the relationship cannot be ended without exacting something from you. Even if the decision is mutual, your feelings will be touched and you must be prepared to cope with emotional disruption.

Because the actual act of terminating a relationship can be especially unpleasant and difficult, some people tend to be unwilling to bring themselves to the act and lock themselves into relationships that are no longer satisfying or fulfilling. But breaking off a relationship is a skill you can learn.

Before you try to write the terminating letter, or plan a final meeting, prepare yourself by learning to employ one or more of the methods suggested below. Depending on your emotional state and the vulnerability of the other person, one method might seem more appropriate than another. But it is likely that you will be well served by drawing upon several.

You may need to ready yourself emotionally through a program of Desensitization and Assertiveness Training. Behavior Rehearsal can permit you to run through the most difficult stages of the process ahead of time and give you glimpses into how you and the other person might behave. A Rewards program (perhaps supplemented by Punishments) could reinforce your decision. And it may help to think about how someone you know and respect might handle a similar situation, so don't discount Modeling as a possibility.

Whatever approach you use, your goal should be to reduce the acrimony and discomfort on both sides. Be firm, but be sympathetic. If you are initiating the break — or merely participating in the decision — you have a responsibility to yourself and to the other person to handle the task both effectively and humanely.

See also:
Disagreeable Tasks and Encounters
Indecisiveness

Techniques to try:
Desensitization
Assertiveness Training
Behavior Rehearsal
Rewards
Punishments
Modeling

TECHNIQUE

Exercise

Exercise is as old as life itself. Movement in response to external stimuli and internal impulses is, in fact, a characteristic of being alive. People in modern society, with its labor-saving devices and relatively effortless means of transportation, simply don't get the amount of movement — exercise — that their bodies require. Lack of exercise can cause both physical ailments and malfunctions — even atrophy of muscle tissue — and may encourage the manifestation of anxiety in response to the common stresses of living.

The article on Anxiety points out that in prehistoric times human beings usually responded to stress in physical ways: fighting or fleeing. But today, encounters that cause stress seldom lead to physical efforts that release tension. Instead, anxiety and all its debilitating symptoms can develop. Exercise is suggested, therefore, as a self-psyching technique to counter anxiety caused by the typical stresses of modern living.

Why you should Exercise. Regular exercise promotes both physical and emotional well-being. An exercise program alternates physical tension with relaxation and makes you feel physically fit. Extremely vigorous exercise may drain off pent-up anger and frustration and free you of accumulated stress. Even exercise to the point of exhaustion, which can change your body rhythms, gives your mind and body a chance to recover from everyday strains and demands. And those who exercise regularly tend to get to sleep more easily, sleep more restfully, and wake up more eager to face the challenges of the day.

Forms of Exercise to consider. Exercises or sports that require significant concentration and freedom from extraneous distractions are particularly beneficial to the body and mind. Jogging, for example, with its repeated rhythmic movements, may provide some of the anxiety-reducing effects of formal Meditation. Those who jog regularly gain such physical benefits as weight reduction, increased strength and endurance, improved muscle tone, and cardiovascular and respiratory health. The psychological benefits of jogging include a greater feeling of calm and well-being, a sense of increased self-assurance, and a diminished susceptibility to fatigue, lethargy, and stress-related ailments.

Formal exercises, like Yoga and the Martial Arts, are effective in teaching you concentration, in helping you locate all the centers of tension in your body, and in promoting complete, controlled relaxation even while you are expending energy in those exercises. They help you free your mind from care by ridding your body of uncontrolled responses to outside stimuli. They increase your self-confidence and self-esteem by providing a systematic demonstration of your ability to perform the demanding tasks of physical exertion and mental concentration skillfully. And you carry over this ability to your everyday actions.

Competitive sports like tennis or team activities can promote physical well-being but are likely to cause as much mental tension and anxiety as they relieve if you do not react well to the strain of competition. The more quiet, controlled, and solitary exercises are recommended as more suitable self-psyching techniques because they supply somatic release while increasing emotional stability and psychological flexibility.

Formal, organized exercise is not the only way to work out the kinks in your mind and body. Calisthenics are worth trying and simple exercises like stretching can be quite useful, if done in a careful, controlled, conscientious manner. Rhythmic exercises such as letting the head roll back and forth and around on the neck involve easy movement and are soothing. Even rolling around loosely on the floor can benefit the old or infirm. And simple shaking is relaxing and physically beneficial. Learn to take a moment out of each hour or so to vigorously shake the tension from your arms and legs — it works.

Some rules for sensible exercise.

1. Consult your physician before undertaking any exercise program.
2. Start slowly: Never throw yourself into exercise without warming up before any one session and progress to more strenuous activities only after conditioning your body through successively more demanding periods of physical exertion.
3. Use prudence in scheduling exercise: Don't begin to exercise until at least half an hour after eating and, at least at the start of your exercise program, don't work out for more than fifteen minutes at a stretch.
4. Remember to replenish your body fluids: Exercise is dehydrating, so about a quart of water or other liquids should be consumed daily by those who exercise regularly.
5. Consider exercise a regular part of self-psyching. Try to

get in some form of exercise that works on your mental and physical tensions at least once a day, though three times a week will suffice, especially at the start of your program.

6. Try to make exercising an enjoyable activity you look forward to: Any exercise program that is onerous, that you look upon as a chore, will be short-lived and runs counter to self-psyching principles of voluntary self-regulation. Work out with people you like, if that will help, or, if you exercise alone, make sure that the surroundings and circumstancs are as pleasant as possible. Pick a place that is conducive, with plenty of air and pleasing sights and sounds; if you are working out indoors, perhaps playing music that encourages and uplifts you will add to your enjoyment of the effort you are making to stay physically and mentally fit.

7. End your exercise as slowly as you begin it: Don't stop exercising abruptly; taper off gradually so that your body and spirit aren't forced too precipitously to return to the normal level of activity required of them.

Make exercise a part of your daily routine. You should find that anxiety, boredom, insomnia and nightmares, bouts of mild depression, fatigue and lethargy — even the minor annoyances that crop up in everyone's day — will trouble you less.

See also:
Martial Arts
Meditation
Yoga

Sources of further information:
Cooper, Kenneth H. *The Aerobics Way*. New York: M. Evans, 1978.

Morehouse, Laurence E., and Gross, Leonard. *Total Fitness in 30 Minutes a Week*. New York: Pocket Books, 1976.

Simon, Ruth Bluestone. *Relax and Stretch*. New York: Walker, 1973.

Wittenberg, Henry. *Isometrics*. New York: Award Books, 1975.

Fantasy

Particularly useful in dealing with Anxiety, Insomnia, Nightmares, Fears and Phobias.

May help counter Psychosomatic Complaints and Pains, Headaches, Boredom, Indecisiveness, Shyness and Inhibitions.

Can be a central element in using techniques such as Desensitization, Relaxation, Autogenic Training, Meditation, Behavior Rehearsal, Covert Sensitization, Modeling, Flooding.

WHAT FANTASY IS

Fantasy is a human birthright, a powerful and precious natural resource. We are the only species that we know of capable of choosing to see things not as they are but as we wish them to be. Fantasizing is not the same as living in a fantasy world. (Fantasizing is a symptom of madness only in the person unable to distinguish what is real from what is imagined.) We are imaginative creatures — in our dreams and daydreams, in the poems and fictions we create, in our plans and theories, in our images of longed-for glory, and in our self-serving re-creations of past defeats.

By using our imaginations we do not merely celebrate unreality, we tap subconscious feelings, ideas, and impulses that are part of our true nature and can help us reach our full potential. Guided, consciously controlled, and creative fantasies can be an integral part of self-psyching, helping us discover ourselves and increasing our well-being and ability to cope.

This article provides instructions for harnessing the power of Fantasy through such means as centering, guided imagery, creative dreaming and daydreaming and for utilizing these means with other self-psyching techniques.

HISTORICAL DEVELOPMENT

People have always been aware of and concerned with the vivid and sometimes disturbing images created in their minds when asleep or awake. Modern psychotherapists, in increasingly calling upon their patients to create and control such images, point to Fantasy as a way to alleviate emotional problems.

Many of the major techniques mentioned in this book — methods developed by behavioral scientists — such as Covert Sensitization, Desensitization, Behavior Rehearsal, and others require the user to imagine situations and events that have happened, will happen, or may happen. This systematic use of imagination is for the purpose of duplicating as closely as possible the same feelings and reactions experienced in actual encounters. The idea is to prepare for difficult confrontations, overcome fears and phobias before real-life practice is attempted, and learn to stave off the anxiety usually experienced during situations one is fantasizing about.

Researchers have also found that directed Fantasy can enable people to counter pain and achieve deep relaxation. Autogenic Training and Meditation require visualizations of bodily processes or certain objects (the visualizations facilitate concentration).

Fantasy is especially useful in self-psyching. It's a technique that is easy to use without a therapist. You proceed at your own pace and you can apply Fantasy in a variety of circumstances, and for a wide range of purposes.

BASIC ELEMENTS OF FANTASY

Keeping a Fantasy log
Learning centering
Using guided imagery
Dreaming and daydreaming creatively
Using Fantasy with other techniques
Encouraging the free play of creative Fantasy

HOW TO USE FANTASY

Keep a Fantasy log. We all have fantasies — dreams, daydreams, vivid wishes that come into our minds unbidden. For several days record these fantasies. You probably have several you can write down already: recurrent dreams, images that pop into your thoughts at odd times, reveries that strike you. Write them down in great detail.

Your log will serve several purposes. It will help you locate problem areas, troubles that you may have no words to describe but that your fantasies or dreams communicate. Fears, inhibitions, feelings of inadequacy, a sense of unfulfillment, frustrations, and indecisiveness — almost anything can emerge in your log if you keep it faithfully and make it detailed enough. Deciphering the log is a matter of being honest about what you see in the most powerful, most deeply felt, or most recurrent themes.

In addition to disclosing problems, fantasies will reveal pleasant, even ecstatic images and sensations. Record them in your log. You may be able to employ them to solve problems through the many self-psyching techniques requiring good, positive subjects to concentrate on.

Be sure to use your Fantasy log to open your dream world to closer examination. Keep the log at your bedside and take pains to recall each night's dreams — making notations immediately on awakening. And certainly record any dream that disturbs your sleep.

If nothing else, keeping a log will force you to put down on paper thoughts that you seldom admit are important to you and yet may be influential in subconsciously motivating your behavior and feelings. Your log will give you messages from your inner self, enabling you to make conscious efforts to seek gratifications and pursue goals reflecting your true desires.

Learn centering. Most of the time our minds and bodies are occupied with responding to the pressures and stimuli from the outside world. And because we carry around the influences of these pressures — usually as anxiety — we are seldom completely free of their debilitating effects. Centering creates a place to which we can retreat at will for peace and quiet, for a respite from outside turmoil.

While there are many methods of centering, the following approach will let you develop the type of center that works best for you.

At a time when you are alone, visualize a stretch of ground with nothing on it. Picture yourself there. Now watch yourself begin building a structure, a building you would like to be in, a place safe from all intrusion. Some people prefer to build fortresses out of enormous blocks of stone — do so if you need that much protection. But a simple thatch hut will do. Visualize the entire construction process. This is important. Seeing yourself build the place will make it more real to you and will make it easier for you to conjure up the image of the place later.

Having built your structure — your center place — tell yourself that you have recourse to it whenever you want serenity and relief from the normal trials of life. You may have built it in one session or many, but once it is built it is important to use it often, to keep the image of it vivid.

Say you are facing a particularly tough business meeting. Go to your center for a few minutes before the meeting. You will feel less inhibited as you bask in the sense of inner strength and confidence your center gives you. Or perhaps you have had a terrible day; your head is spinning, you're tense, and you can't get to sleep. Center. Go to your personally constructed safe and peaceful place. Let your mind fill with the conviction that no problems are admitted into your place, that you only admit peace and serenity. You should be able to relax and sleep free from the tensions you unwound from at your center.

Use guided imagery. Guided or directed imagery is related to centering, but as outlined here it is more sophisticated. A mentally created place is usually involved. In this case, you spend some time imagining an unusually pleasant place that has especially tranquil connotations for you. It can be a real place or a created scene; many people conjure images of pastoral settings, cool forests, snow-covered hillsides, tropical beaches. I use a spot next to a frothing, bubbling creek in rural Vermont.

In painting your mental image of your special place, add as much detail as you can — the more the better. My place is filled with the sounds of rushing water, with the clear image of sun breaking through leafy birch trees to dapple the water and smooth stones. I'm able to feel the fine mist touch my face and arms.

Some practitioners of guided imagery go even further. They people their special places with some fantasy creature to which they go with problems. The easiest way to create such a creature is to get a clear image of your place and then just wait for the creature to appear. Some animal, mythical being (like an elf), or even ordinary person will appear, to become a permanent resident of your imaginary locale. You can, of course, choose what sort of creature you want in your scene, but it is usually best to let it come on its own.

Once your imaginary creature is settled in, you will find it can answer any questions you pose. It will give you advice, make suggestions, counter your own ideas. This creature is a reflection of your hidden inner feelings, your suppressed desires, your unplumbed knowledge, your unrecognized capacities. You in effect talk to a part of yourself you might otherwise have no access to.

The method works. Tell your creature that you are anxious about asking for a raise and you may well be advised to approach your boss at a particular time, in a specific way. Follow the instructions and you'll have overcome an inhibition — and you might just get the raise!

Tell your fantasy friend about tensions and psychosomatic pains. Listening to your creature's comments and instructions could help you identify the source of your pain, pinpoint the center of your tension and its cause, and thus make it easier to focus your efforts at relaxation on those areas of your body that are most tense or painful. And you could receive clues about those situations in your life that trigger tensions and psychosomatic pains.

Some people are uncomfortable at the thought of trying to conjure up a fantasy friend. This isn't a major problem because you don't need an imaginary creature to make guided imagery work. The alternative is to imagine yourself in your special place, relaxing and asking questions. Instead of expecting an answer to come from some figure, you let the answers come to you in the form of feelings, ideas, impressions, or actual words during a conversation you hold with yourself.

The relaxed atmosphere of your special guided imagery place can tap your creativity for such fruitful interchanges with yourself. You can probably answer many of your own questions. For example, if you are indecisive about something, use guided imagery by asking what decision would be best for you. You may get the strong feeling that one course of action is preferable to another, or you may actually hear yourself say, "Buy the sports car, not the station wagon" or "Certainly the job in California is worth considering; you don't want to go through another winter like this one, do you?" Such answers come from your own strongest instincts about matters you haven't been able to resolve. Guided imagery can help you resolve them by giving you access to how you really feel.

Guided imagery need not involve a place. You can use special visualization techniques to deal with pain, tension, and fear. For example, if you have a headache, one guided imagery approach is to visualize the pain as an object, say a big ball or cylindrical container. Form a clear image of this pain-object, then start making it smaller, and watch it slowly but steadily diminish in size until it disappears. Repeated practice of this method can enable you to use it as a sort of self-psyching first aid to extinguish such pain quickly. Likewise, visualizing fears or tensions as objects that you can mentally manipulate can permit their eradication.

Some people find the technique works better if the target problem is visualized as a diminishing flame or as a color (usually red) that is slowly changed to another color (often blue) associated with the lack of pain, tension, or fear.

The more time you spend using guided imagery, the more you will be in touch with the potent forces you've kept hidden. Give yourself a chance to benefit from these forces by taking regular mental journeys, periodic fantasy vacations to the special place you visualize where you can have your questions answered, your stress reduced, your boredom alleviated, your life brightened.

Dream and daydream creatively. Both primitive peoples and modern behavioral scientists have recognized the value of making creative use of dreams and daydreams. The members of the Senoi tribe of Malaysia have mastered one such creative use in a form of dream analysis. In this society, even children learn from their dreams and live with greater freedom and enjoyment as a result. It is the Senoi practice to discuss dreams openly. So when a Senoi child tells of a nightmare about falling out of a tree, he is not told to forget it, that it isn't real and means nothing. Quite the contrary. Dreams are held to be instructive and liberating. The child is told to think about the dream and to try dreaming it again the next night. The idea is not to wipe out the bad memory but to direct the dream to a more favorable conclusion. Falling can be pleasant if it is converted into flying, so the child is encouraged to dream about falling, then fly happily through the dream. The fear of the experience is extinguished; dreams are treated as ways to become more than you are. The method recommends itself to all of us.

The dream records in your Fantasy log can help you use the Senoi approach. Consulting your log, try to re-create your most recent nightmare or disturbing dream as you begin to fall asleep the next night. But prepare before sleep by thinking about what you would like to happen, directing your thoughts to the possible positive outcome that undirected dreams deny you. It might also help to use your Relaxation technique at this time. You could find that you start looking forward to your dreams, are less prone to insomnia, have fewer nightmares, and feel much better in the morning.

Creative dreaming can also be of use in helping you make decisions. By regularly recording your feelings and impressions from dreams you have during major decision-making periods, you may get significant guidance. If the themes of the dreams are consistently negative, you are tending toward a negative decision that reflects how you really feel about the problem. Affirmative themes could tell you that a positive decision on the matter is in your best interest.

In recording and analyzing your dreams it is usually a sound practice to pay close attention to the ideas and positions of others in the dreams. Other people, objects, and even disembodied feelings usually represent your own subconscious desires and attitudes better than anything the image of yourself in your dreams expresses or feels. Be guided by what these others say, do, or make you feel, because through them you can gain insight into your deeper motivations and needs.

Daydreams are privately created interludes of escape — not only from responsibilities and efforts — but from cares and worries. Through daydreams we can gain relaxation, extinguish boredom, increase our feeling of well-being, and demonstrate how inventive our minds really are.

If you already daydream, make the most of your habit. Intentionally construct more elaborate scenarios peopled with individuals you wish to know; picture yourself doing things you've never done; inspire emotions you seldom have. Make yourself the hero or heroine of bold adventures, the inventor of great new devices; see yourself as the envy of all you meet. Direct mini-movies in your mind; write great novels in your thoughts. Make your daydreaming a more regular and systematic practice.

If you seldom daydream, give yourself a chance to unlock the unrecognized potential of your imagination.

Daydreaming is best done when you are alone and undistracted by other, more insistent demands. Just before you go to sleep, while in bed, is one of the best times. Practice then and you will ultimately be able to employ the technique at other times.

Make your daydreams as concrete as possible. Give them as much detail as you can. Try to create a new reality that actually stirs your senses. Make yourself able to feel what something is like, smell the fantasy flowers, hear the sounds of distant trumpets or the call of beckoning sirens.

An accomplished daydreamer may find it easier to solve problems that more rational thinking fails to handle. Day-dreamers seem able to tap the intuitive, nonrational, highly creative part of the brain — the right hemisphere. Day-dreamers let themselves *find* answers to problems instead of forcing their minds down preferred pathways that may not lead to useful answers. The regular practice of creative day-dreaming can increase your self-esteem by demonstrating your own creativity. Also, daydreaming is a ready antidote to boredom. And the freer you feel to daydream the more relaxed you should be, which may immunize you against some stress-related complaints. At the very least, daydream-ing may make you a more interesting and imaginative per-son, a more vital companion.

Use Fantasy with other techniques. Practicing Fantasy will hone your skills in image making, skills needed in using other self-psyching techniques. You will be better able to use De-sensitization if you can fashion a clear picture of all the facets of anxiety-provoking situations. Behavior Rehearsal will be more effective if you can portray the outcome of whatever you attempt. You can overcome habits and compulsions with Covert Sensitization only by being able to form images, sometimes grotesque ones, of the possible consequences of your problems. Imagining how your bodily functions are changing is basic to Autogenic Training; concentrating on vivid images is fundamental in Meditation. Fantasy involves the regular practice of the free play of your imagination required for other techniques.

Encourage the free play of creative Fantasy. The world is a fantastic place. Many of the objects, institutions, and interac-tions that are now commonplace would appear to most people who lived before this century as patent impos-sibilities. We must constantly cope with fantasies-come-true

— why not make concentration on and confrontation with our own fantasies work for us? The regular and free play of the imagination is a liberating exercise that teaches you that there is a "you" separate from your problems, fears, emotions, desires, and symptoms. That separate you directs the building of your special centering structure, your private world of guided imagery. You go outside your everyday self and become aware of the you that is spirit, mind, intellect. The more you use Fantasy, the more you embellish your dreams, daydreams, and imaginings, the more confident and capable the free and independent dimension of your self becomes.

PRECAUTIONS

Because the technique involves regular concentration on certain images, obsessive people may substitute the created images for the usual objects of their obsessiveness. If you have such a tendency, be aware of this danger and look for signs that you are uncontrollably becoming obsessive about the fantasies you have created. Similarly, you want to engage in systematic image formation rather than letting yourself become a compulsive fantasizer. If indications of obsessiveness or compulsiveness appear (see the articles on Obsessions and Compulsiveness), give up this approach and try other techniques. The use of Fantasy can be constructive and creative only if it remains entirely under your control.

If you are troubled by psychosomatic complaints, this technique can pose a hazard for you even while you are using it to liquidate your problem. While you are fabricating fantasy images to counter your psychosomatic pains, you may increase your problem by concentrating more on your emotionally inspired pains than on the images useful in reducing those pains. If this happens, if you don't seem to get any better in one or two weeks of Fantasy practice — or perhaps find yourself getting worse — discontinue the technique and try other approaches mentioned in the article on Psychosomatic Complaints and Pains.

Fantasy formation must be conscious but unself-conscious. It involves a process of letting go, of freeing your inner self to be itself. As Thoreau put it:

If you have built castles in the air you haven't built fruitlessly, that is where they should be . . . now build a firm foundation under them.

The exercises in this article give you systematic means for building firm foundations under your fantasies, for making them serve your self-psyching purposes. But everything begins with your willingness to give the method a chance and to suspend your disbelief long enough to prove to yourself that Fantasy works.

Sources of further information:
Assagioli, Roberto. *Psychosynthesis*. New York: Penguin, 1976.
Garfield, Patricia. *Creative Dreaming*. New York: Ballantine, 1974.
Holroyd, Stuart. *Dream Worlds*. London: Aldus, 1976.
Samuels, Mike, and Samuels, Nancy. *Seeing With the Mind's Eye*. New York: Random House, 1975.
Singer, Jerome L. *The Inner World of Daydreaming*. New York: Harper & Row, 1975.

<hr>

PROBLEM

Fatigue and Lethargy

True fatigue is a biochemical process. Exertion fills the body with the by-products of metabolism and effort, which force the body to signal its need for rest by making you fatigued. Rest restores the proper chemical balance. But psychological fatigue — lethargy, lack of energy, lack of initiative — is a pervasive condition that can be a real problem whose solution is not as simple as getting "plenty of rest."

Some people feel fatigued or lethargic at the prospect of undertaking a disagreeable task. The fear of failure can be disguised as fatigue: One is too tired even to try. Becoming fatigued without having expended much energy at all is sometimes a symptom of the onset of depression. Likewise, anxiety can result in psychological fatigue. And boredom, the lack of sufficient mental and physical stimulation, can make you lethargic.

The first thing to do when gripped by recurrent fatigue is to see your doctor. You may have a real physical problem that should be attended to if you want to avoid serious illness. If you find that you have no physiological ailment, that your emotions and not physical exhaustion are making you listless and dispirited, some self-psyching efforts may be in order.

Sleep is the most logical treatment for physical fatigue. You will be surprised at how a few successive nights of sound, restful sleep can restore you and end much of your fatigue. However, sleeping too much may be a sign that your fatigue and lethargy have an emotional cause.

Practicing Relaxation, Meditation, or The Relaxation Response may fatigue-proof you to a degree by lessening your anxieties and staving off depression by giving you more composure in the face of life's demands. Incompatible Behavior may help you counter minor emotional complaints that inspire fatigue and lethargy.

Paradoxically, Exercise can often remedy or prevent psychological fatigue and lethargy. Although too much exertion does cause physical fatigue, a regular program of Exercise should make you more alert and eager to face life's pressures.

Consulting your Biorhythm chart will alert you to days when your innate character may put you in a slower, more lethargic mode and mood. Thus alerted, you need not become overly concerned. Merely wait for your energies to swing naturally to a higher point in your normal cycle.

Going with the flow — but not abandoning yourself to it — taking things as they come, learning acceptance and compromise, and setting reasonable goals are common-sense approaches that can prevent the type of stress leading to both physical and psychological fatigue.

See also:
Depression
Anxiety
Minor Emotional Complaints

Techniques to try:
Sleep
Relaxation
Meditation
The Relaxation Response
Incompatible Behavior
Exercise
Biorhythms

· PROBLEM

Fear of Disappointing Others

It is perfectly normal to fear disappointing others — letting them down or failing to live up to their expectations. As children, most of us are conditioned to try to please our parents and then our teachers by attempting to do what they ask of us, perform in accordance with standards they set, and follow the rules they lay down for correct behavior. And, as adults, many of us continue in our attempt to be "good boys and girls" by persisting in our efforts to keep from disappointing friends and strangers alike.

But letting someone down is one of the normal hazards of living. Only by spending inordinate amounts of time and energy to please others can we consistently avoid this hazard. The impossibility — and futility — of such an approach is immortalized in the story of the man, the boy, and the donkey: The man, who has agreed with and acted upon successive, contradictory advice about who should be riding the donkey, ends up carrying the donkey. Self-psyching and common sense tell you not to go along with everything that others want you to do.

Fear of disappointing others can incapacitate you; you avoid tasks and situations in which you could fail to satisfy others' needs or desires. Solving this problem involves learning to cope with the discomforts you may now experience because of your fear and learning to prevent others from exploiting your desire not to disappoint them.

See also:
Disagreeable Tasks and Encounters
Fear of Failure
Disciplining Others

PROBLEM

Fear of Expressing Anger

Although feeling angry is a normal and natural response to frustration or mistreatment, many of us find it difficult to express anger openly. We have learned to keep our anger bottled up so as not to hurt or displease others. But when we feel angry and inhibit the feeling, we do ourselves harm — in the form of developing symptoms ranging from physical pain to self-defeating patterns of behavior.

Consequently, the problem is not anger per se, but rather inhibiting anger. And releasing angry feelings is the solution. This doesn't mean blowing up. Loss of control serves no useful purpose and probably indicates that anger has been held in so long that the only way it could get out is in an explosive and destructive display that just causes more problems. Likewise, it doesn't really help to vent your anger at the wrong time or on the wrong object. If someone has been abusive or unfair to you at work and you suppress your justifiable anger until you get home, where you let it out on your spouse, children, or pets, your misdirected and poorly timed release of anger only makes things worse. And the total failure to let such pent-up anger out can actually make you sick, depressed, and ashamed of yourself.

The idea is to stand up for your rights without flying off the handle at every real or imagined provocation, to recognize that anger is not violence and that it is all right to express anger in a controlled manner.

Because inhibition often reflects a fear of loss of control, controlled anger can be good therapy. Start by going through the motions of anger release in private: Imagine yourself telling off your boss; picture yourself socking someone who has offended you; shout out your displeasure with those who have made you miserable. The section of this book on Behavior Rehearsal will guide you in using the process of controlled anger expression.

How you handle anger often is a measure of your ability to identify and express emotion in general. In evaluating the effectiveness of techniques such as Assertiveness Training, consider your progress in expressing anger. You know you are succeeding when you are able to show displeasure, when you are getting angry in appropriate situations. Anger is not a subtle emotion and your practice in expressing it may well be accompanied by vivid physical signs such as getting red in the face, shaking your fist, and even screaming. Moreover, it feels good to get angry.

Some currently popular forms of supervised therapy almost exclusively involve getting angry. Creative Aggression, Bioenergetics, and Primal Scream Therapy involve training in anger release. Shouting, for example, is said to be a way of unlocking repressed anger. Some therapists use mock combat in which patients strike pillows, the floor, or each other (using harmless cushioned bats). Such techniques require expert guidance, whereas self-psyching methods can help you cope with inhibited anger on your own.

See also:
Losing Your Temper
Standing Up for Your Rights
Shyness and Inhibitions

Techniques to try:
Assertiveness Training
Behavior Rehearsal

Supplementary techniques to consider:
Desensitization
Stimulus Control

Sources of further information:
Bach, George R., and Goldberg, Herb. *Creative Aggression.* Garden City, N. Y.: Doubleday, 1974.
Bry, Adelaide. *How to Get Angry Without Feeling Guilty.* New York: New American Library, 1977.
Ellis, Albert. *How To Live With and Without Anger.* New York: Reader's Digest Press, 1977.
Madow, Leo. *Anger.* New York: Charles Scribner's Sons, 1974.

PROBLEM

Fear of Expressing Opinions

There are people who can offer their opinions only with great difficulty. They may know of a fine restaurant but may hesitate to recommend it to others. When asked what they think of some book or movie, they avoid giving a firm evaluation. When approached about a good doctor, the best camera or calculator, an acceptable ski resort, they tend to withhold their ideas even if their knowledge and experience make their opinions valuable. Such people tend to be afraid of disappointing others and of invoking their displeasure or losing their respect if their advice doesn't pan out.

Overcoming such inhibitions will increase your self-confidence and your facility at interacting with others. Everyone has opinions and no one can be responsible for every unfavorable outcome that may result from sharing those opinions. Assertiveness Training provides a progression of simple steps that you can follow to help you liberate yourself from the habit of keeping your opinions to yourself.

See also:
Shyness and Inhibitions
Fear of Disappointing Others
Disagreeable Tasks and Encounters

Technique to try:
Assertiveness Training

PROBLEM

Fear of Failure

To live is to fail — sometimes. Human beings are programmed to attempt many things beyond their capacities. Watch a child learning to walk or a youngster learning to ride a bicycle. They keep falling down, but most get up again and keep trying. How many rockets blew up on the pad in the late 1950s before the American space effort got off the ground and we put men on the moon?

If you have a history of failure, you are likely to have developed a fear of failing again. Consistent lack of success in school keeps many youngsters from pursuing higher education. Failures from the past can haunt you in the present. They can make you anxious and self-conscious enough to imagine that you will fail (or are failing) even at tasks you are equipped to handle. You can condition yourself to believe that you are a loser, a failure. If you persist in this behavior you may fall into a pattern of avoidance and procrastination that fulfills your belief that you must fail.

Self-psyching can give you some new techniques for dealing with both actual and imagined failure and for overcoming your fear of failing. There are techniques that provide options to anxiety, inaction, and noninvolvement. They can teach you to bounce back from failure and not to feel so bad about being only human. You can learn that it is impossible to avoid all failure but that it is relatively easy to stop making yourself unhappy and unproductive because of your fear of failure.

Modeling gives you the example of others who have succeeded where you've failed and a means for making the factors that brought them success work for you. Behavior Rehearsal shows you how to structure your efforts to prevent failure. Desensitization can help you cope with anxiety about failing. Try each or use them in concert.

See also:
Guilt
Inability to Make Requests
Procrastination

Techniques to try:
Modeling
Behavior Rehearsal
Desensitization

PROBLEM

Fear of Recommending

See:
Fear of Expressing Opinions

PROBLEM

Fears and Phobias

Everyone is afraid of something. Even Superman was afraid to be caught in the presence of a particle of matter from his home planet, Krypton, lest he lose all his powers. Some people are afraid of flying, of heights, of being alone, of animals. Fears are not problems if they are reasonable — if they fit the reality of the threat posed by the object of one's fear. Superman's fear of Kryptonite was not a problem but a healthy protective reaction to a substance that was a real danger to him. Likewise, it is foolish not to fear wild animals that might do you grave harm. And high places may be dangerous and should be treated with caution.

But if your fear is unreasonable, you may be suffering from a phobia; that is, you may be afraid of something that can't actually hurt you or your fear may be out of proportion to the real chance that your fear object will bring you harm. Even if you know your fear is groundless your behavior can still be affected: Your activities can be limited by your need to avoid the object of your phobia.

Whether self-psyching will help you overcome your fears, or whether professional assistance is required depends on the nature of your problem and the pervasiveness of your responses to your fear object. If you fear something (or everything) so much that you spend a major proportion of your time and energies organizing your life to prevent exposure to what you fear, you probably would profit from professional help. Fears of lesser extent may sometimes diminish by themselves over time and usually respond to self-psyching.

So many debilitating fears afflict large numbers of people that each has a scientific name: Agoraphobia is the fear of open spaces; claustrophobia, the fear of enclosed spaces; fear of high places is acrophobia and of water, hydrophobia. Howard Hughes was supposed to have been terrified of filth and of being infected by germs (mysophobia and hypochondriacal phobia).

I knew a woman who was deathly afraid of spiders and similar multilegged beasts. She was forced to take biology in college but had her mother go through her textbook and paste blank paper over every picture of insects, lobsters, and so on. Ironically, when she later married and moved to her husband's home in Lebanon she was exposed to such creatures in the flesh, having to cope with giant scorpions in her slippers and spiders beneath her bed clothes. Facing the real thing, her phobia was undermined because she saw that her worst fears could be survived, and even though some animals of this sort are really dangerous, she learned to handle the danger realistically, without panic. In one setting, she had reorganized her life to avoid the mere sight of her fear objects; in another setting she was forced to confront her fears and thus learned to overcome them. Her experience was an uncontrolled version of the technique known as Flooding.

This example should be both instructive and encouraging. It shows that even long-standing fears can be overcome. From the perspective of behavioral science, it is not even important to discover the underlying cause of the phobia (which might be some early trauma involving the feared object, anxiety caused by symbolic connotations, or a combination of these and other factors). What you are aiming at is the removal of the symptoms of the phobia: You want to gain the ability to live without fear even when exposed to the object or event or situation that frightens you. And if self-psyching techniques can have this effect, they are well worth trying. But if they fail to give relief, seek professional aid — just as the woman described was ready to do before the rush of events (Flooding) liquidated her fears.

The techniques suggested below are designed to help you overcome specific fears so that you can fly without feeling tension and stress, enjoy the company of large groups of people, ride in elevators alone, or do whatever it is that your fears now prevent.

Desensitization, which works so well for most forms of anxiety, has proven effective with a remarkably high percentage of people suffering from fears and phobias. Try it first. You might also wish to try Flooding, which is a faster, more demanding method than the step-by-step approach used in Desensitization. Modeling also may work: You learn vicariously through someone you know who is able to cope with the object of your fear. By employing Fantasy you can generate images, feelings, and impressions that promote a sense of well-being, and thus counter your fears. If your fear involves having to deal with certain people or types of people, Assertiveness Training could help. Finally, Stimulus Control, Changing the Sequence of Events, and Rewards and Punishments might teach you to modify your behavior to reduce your phobic reactions in given situations.

It is not what you fear that is your problem, it is the extent to which your fears upset you and disturb your way of life. Self-psyching won't help you avoid what you fear — it will help you become less afraid.

Techniques to try:
Desensitization
Flooding
Modeling
Fantasy
Assertiveness Training
Stimulus Control
Changing the Sequence of Events
Rewards
Punishments

Sources of further information:
Fensterheim, Herbert and Baer, Jean. *Stop Running Scared*.
New York: Rawson Associates Publishing Inc., 1978.
Marks, Isaac M. *Fears and Phobias*. New York: Academic Press, 1969.
Smith, Manuel J. *Kicking the Fear Habit*. New York: The Dial Press, 1977.

PROBLEM

Feelings of Inadequacy

You may actually be inadequate in some way. None of us excels at everything. You may have a job that is too much for you, not be able to deal with the demands of marriage and family life, undertake projects beyond your capacities. Your situation is like the old joke in which the psychiatrist tells the patient that he doesn't have an inferiority complex, he's just inferior.

The first step in dealing with such a problem is facing the facts. There is no law that says we will all be able to perform adequately at whatever we try. You can live with a measure of inadequacy — we all do. Covert Sensitization and Flooding can show you that the implications of your inadequacy are not as great as you may imagine. Modeling could inspire you to find the resources in another person's behavior that you can adapt to yourself.

If much of your sense of inadequacy is imagined, if you simply put yourself down all the time, you need some self-psyching tips. Employ Assertiveness Training to gain self-confidence. Restructure your approach to what you do by improving work habits with Stimulus Control, Rewards and Punishments. And you can learn to stop bad-mouthing yourself with Thought-Stopping.

Techniques to try:
Covert Sensitization
Flooding
Modeling
Assertiveness Training
Stimulus Control
Rewards
Punishments
Thought-Stopping

PROBLEM

Floods of Unwanted Thoughts

When you've just ended a particularly busy and demanding day or when you're facing the beginning of one, you may find your mind racing with ideas and impressions over which you seem to have little control. You are not experiencing simple confusion or disorganized thinking but the involuntary, unregulated functioning of normal mental processes. Even though you may want a respite from matters of legitimate concern, your mind takes charge and continues its fruitless rumination that can distract you from other thought and action. Such mind racing can regularly inhibit sleep.

If floods of unwanted thoughts wash over you for days on end, if you habitually allow your mind to race unchecked, you can develop a form of obsessiveness that requires professional therapeutic intervention. The Thought-Stopping technique can quickly alleviate the problem for most people, restoring calm and control, improving concentration, and eliminating this cause of insomnia.

See also:
Disorganized Thinking
Obsessions

Technique to try:
Thought-Stopping

TECHNIQUE

Flooding

Particularly useful in dealing with such problems as Fears and Phobias, Compulsiveness, Obsessions, Disagreeable Tasks and Encounters, Shyness and Inhibitions.

Supplementary or alternative techniques: Desensitization, Modeling, Behavior Rehearsal.

WHAT FLOODING IS

With this technique you force yourself to experience the most unpleasant feelings you associate with your problem. In the process, you should discover that you won't drown in your problem. By facing that which you fear, by flooding yourself with the very feelings you have been guarding against, by seeking out whatever you have been avoiding, you not only learn to cope with your problem, you also rise above it so that it is no longer a problem at all.

HISTORICAL DEVELOPMENT

Controlled, systematic Flooding is a recently developed therapeutic technique. Used as an alternative to methods requiring more time and effort, it is equally effective in breaking down the highly resistant behavior patterns that people fashion to protect themselves from having to face what they fear or dislike. It is based on theories of learning and conditioning that view neurotic behavior as a repetition of "successful" efforts to keep anxiety at bay. Like the man in the old joke who snaps his fingers constantly to keep elephants away and is sure the method works because he never sees any elephants, many people adopt forms of behavior that are symptoms of their struggle to handle psychological difficulties.

Flooding is aimed at removing the symptoms that have become troublesome enough in themselves to require attention. It attacks the finger snapping, not the sources of one's fear of elephants. It recognizes the basic behaviorist principle that there is little point in looking for subconscious causes when you can successfully modify behavior to remove symptoms and make a person feel and act better.

Flooding has had its most consistent success in the treatment of fears and phobias. As an early demonstration of its clinical utility, E. R. Guthrie helped a teenage girl overcome her fear of cars in one session. He made her sit in the back seat of a moving automobile for four hours. At first, she experienced outright panic; her worst fears were being realized. But soon she stopped being afraid, because it became obvious that riding in a car was not as bad as she had psyched herself into believing it was. By the end of her initially nightmarish trip, her fear had dissipated, never to return.

Guthrie had demonstrated that by being forced to confront a fear, people could experience a greater and more lasting reduction of anxiety than was achieved by their typical avoidance behavior. Avoidance of riding in cars is a psychologically inefficient way to handle the fear of automobiles because it is temporary at best, keeps one from facing and finally defeating the problem, and can disrupt one's life. Flooding is a valuable means of altering such behavior by making it unnecessary. Flooding breaks the conditioning pattern that results in reliance on bad habits and unproductive behavior to prevent anxiety. After a person faces and survives the anxiety, the problem behavior is no longer necessary because it no longer protects anything — the worst has been faced, the barriers have been breached.

Since Guthrie's work in the 1930s, Flooding techniques have been further refined. Thomas G. Stampfl and Donald J. Levis have done considerable clinical work with a variation of Flooding they call Implosive Therapy.

BASIC ELEMENTS OF FLOODING

Identifying the problem (see Introduction)
Setting a goal (see Introduction)
Confronting the problem head-on:
1. In your imagination (best to try first)
2. In real life (after trying fantasy Flooding)
Monitoring your behavior to detect improvement (see Introduction)
Repeating the technique with other problems

HOW TO USE FLOODING

Identify the problem. Using the instructions in the Introduction, determine what it is you fear or feel anxious about; what task, obsession, compulsion, or situation seems to disrupt your normal functioning by inhibiting your freedom of action. Perhaps you are afraid of flying, of spiders, of failure; maybe you cannot face the prospect of examinations in school or reports at work, cannot bring yourself to ask someone for something or to break off a relationship, are impatient or uncomfortable if everything in your home or office is not always in its place or if common activities are not carried out in precisely the same way every time.

Set a goal. Plan to spend twenty to thirty minutes twice a day for several days employing the Flooding technique. Stay with it until you find that you must work very hard to create the same level of anxiety you first experienced with the method or until it becomes obvious that your anxieties are undiminished and so distressing that the method is clearly making your problem worse, not better. Give the technique the better part of a week for a fair test on one problem. And be sure to tackle only one problem at a time.

Confront your problem head-on. Say your problem is a fear of being tested, having to show whether or not you know or can do something. This is a fairly common complaint among college students. I had a roommate, a brilliant sixteen-year-old sophomore math wizard and chess champion, who became so anxious before some examinations that he became nauseated and even fainted on a few occasions. Flooding might have been of help to him.

1. *In your imagination:* Using Flooding to overcome a fear of tests should begin with your imagining the worst possible consequences of feared events. Alone, in a quiet place, vividly imagine what could happen as a result of failing a test or even failing to take the test. Without any gradual buildup through less frightening aspects of the problem, picture — experience — what would happen if you showed that you didn't know the answers or were afraid to be tested. See your test paper with a big fat F on it; think of what your parents will say when they learn you have failed. Hear them berate you for having wasted all their hard-earned money on your education and run down the list of all the things they went without so that you could get a degree. See yourself in the dean's office. They are telling you that you will be forced to repeat the course or even that you will have to leave school. Think of the public humiliation to follow: Everyone now believes you're stupid and inept.

   You can play out a similar scenario in fantasy with your demonstration of a lack of preparation and knowledge while delivering a business report. Picture what your boss will say, how your colleagues will react, how bad you will feel.

   The procedure never varies: You must unflinchingly confront what you fear most and hold the most unpleasant images in your mind until you feel real anxiety and then continue experiencing the anxiety until it starts to diminish. (See the article on Anxiety for various signs of being anxious.) Stay in mental and emotional contact with what you fear until you are less afraid. And you'll feel this lessening of fear as you find that your avoidance of that which you fear has maintained it as a fear object. Forcing the fear into the open and creating the very anxiety you have been trying to avoid should remove the feared object's potential for causing continued fear and avoidance behavior.

The method works similarly for obsessions and compulsions, which are usually sustained by your fear of some terrible consequences that never materialize. Flooding takes the hidden fears perpetuating obsessions and compulsive behavior out of hiding and reveals them for what they are: truly frightening, but extremely unlikely. By mentally confronting and accepting the consequences of giving up your compulsions or obsessions, you become less anxious.

2. *In real life:* This requires a greater willingness to confront problems head-on. It's a good idea to try fantasy Flooding first: In a real-life confrontation the anxiety that must be generated may force you to try escape maneuvers that can negate the effects of Flooding. For example, if you place yourself in contact with snakes or something else you fear, you can increase anxiety to Flooding levels but you may end up by running away and thus reinforcing your dread by proving that you can't handle it.

The idea is to try only those problems you have good reason to believe you can master. By confronting the problem first in your imagination, you give yourself a chance to succeed by adequately assessing your capacity for coping with the anxiety involved.

Whether you use fantasy or the real-life approach, take pains to give the technique a fair chance by promoting real anxiety that you can willingly face long enough to discover that it can and will subside.

Monitor your behavior to detect improvement. Following the guidelines in the Introduction, keep a record of how you behaved and felt before and after employing Flooding. Have you altered your problem behavior, overcome some fear, reduced your compulsiveness? If you see no appreciable changes the technique is not suited to your problem. If you notice real improvement, move on to other problems.

Repeat the technique with other problems. If you have been successful in your use of Flooding for, say, test phobia, try it with compulsive neatness, or the inability to face certain people or situations.

Try one problem at a time, first in fantasy, then, if necessary, in real-life encounters. Real-life Flooding often may not be necessary, because if the fantasy approach worked well, encountering what you had feared in a real-life setting should generate little anxiety. And repeated contacts with what you feared will only reduce anxiety further.

PRECAUTIONS

The greatest problem with Flooding is that it may not work at all. It may actually make things worse as the anxiety it requires you to generate and confront prompts you to avoid similar encounters in the future, thus ingraining more deeply the very patterns of behavior you were trying to change. The technique was designed for use by a therapist who carefully controls your confrontation with your problem, giving you confidence that you can face and overcome it. So if you find that you are unable to deal with such problems by yourself and handle the anxiety on your own, a more gradual, less threatening method like Desensitization may work better for you. And if your problems are the result of fears and conflicts so deeply buried that you cannot come to grips with them, you may require the assistance of a trained therapist.

But self-applied Flooding can work for a great many people. As an experiment, knowing you can back out if things get too rough, it's certainly worth a try.

Sources of further information:

Guthrie, E. R. The Psychology of Learning. New York: Harper & Brothers, 1935.

Morganstern, K. P. "Implosive Therapy and Flooding Procedures: A critical review." Psychological Bulletin, 1973, 79, 318-334.

Stampfl, T. G., and Levis, D. J. "Essentials of Implosive Therapy: A learning-theory-based psychodynamic behavioral therapy." Journal of Abnormal Psychology, 1967, 72, 496-503.

PROBLEM

Forgetfulness

Forgetfulness can, of course, be a sign that you have a bad memory — a vaguely annoying trait to yourself and others. It can also indicate that you don't want to remember certain things — a fear-induced symptom of your reluctance to deal with people, tasks, or problems. Such willful or reflexive forgetfulness may respond to self-psyching techniques designed to help you overcome fears, anxieties, and inhibitions that block your memory of what you have to do.

The articles on Disagreeable Tasks and Encounters, Shyness and Inhibitions, and Fears and Phobias contain numerous suggestions for techniques that may be useful in coping with emotionally based forgetfulness. Methods such as Relaxation and Desensitization can prepare you to deal with encounters whose stress quotient is high enough to force you to forget to face them at all. Behavior Rehearsal also gives you a chance to reduce the amount of anxiety you might experience and thus makes you more willing to get involved with people or tasks you'd rather forget. Stimulus Control, Rewards, and Punishments can teach you to associate important events with certain stimuli and supply incentives for remembering.

By practicing such techniques, you should soon discover that you forget less because you have less reason to forget. What has been distressing to you in the past is now in manageable form. Likewise, you should find out how much of your forgetfulness is based on fear or inhibition and how much is your poor memory's reticence.

See also:
Disagreeable Tasks and Encounters
Shyness and Inhibitions
Fears and Phobias

Techniques to try:
Relaxation
Desensitization
Behavior Rehearsal
Stimulus Control
Rewards
Punishments

PROBLEM

Frustration

Frustrated needs, desires, plans, or actions can make you feel angry, helpless, sad, guilty, and depressed — frustrated. Coping with the problem has two aspects: easing the feelings of frustration and overcoming the causes of frustration.

Practicing Relaxation or Meditation can soothe your frustration and may even increase your customary composure sufficiently to prevent frustrating experiences from bothering you as much as they did in the past. Other techniques, mentioned in the articles on Fear of Expressing Anger, Guilt, and Depression may also help you ease feelings of frustration.

One cause of frustration may be your inability to carry out your own plans. Assertiveness Training is designed to help you better formulate the means to your ends, and could give you the confidence to pursue your wishes and needs. Employing Stimulus Control, Rewards and Punishments may enable you to improve your performance of various tasks so that you can achieve what you wish more often.

Nothing can guarantee that you will always get what you're after. However, these self-psyching techniques can pave your way to overcoming aspects of your own behavior that may be laying you open to unnecessary frustration and can reduce the impact of frustrating experiences that arise from developments over which you have no control.

See also:
Fear of Expressing Anger
Guilt
Depression
Work and Study Habits

Techniques to try:
Relaxation
Meditation
Assertiveness Training
Stimulus Control
Rewards
Punishments

Grief

Grief is a normal and beneficial reaction to great loss, a cathartic emotion that releases tension and helps you make the transition to a new stage of life. Virtually every culture has elaborate customs and ceremonies to channel grief into appropriate expression when death robs people of a loved one. Mourning helps you get through the initial shock of your loss.

But if a death, divorce, loss of a job, or any other major change in your life brings on a sadness that lingers long after formal mourning or an ordinary period of adjustment has passed, you may be falling into depression. Major depression requires professional therapeutic intervention. Milder sadness could be helped by self-psyching techniques listed in the articles on Sadness and Minor Emotional Complaints.

See also:
Sadness
Depression
Minor Emotional Complaints

Guilt

Occasional guilt feelings are healthy and even admirable responses to improper behavior. If you fail to keep your word, if you disappoint or insult someone unnecessarily, if your selfishness causes another person harm or loss, then you *should* feel guilty. The feeling might teach you how to get along with others. Let the feeling touch you and honestly accept your responsibility for the act and the feeling it has generated in you. Then try to avoid both the transgression and the guilt in future interactions.

One form of guilt, which psychoanalysts regularly treat, is rooted in childhood traumas. Self-psyching is not intended to deal with this problem. But many people often feel guilty for no apparent reason and their guilt, which is embedded in a matrix of anxiety and depression, can be set free and relieved with some of the techniques suggested in this book.

Anxiety is pervasive, and, looked at in one way, is a fear of injury or loss. Such fears can produce resentment, frustration, and anger. These feelings, if repressed, can produce guilt. In your anxiety about life in general and the demands of life in particular, you may be generating this sort of guilt. An undiminished guilt eventually shows up in the symptoms of depression. (See the article on Depression.)

Covert Sensitization and Desensitization can help you uproot anxiety-based guilt by showing you that your fears aren't as terrible or as insurmountable as you believe. Desensitization can be especially helpful in proving to you that you can function effectively despite your guilts and the depression they may have inspired.

Assertiveness Training is useful in teaching you that the pursuit of happiness is your right. You can fulfill yourself without feeling guilty. This technique gives you the guidance in maintaining and expressing your autonomy in the face of other people's efforts to stir up guilt feelings in you, just because you have your own legitimate needs and desires.

Modeling can contribute to handling guilt. With this method you discover how to duplicate the successful behavior of people who seem able to function without the guilt and anxiety that may be plaguing you.

And if your guilt is attributable not to what you may have done to others but to what you do to yourself — engaging in Nervous Habits, for example — check the techniques suggested in that article to help you.

Guilt is essentially a philosophical and ethical matter. Behavior that may produce guilt in one person may have no such impact on another whose values and outlook are different. It is also a cultural phenomenon. Actions that prompt guilt in one society go unnoticed and produce no guilt among other groups of people with different customs.

Yet guilt feelings, when they do occur, have the potential to disrupt normal functioning and increase stress, anxiety, and depression. They cannot be ignored and you can deal with them by facing their reality and doing everything possible to reduce their destructive effects. Self-psyching can play a role in handling this common problem.

See also:
Anxiety
Depression
Nervous Habits

Techniques to try:
Covert Sensitization
Desensitization
Assertiveness Training
Modeling

Sources of further information:
Lewis, Helen B. *Shame and Guilt in Neurosis.* New York: International Universities Press, 1971.
Piers, Gerhart, and Singer, Milton B. *Shame and Guilt.* New York: W. W. Norton, 1972.

Hair Pulling or Plucking

Some people cannot resist the urge to pull at their hair. Some even pluck out individual strands. Many men with new mustaches always have their hands near their mouths, stroking, pulling, and even plucking at the whiskers.

Hair pulling is common among men and women who are losing their hair — starting with the desire to check how much is left. Itchy scalp — a very common problem — can trigger hair pulling and also involve scalp scratching.

If you have determined that you do not have a physical ailment best treated by a dermatologist, or if pulling and scratching have produced an infection that is being treated but is only the most obvious result of your underlying habit, you may want to consider self-psyching. A technique such as Thought-Stopping, for instance, can help you break the habit by creating a new reflex that is strengthened with repeated practice and reinforced with concurrent Relaxation exercises. You can thereby build a new pattern of habitual behavior from which hair pulling is absent.

See also:
Nervous habits

Techniques to try:
Thought-Stopping
Relaxation

Headaches

Most headaches respond adequately to aspirin or other over-the-counter pain killers. But recent discoveries that relate physical ailments to psychological states indicate that some headaches may best be treated by attacking the emotional and behavioral problems underlying headaches. You can use certain self-psyching techniques to bring relief from your pain.

In both experimental and clinical settings, migraine headaches have been controlled with Autogenic Training and Biofeedback. Patients have learned to alter their blood flow to reduce the dilation of cranial arteries that causes such headaches. Many people have successfully employed this approach outside the lab using their own Autogenic Training routine, which requires no machinery, or by obtaining their own Biofeedback device for use at home.

Tension headaches respond favorably to Relaxation methods and to Biofeedback, both of which help reduce tension and stress. Such headaches often result from the habit of constantly grinding one's teeth (bruxism) or otherwise keeping pressure on the muscles of the face and scalp. Relaxation and Biofeedback, as well as Negative Practice to break the habit of bruxism, are worth trying if you suffer from tension headaches.

Although consultation with a physician is, of course, the sensible course for those with long-standing headache problems, it cannot hurt to familiarize yourself with those self-psyching techniques that have brought relief to others.

See also:
Psychosomatic Complaints and Pains
Teeth Gnashing

Techniques to try:
Autogenic Training
Biofeedback
Relaxation
Negative Practice

Sources of further information:
Diamond, Seymour, and Furlong, William B. *More Than Two Aspirin: A Complete Guide to Identifying, Understanding*

and Solving Your Headache Problem. New York: Follett, 1976.

Freese, Arthur. *Headaches: The Kinds and The Cures.* New York: Schocken Books, 1974.

PROBLEM

Helplessness

Some people get so down on themselves that they come to believe that they have no control over their own experiences: Whatever happens to them — good or bad, success or failure — doesn't seem to arise from their own actions or desires. Such helpless feelings are a form or symptom of a depression in which the unpredictability of the course of one's life overwhelms one's capacity for coping normally.

Major crises and setbacks such as the death of a loved one, breakup of a marriage, loss of a job, or bankruptcy can bring on the helpless feelings. But the accumulation of even minor pressures and stresses can also produce helplessness. The degree of one's ability to handle stress and anxiety determines what promotes helplessness severe enough to disrupt one's life.

The article on Depression offers several techniques that may permit you to deal with helpless feelings, though acute depression of any kind is a matter best left to the care of trained professionals. Reading that article will help you decide how severe your problem is and whether or not the self-psyching methods will give you sufficient relief. And the article on Hopelessness gives you a glimpse into this most extreme form of helplessness.

See also:
Depression
Hopelessness

PROBLEM

Hoarding

See:
Compulsiveness

Hopelessness

Hopelessness is the most extreme form of helplessness, that aspect of depression characterized by a belief that you have no way to influence events or control the direction of your life. Some researchers contend that hopelessness is the cause of many unexplained sudden deaths among infants and even adults. So-called crib deaths may result from the newborns' diminution of life force, which is sapped by an intuitively felt failure to influence the world around them. Experiments with lab animals deprived of the ability to influence their environment have produced similar sudden deaths that could be attributed to terminal hopelessness.

If you are prone to such an acute form of depression, professional intervention is indicated. Self-psyching can do nothing to aid anyone so gravely afflicted. But reading the article on Helplessness and Depression could broaden your understanding of the symptoms that may be precursors to hopelessness, and techniques are suggested for alleviating those problems.

See also:
Helplessness
Depression

PROBLEM

Hostility

People who always seem to be angry, who seldom smile, and who frequently strike out — verbally or physically — at others are hostile individuals; hostility is a dominant element in their personalities. Such people are not likely to try, nor would they be much helped by, self-psyching. They require professional help from a trained therapist. If hostility is so pervasive in your life that your angry feelings and thoughts keep you from holding jobs, making friends, and being happy, you have a serious problem worthy of expert attention.

But if you only occasionally find your anger so powerful that it frightens you and threatens your normal functioning, you might profit from trying the techniques mentioned in the articles on Losing Your Temper, Fear of Expressing Anger, and Crying. Those techniques work for people who exhibit anger as a normal response to ordinary and justifiably infuriating situations and events.

See also:
Losing Your Temper
Fear of Expressing Anger
Crying

Imagination

See:
Fantasy

Inability to Make Requests

If fear or embarrassment has ever kept you from asking for a raise, promotion, date, loan, or favor, you are not alone. Many of us find reasons to avoid making requests, preferring to do without rather than risk a refusal. And even if you build up the courage to make your request, you may discover that it is made too late, as happens when you ask for a promotion and find that someone else got it because your boss didn't know you had wanted the better job.

This inability to make reasonable, well-timed requests and to make them forcefully and convincingly cheats us of our fair share of the good things in life. Overcoming this problem starts us down the road to greater self-assurance, self-satisfaction, fulfillment, and self-control.

Assertiveness Training can enable you to overcome the inhibitions that may be keeping you from making legitimate requests of others. Behavior Rehearsal teaches you to approach the task of asking for something with a greater expectation of maintaining control of yourself and getting a positive response. Similarly, Modeling shows you how others get their requests fulfilled. And Desensitization helps remove anxiety that may be keeping you from making requests.

See also:
Shyness and Inhibitions
Fear of Failure
Roadblocks to Successful Self-Psyching (in Introduction)

Techniques to try:
Assertiveness Training
Behavior Rehearsal
Modeling
Desensitization

TECHNIQUE

Incompatible Behavior

Particularly useful in dealing with such problems as Nervous Habits, Minor Emotional Complaints (the Blues and the Blahs, Sadness, Fatigue and Lethargy, Boredom, etc.). Can help in establishing Good Habits.

May also play a role in overcoming Smoking, Overeating, Problem Drinking. But in trying to handle such addictive behavior, Incompatible Behavior should be used in conjunction with other approaches suggested under the particular problems. And, of course, in severe cases, treatment may be necessary.

Supplementary or alternative techniques: Negative Practice, Thought-Stopping, Rewards, Stimulus Control, Relaxation.

WHAT INCOMPATIBLE BEHAVIOR IS

An incompatible behavior is any action that by its performance makes another action impossible or at least difficult to execute. As a self-psyching technique, it involves doing something that prevents the occurrence of a behavior you wish to change or eliminate. The technique also encompasses thought and emotion — for example, thinking a cheerful thought can make it all but impossible for you to feel unhappy.

HISTORICAL DEVELOPMENT

Behavior therapists and researchers have found that certain problems can be eliminated by replacing unwanted actions with others that may be more desirable or even neutral. The only requirement is that the replacement behavior make the problem harder or impossible to perform. Common sense suggests that you can't do two contradictory things at the same time: You can't smile while you frown; you can't walk while sitting.

The mutual exclusiveness of certain actions is the foundation of the Incompatible Behavior technique. Its effect is related to Desensitization's ability to counter anxiety with relaxation. But Incompatible Behavior is a more narrowly focused method, best suited to combating undesirable habits and clearing the way for new and better habits.

BASIC ELEMENTS OF INCOMPATIBLE BEHAVIOR

Identifying the problem (see Introduction)
Setting goals (see Introduction)
Selecting an appropriate incompatible behavior
Practicing Incompatible Behavior
Monitoring your behavior to detect change (see Introduction)
Employing the technique with other problems

HOW TO USE INCOMPATIBLE BEHAVIOR

Identify the problem. It is imperative to correctly identify the behavior you wish to change. Pinpoint your problem by observing your behavior before you attempt any modification of it. Count how often and for how long you bite your nails or crack your knuckles each day. Such specific information helps you decide what problem to attack and is the basis for measuring later improvement.

Set a goal. If you are trying to break a nervous habit, you can expect to observe progress within a couple of weeks. That should be your goal so commit yourself to trying the technique for at least two weeks.

No formal practice sessions of a particular duration are called for. Repeated, regular use of the technique — as often and for as long as is convenient — is what you must plan on.

Select an appropriate Incompatible Behavior. Be sure to select an appropriate incompatible behavior. Although it is advantageous to pick desirable behaviors to counteract undesirable ones, this is not required for breaking old habits. A related action, even a purely neutral one, will work as long as when you are performing it you are prevented from engaging in the habit you wish to change.

If you have the habit of scratching yourself, an Incompatible Behavior is patting. That is, whenever you find yourself scratching or feeling the impulse to scratch, pat (or rub or stroke) the area instead. The scratching urge will be satisfied, but you won't get scratched and you will·be disrupting the habitual pattern of scratching almost reflexively in certain situations. And it is unlikely that you will develop a new patting habit to replace the scratching habit, because, unlike a nervous habit, your use of Incompatible Behavior is a conscious and controlled activity of limited duration, not a reflexive act developed over a long period.

Practice Incompatible Behavior. Once you have identified your problem and selected an appropriate Incompatible Behavior, you must take advantage of every opportunity to practice. Pay particular attention to occasions on which you most commonly engage in the target behavior. For example, you may habitually crack your knuckles during business meetings or lectures, while watching television or studying. Nervous habits involving use of your hands can be broken by giving your hands other tasks. Doodle, play with a pencil, make paper airplanes — do anything socially acceptable that prevents the knuckle-cracking process from beginning. Something as simple as opening and closing your hands, making a fist, or holding an object might work. (If you are also trying to cut down on your smoking, don't hold onto a cigarette.) It's a matter of retraining your reflexes, of choosing an activity that you can consciously control and can discontinue when the target habit is broken.

Not only will you be able to stop a troublesome habit once it starts, but ultimately, by altering the conditioning that makes habits so tenacious, you will weaken the impulses that provoke and sustain habitual behavior.

Monitor your behavior to detect change. Following the instructions in the Introduction, check your progress. If you continue to practice this technique on any one problem for about two weeks you should observe significant modification of your target behavior.

Employ the technique with other problems. If, for example, you are successful in breaking a nervous habit like knuckle cracking or nail biting, then consider using the approach on other habits or on minor emotional difficulties.

Say you now want to counter the blues and the blahs; begin by making it part of your daily routine to smile in situations that normally cause you to frown. Every morning, while making up or shaving, look at yourself in the mirror, smile, even make funny faces — laugh if you can. Because of the connection between the mind and the body, between thoughts and emotions and bodily feelings, you should find it very hard to feel sad when you are making the outward, physical gestures of happiness. Look happy and you will feel happier; put on a happy face and it will be harder to think unhappy thoughts. Likewise, if you trot, run, or walk briskly — rather than drag yourself along — you should elevate your spirits and increase your energy level. Try it: you have nothing to lose but your lethargy.

If you are trying to develop new habits, use the Incompatible Behavior technique along with a positive-reinforcement technique: Reward yourself for behavior changes. Arrange to give yourself a suitable reward as soon as possible after successfully engaging in the new habit. (You might reward yourself each time you use Incompatible Behavior to successfully counter an undesirable habit.) See the section on Rewards for further details.

PRECAUTIONS
Certain habits, like smoking, overeating, or problem drinking, can be partially combated with Incompatible Behavior. The old method of chewing gum whenever you feel like smoking does have some merit. But unlike some nervous habits that you want to get rid of because they have obvious and immediate ill effects, habits like smoking probably furnish considerable pleasure, are deeply embedded in your social life, are reinforced each time you smoke, and may even serve you as well as trouble you. As the articles on these problems point out, more potent means may be required to curtail such habits.

It is true that minor emotional difficulties — sadness, boredom, Sunday-night tensions, mid-week letdown, unwillingness to face the daily grind — may respond to the Incompatible Behavior technique. Smiling, laughing, playing, being active, and involving yourself in joyful pursuits are incompatible with frowning, crying, despondent withdrawal, surrender to pessimism, and just plain feeling sad. But more severe anxiety or depression calls for the use of other techniques specifically intended to alleviate emotional distress. And deep depression or outright panic requires professional assistance.

Sources of further information:

Robbins, Jhan, and Fisher, Dave. *How To Make and Break Habits.* New York: Peter H. Wyden, 1973.

Watson, David L., and Tharp, Roland G. *Self-Directed Behavior: Self-Modification for Personal Adjustment.* Monterey, Calif.: Brooks/Cole, 1972.

<hr>

PROBLEM

Indecisiveness

Making decisions can be a problem if you have too many choices. Unlike children who cannot decide which of the 31 flavors at Baskin-Robbins to buy, most adults have developed favorites that keep them from being distracted by licorice-flavored ice cream when they know they like chocolate. But there are grownups who don't yet have a clear enough idea of their own preferences and whose indecisiveness often results in their doing what other, more decisive people want — they go to movies others choose, eat at restaurants others in their party select, even let someone else's forceful opinions influence what they will pick from the menu.

Indecisiveness can also be a problem if you are afraid or unwilling to take responsibility. An example of this is when a couple waste and frustrate themselves fretting over both trivial and significant decisions. Trying to pick a TV program to watch can be as taxing as deciding where to take a vacation, because neither partner wants to be responsible if the decision turns out wrong.

In most social, personal, and professional situations you will be called on regularly to make decisions. Success in these areas can depend on your ability to make decisions — not necessarily to always make the right decision but able to make a decision.

That you must make a decision also means having choices, options. If decision making is tough for you, try this approach. First rank your choices, considering whether or not each alternative will produce the results you want or need and how much effort, time, money or risk will be involved. Make a list of your choices, ordering them according to whether your decision depends most on making a quick and easy choice, a costly or risky one, or one that will require a great deal of time to implement. Now see which ones you might try first. Obviously, you won't want to try a complex or irreversible option right away if you have other choices, nor would you decide on a course of action taking days or weeks if action is needed in minutes or hours. By balancing the factors that led you to identify and rank your options, you may come up with a sensible decision-making plan.

If you still have trouble deciding, even after laying out all the choices — and you very well might — then a more elaborate self-psyching program is in order.

Assertiveness Training could give you the confidence needed to exercise autonomy and face decision-making responsibilities. Changing the Sequence of Events could break down your habitual pattern of avoiding decision making. Rewards, Punishments, and Stimulus Control may provide incentives for deciding more effectively and enable you to modify your behavior and habits so that you are more likely to make decisions.

Becoming a better decision maker is a worthwhile enterprise. Life can be richer and more exciting when you gain this fundamental ability. Think about how many of the little things, the pleasant aspects of life, involve decision making. Just try playing gin rummy or even pushing a shopping cart through a supermarket if you can't make decisions. Even if you make a lot of bad choices in life, it is better to be able to make them than to have other people or mere accident and circumstances make them for you.

If the fear of being wrong is at the root of your indecisiveness, it is valuable to remember that few decisions are ever final and irreversible and that you are unlikely to make many decisions that are entirely wrong. Knowing that you will probably be at least partially right in most decisions and that you may well get a chance to revise many decisions should encourage you to make choices more freely. By employing Desensitization, you can make it easier to overcome the fear of a wrong decision, a fear that may be contributing to your indecisiveness.

The decision-making process is inescapable: Every decision can create the need for making yet others. So you might as well learn to be an effective decision maker. It's not that hard a skill to acquire.

See also:
  Procrastination

Techniques to try:
  Assertiveness Training
  Changing the Sequence of Events
  Rewards
  Punishments
  Stimulus Control
  Desensitization
  Fantasy

PROBLEM

Inefficiency

See:
  Work and Study Habits
  Procrastination

PROBLEM

Inhibitions

Assertiveness Training is the specific technique for overcoming inhibitions and getting more out of life by getting more into life. Other techniques mentioned in the article on Shyness and Inhibitions can support your efforts to learn how to do much of what you now seem reluctant to hazard.

See also:
  Shyness and Inhibitions

Technique to try:
  Assertiveness Training

PROBLEM

Insomnia

We need sleep for good physical health and dreaming for good mental health. People who suffer from genuine insomnia experience extended periods of sleep deprivation, inability to get to sleep or stay asleep, and inability to get sufficient periods of mind-cleansing dreaming. But such people are actually few in number. Most people who think they are insomniacs actually get plenty of sleep between periods of tossing and turning. And the old-fashioned notion that everyone must get in a solid eight hours has been disproven.

Different people need different amounts of sleep. Some need as much as twelve hours; others sleep little more than a few hours a day and have full and productive lives. And older people need far less sleep than they did when they were young.

Notwithstanding these facts, if you are disturbed because you cannot seem to get to sleep when you want, there are methods for preparing yourself to get to sleep easily and stay asleep through fairly long periods of uninterrupted rest, with emotionally beneficial dreaming thrown in.

Relaxation techniques in the evening can reduce physical tension and emotional stimulation. Meditation exercises can have the same effect. If anxiety about events of the day or about forthcoming encounters keeps you awake, a session of Desensitization (along with Relaxation) is highly effective. If floods of unwanted thoughts keep you awake, Thought-Stopping works very well. If nightmares interrupt your sleep, controlled Fantasy can give you control over your dreaming, allowing you to sleep longer and even convert recurrent nightmares into pleasant and uplifting dreams that restore you while helping you learn more about yourself. However, controlling anxiety about the day's events or impending responsibilities may not be enough to help you get to sleep.

Environmental stimuli and your own physical condition and habits can also interfere with sleep. Insufficient Exercise can promote insomnia, so getting adequate physical activity on a regular basis is advisable if you want to go to bed really ready to sleep and rest. Stimulus Control may contribute to combating insomnia caused by sleep-robbing distractions such as arguing with your spouse or snacking uncontrollably before retiring. Negative Practice can help you overcome nervous habits that may be preventing you from getting to sleep or sleeping restfully. And with Self-Hypnosis you can relax your mind and your body.

The old standby of counting sheep has much to recommend it, inasmuch as it involves focused concentration and a rhythmic repetition similar to that used in forms of Meditation. Use such ancient approaches or the more contemporary means of smoking pot or getting a bit drunk, if such measures work for you. There are no certain methods for everyone, but the self-psyching techniques suggested here have the merit of being systematic, easy to learn and employ, and focused on particular aspects of your problems with sleep.

See also:
Sleep
Nightmares
Nervous Habits

Techniques to try:
Relaxation
Meditation
Desensitization
Thought-Stopping
Fantasy
Exercise
Stimulus Control
Negative Practice
Self-Hypnosis

Sources of further information:

Freemon, F. R. *Sleep Research: A Critical Review*. Springfield, Ill.: Charles C Thomas, 1972.

Rubinstein, Hilary. *Insomniacs of the World, Goodnight*. New York: Random House, 1974.

Thoresen, Carl E., and Coates, Thomas J. *How to Sleep Better*. Englewood Cliffs, N. J.: Prentice-Hall, 1976.

PROBLEM

Interviewing for Jobs

See:
Disagreeable Tasks and Encounters

Knuckle Cracking

This habit is fairly common among children, who usually practice it consciously to get attention. Among adults it is typically an uncontrollable habit that annoys other people, and can injure the delicate structures of the hand and may promote future arthritic problems. From the perspective of self-psyching, the principal problem this habit creates is guilt over the lack of self-control it indicates. It can be dealt with rather easily using one or more of the techniques suggested in the article on Nervous Habits.

See:
Nervous Habits
Guilt

Lack of Concentration

See:
Disorganized Thinking
Floods of Unwanted Thoughts

Lack of Privacy

You have a problem if you allow others to rob you of your privacy. It is unreasonable to feel guilty or embarrassed about preserving the sanctity of the place in which you work, study, or live. It is unnecessary for you to be the one whose office is always crowded with people. The intruders are the offending parties, and if they are offended by your displeasure at being interrupted, the offense is compounded. Such people, by taking your time and breaking your concentration, are depriving you of things of tangible value to you. Putting up with their larceny makes you an accomplice. You wouldn't help a burglar carry away your stereo set; don't let a time thief steal something of far greater value: the privacy you need to carry on the business of living or the solitude that can give your life added joy and meaning.

Assertiveness Training is ideal for this problem. Practice it and you should be able to discourage most intruders without losing your composure or their friendship. It can teach you to modify your responses so that you don't reflexively go along with intrusions, choking down your resentment and feeling guilty for even wanting to mention that the intruder has disregarded your feelings. The technique makes those very intrusions stimuli for new reflexes, through which you easily and automatically express the way you feel and the way you think things should be.

Try this form of self-psyching and you can quickly discover how much more you can accomplish in a work day or an evening of study. And your knowledge of how it works and your practice of it will give you important new skills in dealing with related problems, such as standing up for your rights, handling disagreeable tasks and encounters, and overcoming inhibitions and shyness.

Techniques to try:
Assertiveness Training
Behavior Rehearsal

PROBLEM
Lack of Self-Confidence

See:
Shyness and Inhibitions
Standing Up for Your Rights

PROBLEM
Lethargy

See:
Fatigue and Lethargy

PROBLEM
Loneliness

An excellent way to handle loneliness is to convert it into solitude. If you find yourself alone much of the time, take advantage of the situation to do things that only solitude permits. Engage in solitary hobbies like painting, serious reading, or creative writing. But if you desire increased involvement with others, more social activities, you can learn to be more outgoing and need not put up with being alone so often. The articles on Making Friends and Inability to Make Requests will guide you to self-psyching techniques that can help you break your interludes of unwanted solitude. The article on Shyness and Inhibitions may prompt you to break out of the shell that may be sustaining your loneliness.

See also:
Making Friends
Inability to Make Requests
Shyness and Inhibitions

PROBLEM

Losing at Sports and Games Without Anxiety

See:
Fear of Failure
Compulsiveness
Guilt

PROBLEM

Losing Your Temper

Giving vent to uncontrollable anger is usually an inappropriate response to the pressures of daily living. When you fly off the handle, reflexively saying or doing harsh or harmful things, you seldom get what you want and you usually force the objects of your rage — other people — to react more emotionally than they'd like to. Everyone loses when you lose your temper.

The opposites of shy and meek people who must learn to release their feelings and assert themselves, those who lose their tempers too often must learn to keep their emotions in check. Unnecessary embarrassment, guilt, and even depression are the unavoidable outcomes of unrestrained anger.

If losing your temper is your typical response to the frustration and stress of modern life, you might consider employing some of the following techniques. The regular practice of Relaxation can raise your threshold of frustration tolerance. Desensitization and Behavior Rehearsal can help you defuse your anger before you face stressful encounters and reduce your expectations of anxiety, anger, or frustration.

In situations where you feel you are getting close to uncontrollable anger, employ Relaxation or Autogenic Training to reduce your emotional level and give you a degree of tranquility that will enable you to stay in control.

Losing your temper is almost always a regrettable experience. It has cost people friends, business success, jobs. At the very least it forces them to apologize repeatedly for their behavior and feel guilty for having to do so. It causes unhappiness and diminishes self-esteem. Learning to control your temper — certainly not to stifle it entirely and turn yourself into a spineless cipher — is a valuable exercise in self-psyching and self-improvement.

See also:
Fear of Expressing Anger
Guilt
Disagreeable Tasks and Encounters
Hostility

Techniques to try:
Relaxation
Desensitization
Behavior Rehearsal
Autogenic Training

Making Friends

If you are shy, retiring, or inhibited you aren't the only one who has trouble making friends. Even ordinarily outgoing people can find themselves in circumstances in which they have to work at making new acquaintances and building new friendships. If you have moved to another city, changed schools, or started another job, probably you left most of your old friends behind and have had to start all over in your efforts to get to know strangers better. And if you merely feel that you don't have enough friends now, that not enough people know you, that you want to widen your circle of friends by meeting new people, you are in almost the same position as someone with no friends at all.

To find people with whom you share interests you might begin by examining your own activities, ideas, and aspirations: Compile a list that will profile your character traits. Use this list to guide you to people who might be most compatible with you and thus most likely to become your friends. Potential friends need not match your profile exactly — few will, and even those who come close may be hard to get close to because of their own personality traits. You don't want carbon copies of yourself for friends, merely people with whom you have enough in common to base a friendship.

Venture into other areas of activity in your search for new people to meet. Among the people you ordinarily spend time with — at work or school — you may well encounter some compatible individuals. But outside the orbit of your daily routine there are probably thousands of people with interests and backgrounds similar to yours. Take courses in subjects you like; join organizations that attract individuals with philosophies like your own. Go where people meet and converse and you may just find others like yourself, people looking for friends like you.

Of course, many of us miss opportunities for real friendships with people we already know. Why not let such people get to know you better? If shyness is part of your problem Assertiveness Training and Behavior Rehearsal could help you become more outgoing and make contacts more effectively. And Desensitization can defuse the anxiety that may be keeping you from approaching potential friends, whether you know them or not.

Friendship is not something that you can expect to have thrust upon you or that you can thrust upon others. It takes effort; it requires a degree of commitment and selflessness. Just giving of yourself will do more to gain you new friends than all the plotting, planning, and waiting you may already have done.

See also:
Shyness and Inhibitions

Techniques to try:
Assertiveness Training
Behavior Rehearsal
Desensitization
Modeling

PROBLEM

Managing Time

See:
Work and Study Habits
Procrastination
Tardiness
Punctuality

PROBLEM

Marital Problems

The difficulty of getting along with your spouse may be of sufficient magnitude to require a trained counselor or therapist. But because marriage is in many respects a microcosm of society, reflecting many of the difficulties and demands of social life, several of the techniques in this book do apply to marital problems that arise when two people interact continually.

Assertiveness Training could help you make your needs known to your spouse, help you speak up more consistently and clearly to improve communication, and aid you in working out solutions to conflicts. Rewards, Stimulus Control, Changing the Sequence of Events, and even Punishments might give you guidance in breaking existing troublesome patterns of behavior such as sulking, bickering, overresponding to criticism, being hypercritical, arguing constantly about money, sex, and so on. And Desensitization, Behavior Rehearsal, and Modeling can help you prepare for interactions you find difficult. Try some or several of these methods and monitor the changes in your marital situation.

See also:
 Conflict Avoidance
 Sexual Hang-ups
 Accepting Criticism and Criticizing Others
 Disagreeable Tasks and Encounters

Techniques to try:
 Assertiveness Training
 Rewards
 Stimulus Control
 Changing the Sequence of Events
 Punishments
 Desensitization
 Behavior Rehearsal
 Modeling

TECHNIQUE

Martial Arts

Learning one or more of the Martial Arts — Kung Fu, Karate, Aikido, and Zen Archery, for example — may be considered an adjunct to self-psyching, though such disciplines require involvement with a group and instruction from an acknowledged master.

Such activities and skills are recommended because each requires a degree of concentration and application that counteracts the stress responses at the root of anxiety. You will be training your body to ignore anxiety-provoking outside pressures and distractions. At the same time you will be conditioning your reflexes, both physical and emotional, to respond logically, directly, and with appropriate outlays of energy and concentration to the pressures of everday life. And achieving excellence in such pursuits is bound to increase your self-confidence. Even if you never have to strike out at a mugger, your body will have been programmed to handle the subtler psychological attacks that the untrained person responds to with inappropriate fight-or-flight reactions.

Why Martial Arts are worth learning. The greatest attraction of Martial Arts to anyone involved in self-psyching is their unique combination of exercise and meditation. By learning any one of them you have the opportunity to train yourself to gain the physical benefits of exercise while achieving the tranquility that comes to the accomplished meditator.

A student of one of the Martial Arts should find it far easier than most people to fight off anxiety, maintain self-control and self-confidence, handle such common problems as insomnia, frustration, anger, fatigue and lethargy, and cope with typical nervous habits arising from nervousness and improper channeling of stress. If you are already a Martial Arts student, your involvement in self-psyching should be quite profitable. You do not, of course, have to study these arts to use self-psyching, though conscientious practice of self-psyching may well make you a person more likely to benefit in turn from Martial Arts training.

See also:
Exercise
Meditation

TECHNIQUE

Meditation

Particularly useful in dealing with such problems as Anxiety, Minor Emotional Complaints, Insomnia, Frustrations, Losing Your Temper, Fatigue and Lethargy.

May play a role in coping with Psychosomatic Complaints and Pains and breaking such habits as Smoking and Overeating.

Supplementary or alternative techniques: Relaxation, The Relaxation Response, Biofeedback, Desensitization, Prayer, Fantasy.

WHAT MEDITATION IS

Meditation is a technique for overcoming the sensory and intellectual distractions that often crowd our waking hours, disturb or discourage sleep, and stimulate tension, stress, and anxiety.

You won't find a fully satisfying definition of Meditation in any dictionary. It is a process, an action, a mental and physical phenomenon that all who practice it claim must be experienced to be understood and appreciated. Fortunately, it is easier to meditate than to define the word. So the bulk of this article is devoted to instructions for using some of the many methods available.

HISTORICAL DEVELOPMENT

Meditation is probably as old as humanity. In a sense, any being capable of focusing on a single object is equipped to meditate. The predator intently stalking its prey, the hunting dog on point, the monk deep in contemplation, the scientist lost in thought are all cut off from the normal sensitivity to outside distractions.

Meditation involves a single-mindedness that at once produces both relaxation and heightened awareness. This awareness is central to the process as practiced by human beings. At first, meditators center their awareness solely on the object of their concentration. But ultimately, according to some meditators, real time and space are transcended in a way that expands awareness to encompass new knowledge of the self and of reality.

If all this sounds more than a little mystical, it is with good reason. Meditation and mysticism have an ancient, intertwined history. The age-old human search for meaning beyond what is revealed to the senses — a quest carried on both within and outside formal religions (prayer is a form of Meditation) — has often involved experiences termed mystical.

Meditation of one kind or another has been practiced in virtually every culture. In fact, only Western, industrialized societies of the last century or so minimized its utility. Science, technology, and commerce became our reality and there seemed little place for the reality glimpsed by meditators. But recent developments — from scientific breakthroughs into the way the brain functions to the drug culture of the sixties and the spread of movements like Transcendental Meditation in the seventies — have reawakened Western interest in what Meditation is and what it can do for us.

There is some evidence that Meditation has physiological benefits. Laboratory tests on people who have meditated for years and on volunteers who were taught to meditate in order that their responses might be measured have suggested that Meditation produces effects almost exactly the opposite of those generated by stress and anxiety. Meditation seems to lower the consumption of oxygen and the discharge of carbon dioxide as part of a general reduction in metabolism and respiration rates. The blood chemistry is changed in ways promoting relaxation and a sense of well-being. The heart rate slows and production of alpha brain waves associated with deep restfulness increases. These, along with other changes in the various systems of the body, seem to make meditators uncommonly able to cope with anxiety-provoking stimuli. And, after long experience with the practice, meditators have been found to remain relatively relaxed and anxiety-free for a considerable time, despite exposure to the same pressures that send nonmeditators into bouts of anxiety.

Meditation, therefore, may be a sound, simple, and practical method for inoculating oneself against the distress and discomfort of anxiety.

Scientific studies have also provided evidence that Meditation can help in dealing with a number of other complaints. Drug-users, smokers, drinkers, and overeaters who have become meditators have had greater success kicking their habits. Meditation seems to help people reformulate their needs and restructure their emotions so as to diminish dependence on agencies outside themselves. Meditation can therefore be at least an adjunct to any program of behavior change aimed at altering troublesome habits.

Insomnia is far less of a problem for meditators, so sleep problems might be attacked with this technique. Similarly, proneness to fatigue and lethargy appears to diminish: Meditation involves periods of profound rest — deeper, in most cases, than that achieved through hours of sleep — which gives meditators greater energy and endurance.

Meditators also seem unusually able to tolerate frustration, have fewer problems with obsessions and compulsiveness, and find themselves able to be assertive without becoming angry or aggressive. And research indicates that Meditation could lessen the likelihood of suffering from certain illnesses at least partly attributable to stress: panic attacks, certain skin ailments, asthma, hypertension, forms of arthritis, some ulcers, and susceptibility to infection.

BASIC ELEMENTS OF MEDITATION

Deciding whether or not to become a meditator
Setting goals (see Introduction)
Continuing current practices conducive to Meditation
Practicing formal Meditation
1. The right place
2. The right time and proper duration
3. The correct posture
Choosing what to meditate on
1. Objects
2. Ritual movements
3. Sounds
4. The breath of the meditator
5. The imagination
Checking to see if Meditation is working for you

HOW TO USE MEDITATION

Decide whether or not to become a meditator. Meditation should not be thought of as a miracle cure. Some people have great difficulty meditating or obtaining the beneficial effects that others report. And some problems are too far advanced or too grave to be dealt with without professional assistance. But for average people with some of the typical problems of life, Meditation can provide not only physical rewards but also psychological and spiritual benefits.

Everyday life provides few chances for giving our minds and spirits genuine rest. The way we live makes it terribly difficult to achieve the insights that come from quiet contemplation and the experience of escaping the turmoil created by all the distracting sights, sounds, ideas, demands, and sensations that constantly bombard us. Meditation furnishes one way to gain that rest, to make that escape, to find that place within ourselves where we can discover who we are, what we want and need, what our real capabilities are, and what is truly important to us at the deepest level.

Most Meditation forms are easy to learn and practice without a teacher. And because relatively little time is required,

Meditation can readily become a regular and permanent part of a self-psyching repertoire.

Set goals. Once you have decided to begin meditating, resolve to continue the practice regularly until you witness appreciable improvement in the way you feel and behave. Allow for at least one (preferably two) fifteen- to twenty-minute session per day for a minimum of a month. After a month, if you have noticed improvement, resolve to make Meditation a permanent part of your life.

Continue current practices. You may be something of a meditator without knowing it. If you have a hobby that totally engrosses your attention, those moments when you are thinking of nothing else but the objects and actions involved in your pastime manifest a form of Meditation.

Say you are a weekend painter. You set up your easel in a quiet spot and start mixing your paints. You study your subject, noting every line and color. Your mind and heart are locked into what you are doing. There are moments when you think and feel nothing that is not part of the act of painting, moments when you are liberated from outside distractions.

Even if you achieve this altered awareness state for only a few minutes out of every hour you devote to such a hobby, those minutes are meditative and probably supply most of the refreshment and relaxation you obtain from your pursuit. When you return to your other activities with a keener awareness, a sense of accomplishment, a measure of physical and spiritual renewal, it may well be because you meditated — however unknowingly. The fact that an unusually large percentage of professional painters — and photographers, architects, designers, and others engaged in occupations requiring long periods of quiet attention and contemplation — live long lives of relative good health and comparative tranquility seems to argue for Meditation.

Even hobbies requiring physical exertion may involve some elements of Meditation. Full commitment of your energy and attention to a sport (tennis, handball, golf) requiring long periods of concentration on the game, to the exclusion of work and home worries, can recharge your emotional batteries in much the same way that quiet pastimes like painting and formal Meditation do.

Therefore, the first instruction for those wishing to meditate is that they seek out or continue to engage in activities that encourage concentration, full involvement, and freedom from the everyday concerns and distractions of their lives. A number of activities qualify. For instance, reading, no matter what the content of the book, can certainly require intense concentration, and the regular, repetitive, rhythmic act of scanning and turning the pages can be like some forms of meditative practice. Pick an activity you like and make it a part of your daily, or at least weekly, routine. This is the simplest introduction on how to meditate.

Formal Meditation requires more concerted planning, but nothing terribly difficult, unless you wish to become an initiate of one of the Eastern disciplines that can demand a lifetime of training and dedication!

Practice formal Meditation.

1. *The right place:* All you need is a relatively quiet place in which you are willing to spend a short period alone once or twice a day. Many meditators choose the bathroom, which is probably one of the last precincts of privacy left in our open and interacting society. A corner of the garage, a spot in the backyard, your office or bedroom, a parked car, anywhere will do if it's a place where you will not be disturbed and where you can get physically comfortable.

2. *The right time and proper duration:* Fifteen to twenty minutes is about the right duration for any one session. Time of day is not that important, though many meditators find once in the morning and once early in the evening optimal. (Some research has shown that it may be hard to get maximum physical benefits if you meditate within two hours of a meal: The digestive process seems to counter some of Meditation's physiological effects.) Try various times and check the effects over a few weeks until you find a time that works best for you and fits into your schedule.

3. *The correct posture:* It is most important to begin in a relaxed and comfortable position. This may mean loosening or removing any clothing that might distract you. Your exact posture is up to you — based on your own feelings and trial-and-error experience. You can sit in a chair or use the so-called Lotus position, in which you sit cross-legged on the floor. The Lotus position, with the back straight or slightly arched, is comfortable with-

out being conducive to sleep, which is why so many meditators have used it over the centuries.

It is usually not advisable to meditate while lying down, and certainly not in your bed just before you are ready to fall asleep. Meditation requires you to be relaxed — but *fully awake* and aware. Your goal is to gain a deeper awareness of yourself, to relax and refresh yourself for subsequent waking activities, not to put yourself to sleep. So even though Meditation can help you sleep better by making you less prone to the tensions and worries that may have been robbing you of sleep, the technique is not to be used to turn off your body and mind. Select a time, place, and posture that permit focusing your concentration, not obliterating it.

Choose what to meditate on. What should you use as the focus of attention in order to free your mind and senses from outside distractions? You may use an object for visual contemplation, ritual movements you make, a sound that comfortably blocks out other sounds and thoughts, the rhythm of your own breathing, compelling thoughts or images, or a combination of some of these — anything that absorbs you sufficiently so that it and only it occupies your consciousness for the interlude of your session.

1. *Objects:* Many meditators find it easiest to focus on objects. You might begin your training with this ancient technique.

   First, select an object — preferably something simple, small, and portable, like a bit of stone or wood, a sea shell, or similar object.

   Assume your Meditation position with the object placed in line of sight a few feet or a few inches from you — depending on its size — so that you can see all its details. Gaze at the object throughout your session. Keep out distracting thoughts and feelings by focusing your attention on the object. Certainly you will be distracted — especially as you are beginning as a meditator — but by returning your attention to your meditation object you will overcome distractions. Think of the object as a beacon in the darkness, as an island in the stormy sea of sensory input, as a refuge from intrusions on your consciousness. As your object gains these attributes, you gain the peace of mind that comes from periodic freedom from distraction and sensory bombardment.

You may find that meditating upon an object can be facilitated by handling it as well as looking at it. Feel and fondle the object. Examine its every characteristic. Learn so much about it that you could identify it out of a group of similar objects in total darkness. Think of nothing else but the appearance, size, and texture of your object. Get so involved in it that it becomes a mini-universe in which you might dwell for the duration of your session.

Manufactured items are more difficult for beginners than natural objects. Even something as simple as a piece of cloth can evoke images of the process that created it, of the people who worked on it, of the things it might be made into. Keep your Meditation pure and simple — at least until you have had many weeks of success with the technique — by using objects with pleasing lines and colors but without distracting connotations. Keep your object simple and self-contained. Choose something like a leaf, a touchstone, or a bit of broken branch.

Gazing at, and especially handling, objects is a form of Meditation involved in many religious practices in which the devout concentrate on sacred images, statues, relics, paintings, rosaries, or prayer wheels. It is a simple yet highly effective technique that can be learned quickly. You might even find it helpful to carry your object around with you and touch it and contemplate it in moments when you wish to restore your emotional equilibrium.

As you get better at object-centered Meditation, you may want to try variations used by advanced meditators.

In one variation, still using your original object, you train yourself to contemplate all features of the object with your eyes closed, picturing it in your mind. Do this with the object in front of you so you can switch from imaginative to real visualization from time to time.

Another variation involves contemplating some portion of a larger object — like parts of a room, such as the wall, floor, ceiling, or door. Focus on a doorknob, a pattern in the plaster or rug, anything that has a uniquely compelling shape and details (or, perhaps, lack of details). All that matters is that you are able to rivet your attention on that thing and that you find it easy to return your concentration to it whenever you are distracted while meditating.

An ultimate variation would be finding that your skill has increased to the point where no real object is needed, where you are able to conjure up a remembered object or even create an imaginary one and focus on that. This is a major breakthrough for meditators. After many weeks — or even months — of success with real objects, try constructing a unique image or pattern that you will use as your object. Known in the East as *yantras*, these mental images might be floral patterns, a series of lines, patches of light and darkness, particular shapes combined in a special way. They may be varied or improved over time. Whatever your yantra is, it is yours alone. You will always be able to summon it up during Meditation and it will permit you to concentrate and relax by blocking out distractions and disturbances.

Another variation recommended by many meditators involves using the flame of a candle to center on. There is something about a dancing flame that holds one's attention remarkably well. This is both good and bad, especially for beginners. If you have had little experience with Meditation, you can become so captivated by the flame's movements that you may go into a sort of trance, a mild hypnotic state in which you don't experience things at all but are merely turned off for a time, feeling a bit dizzy and disoriented rather than relaxed and aware. The contemplation of flowers or floral patterns can also produce such effects.

Meditation should increase your awareness of yourself — of aspects of your being, and of all existence. It can't do this if you are mindlessly mesmerized and your awareness blunted. Still, contemplating a candle flame is effective once you know what you are doing. Try it as you would other objects — using both your eyes and your mind's eye — and measure the impact.

Object Meditation has almost endless variations. You may wish to contemplate a scene or a person's face (though these are fairly complex and potentially distracting practices because of all the connotations possible). You may even learn to meditate on nothing at all.

Mentally gazing at nothing means closing your eyes and "looking" at a spot directly in front of you, between your eyebrows. The effects of this sort of Meditation can be quite profound, increasing alpha brain waves more than other variations do. Pictures of Eastern holy men which show them looking cross-eyed, portray them gazing meditatively in this fashion.

Perhaps the simplest and quickest way to achieve the effects of meditating on "nothing" is through use of the so-called *ganzfeld* effect. All you have to do is cut a Ping-Pong ball in two and place the halves over your eyes, held in place by clear tape. It has been found that with nothing to see but the uniform white of the Ping-Pong ball halves, the mind automatically switches into deep relaxation with prodigious production of alpha waves. This is the *ganzfeld* or whole-field effect. Be sure to face a fairly bright window or stare in the direction of a lamp. This will illuminate the field so that you see a uniform white.

From personal experience with this method, having first been exposed to it as the subject of an experiment while in college, I can both recommend it and note its dangers. It is simple and quickly effective. But it can cut you off from outside stimuli so completely that you lose track of time and might remain in a meditative state for longer than is advisable, may go into a trance, or may simply fall asleep — in the middle of the day. Like so many "automatic" methods, it leaves insufficient room for control and self-monitoring, so it is best thought of as a supplement to other Meditation methods, to be tried experimentally and only occasionally.

Object Meditation is relatively easy, but there are other approaches beginners may try.

2. *Ritual movements:* Meditation need not be a sedentary act. Your own movement may be the focus of attention, occupying your mind and body to such an extent that your physical and psychological balance is beneficially affected.

You can get a good understanding of movement Meditation by looking at the faces of couples on a discotheque dance floor. Some seem to be in a trance. The music pounds out a steady beat; light shows paint the walls — perhaps even the ceiling and floor — with living color. All thought is blocked out except that which centers on the music and the dance. You are seeing something approaching mass Meditation. How can the noise and action of dancing approximate the benefits of quiet, solitary contemplation? It all comes down to the fact that when people give themselves over entirely to an experience they can shut out distraction and worry and come away relaxed. Such dancing relaxes even as it exhausts.

However, the person who would really rather be doing something else will get little from dancing. Those who dislike the sights, sounds, and movements of such dancing and who consider the other dancers exhibitionists, will probably come away from the experience feeling tense and unhappy.

In the same way, while some square dancers may get a measure of Meditationlike benefits (as they concentrate on coordinated movements and the caller's instructions) others who try to square dance but don't really like it will get none.

There are even religious forms of dance — from the ancient dervishes of the East to individual and communal dances in both Christian and non-Christian fundamentalist sects. Such dancers move in joyful response to their faith, with energetic devotional concentration.

Less strenuous movements than dancing requires can have some benefits. Sitting quietly in your Meditation posture, you can move just your fingers — touching each in turn with the thumb — and by concentrating fully on the movements you can shut out distractions and anxiety-provoking thoughts. You might merely tap your palms rhythmically against your thighs or devise your own meditative movements — anything that is fairly easy to do and which readily captures your attention.

Meditating on movements is related to the use of rosaries, crossing oneself, rhythmically rocking as you pray, and many similar rituals found in religious practices throughout the world. Such movements focus one's attention on devotional thoughts. Likewise, secular meditators can employ movements — alone or in conjunction with contemplation of sights or sounds — in their search for greater peace and a sharper vision of inner realities.

Even readers who have no desire to become meditators of any sort can share in the benefits that result from ritual movement. If you jog regularly you probably know that it is good for you (see Jogging in article on Exercise). You have no doubt learned that even short periods of jogging, during which you seemed to sense nothing but the sound of your feet pounding the ground and the taste and touch of the air, left you feeling terrific. (But you have probably also discovered that jogging while your mind was filled with business worries or thoughts of personal problems gave you little relaxation and no exhilaration. Jogging and fretting at the same time is merely moving misery.) Try jogging, dancing, ritual movement of any sort and you will profit greatly if you free yourself of distraction by concentrating on the movements.

3. *Sounds:* Using sounds as the focus of Meditation is perhaps the most widely practiced technique in America today. This is because of the phenomenal growth of Transcendental Meditation, or TM, in just the last few years. TM uses sound, in the form of a *mantra*, as the focus of Meditation. The mantra is a word or phrase given to each initiate by the instructor. It is supposed to be kept secret and each is claimed to be a formula uniquely suited to its user. The details of TM, including some of the controversial aspects of this approach, are covered in articles on Transcendental Meditation and The Relaxation Response. But much of the following information on meditating with sounds also applies to TM.

The sound you use may be uttered by you or produced by your environment. In the latter case, the more natural the sound the better — wind in the trees, the rhythmic pounding of the surf, rain on the roof. If you live near the beach you would do well to find a secluded spot and spend fifteen minutes or so letting your concentration on the sound of the waves wash away the anxiety you have accumulated during the day. A bubbling brook works as well; even listening to the muffled roar of passing traffic on a nearby highway will do (but keep your mind off trucks, air pollution, and the gas shortage).

If you don't have a readily available source of such

sounds and would like to meditate more frequently than those times when it happens to be raining or the wind is stirring the trees, learn to meditate on remembered sounds or create your own sounds.

Almost any neutral, fairly monotonous sound will do, so long as it is easy to produce. The simplest way is to meditate in the bathroom, while showering or letting the tub fill for your bath. Begin by assuming your meditation posture and focus on the sound of the falling water. For the first few sessions leave the water on all the time. Then try it with the water on for half the time and off for the rest of your session, while you try contemplating your memory of the sound. Your recollection should be quite vivid after several such sessions of listening to nothing else. And the sooner you find yourself able to concentrate on the memory of the sound, the sooner you can stop worrying about your impact on the water shortage.

Don't be troubled if other sounds sometimes intrude. As long as you bring your attention back to your target sound you will recapture the thread of Meditation and gain the benefits of the experience. Meditation doesn't have to be perfect; you merely try your best and use your sound, sight, movement, or other focus of attention to help you regain your composure, concentration, and freedom from anxiety-provoking stimuli. The process doesn't destroy all distractions; it does increase your ability to cope with them.

Another way to focus on sound is to select a mantra for yourself — a single word, two words, even nonsense syllables. Lawrence LeShan, author of How to Meditate, produces mantras by picking out names at random from the phone book and linking the first syllables of two of them. What's important is not the word chosen but the fact that you conscientiously focus on it. It's up to you to borrow from Eastern tradition and use Om, Aum, or Hare Krishna or choose Bemu, Jola, or some other made-up sounds.

You can actually vocalize the sound during all your sessions or you can try to learn to merely think the sound. Thinking the sound is especially useful in situations in which you have some time to meditate but less than complete privacy. By having your sound firmly set in your mind, you can call on it for those moments on subways, before meetings, or whenever you need a meditative uplift and psychic restoration.

During formal Meditation sessions, if you feel you are losing the effectiveness of a sound that you are merely thinking of, voice the sound during several successive sessions to restore its potency and deepen its impression on your mind.

Some people find it effective to focus not only on their chosen sound but also on the rhythm of their breathing. They practice saying (or thinking) their mantra on each exhalation of breath. This sets up a simple and sure pattern that facilitates concentration.

Perhaps the simplest way to use a mantra is with a system developed by Herbert Benson. The method involves the use of "one" as a mantra expressed subvocally each time one breathes out. (See article on The Relaxation Response for a full discussion.)

4. *The breath of the meditator:* It is even possible to use nothing but your breath — its sound, rhythm, and depth — as a focus of attention: Meditative exercises involving use of the patterns of breathing can be quite difficult for beginners. There are numerous forms, most of which require the instruction of experts. Simply viewed, these techniques call for you to establish a pattern of breathing that might range from your natural rhythm to one based on an arbitrary number of repetitions of your mantra. The concentration required can be so formidable that relaxation is actually undermined. And when the breathing pattern used is not the normal one, beginners can find themselves constantly returning to their natural rhythm or even gasping for breath. A certain degree of panic may even intrude and totally negate the purposes of Meditation. Meditation by breath control and breath focus is therefore not suitable for most beginners.

5. *The imagination:* For more advanced meditators, thoughts may replace sights, sounds, or movements as a focus of attention. Focusing on your thoughts is tricky: The mind is such an intricate and rapidly operating mechanism that it is difficult to suppress thoughts and images of a disturbingly distracting nature. To overcome this problem, the thoughts used should center on very simple and neutral subjects. It is no good to medi-

tate on the various portions of the anatomy of the opposite sex. This is pleasant, but hardly relaxing. It doesn't help your effort to reduce distraction and anxiety if you meditate on thoughts and fantasies involving people, places, events, or objects with connotations that can trigger worries and concerns.

Thought Meditation can work if you focus, for example, on the mental image of clouds scudding across a pure blue sky or on similarly pleasant but neutral scenes. (See Fantasy for constructive ways to use the contemplation of such visions to handle specific problems.)

You could also visualize a simple shape, say a circle, and concentrate on it as your imagination changes it into a square or a triangle. Some meditators close their eyes and mentally picture a shape that they see steadily diminish until it is totally gone and nothing remains. Creation of that "nothing" — a meditative void — is a skill much prized by meditators. They see it as a sign that you have turned off your conscious mind and freed your inner awareness. Achieving a contemplative void, even for a short period, should provide you with evidence that Meditation is working as it should.

Whatever technique helps you close out the world and open yourself to yourself, use it and use it regularly. You may start with, say, Meditation on movement, add a mantra to it, and then try thoughts and imagination. Give yourself a chance to derive physical and psychological benefits — but feel free to give up any method you don't feel is right for you or isn't producing sufficiently dramatic results after several weeks' practice.

Check to see if Meditation is working for you. Meditation works, but only you can make it work for you. You can check on its efficacy. Give the method a fair chance. Try it for a month, ideally twice every day for fifteen to twenty minutes. You should find yourself more relaxed at the end of a session than before it; your feeling of relaxation should be greater after each succeeding session. It should become increasingly easy to achieve that feeling of relaxation and contentment. And as you get more accustomed to the practice, you will not be as easily distracted during a session, you will become more quickly relaxed, and you will enjoy the benefits of the meditative experience for longer periods between sessions.

While you may not feel any physiological changes right away, closely monitored tests have indicated that changes are usually achieved to some degree despite the lack of our subjective awareness of them. If you demand fully objective verification — with mechanical tests of alpha wave generation, skin resistance, metabolism, and the like — a physician or university psychology or medical department can administer these tests. Notwithstanding such confirmation, if the technique is actually working you'll know it best by how your feelings and behavior have been affected. If it works you should have met some of your goals for behavioral and emotional modification.

PRECAUTIONS

Certain precautions should be taken to prevent misusing the method in ways damaging to your efforts at self-improvement and self-control. Whatever you do, don't continue using a form of Meditation that for any reason — or even for no apparent reason — feels wrong or produces effects you don't like. Some people begin Meditation with high hopes only to find that the results displease them. They can't tolerate the concentration and exclusion of outside sensory input. Others go too far and enter a trance, reducing their awareness rather than enhancing it.

Meditation is not a cure-all and not a psychological first-aid kit. It is a program of mental and emotional conditioning to strengthen your capacity for coping with the stresses of everyday living. It is exercise for your mind that also benefits your body. Its specific functional goal is to enable you to relax and concentrate during a session. This relaxed concentration, made possible by focusing on an object, movement, sound, and so forth, holds out distracting and anxiety-provoking stimuli. Once you have learned and practiced Meditation sufficiently, your conscious mind should reach that blank state or void that permits you to regain composure and a deep awareness of what you are, how you truly feel about yourself, what the world is, and what in it matters most to you.

Meditation is a potent and useful practice. It is also a doorway into new realms of reality and levels of awareness that some of us cannot tolerate experiencing or do not choose to experience. If you find this to be the case, Meditation is not your bag and you are advised to use simple Relaxation exercises, Desensitization, and some of the other techniques that can reduce your anxiety or help you cope with various problems.

Try Meditation, but don't feel you have to buy it unless it is entirely to your liking. And certainly don't stay with it if, after fair testing, you find that it makes you more nervous, less able to cope, and suspicious of your capacity for self-psyching.

See also:
Transcendental Meditation

Sources of further information:
Carrington, Patricia. *Freedom in Meditation: Getting the Most out of Meditating*. New York: Doubleday, 1977.

Eastcott, Michael J. *The Silent Path – An Introduction to Meditation*. New York: Samuel Weiser, 1969.

LeShan, Lawrence. *How to Meditate*. New York: Bantam, 1975.

Naranjo, Claudio, and Ornstein, R. E. *On the Psychology of Meditation*. Baltimore: Penguin, 1977.

White, John A., Ed. *What is Meditation?* New York: Doubleday, 1974.

PROBLEM

Meeting New People

See:
Making Friends
Shyness and Inhibitions
Disagreeable Tasks and Encounters

PROBLEM

Minor Emotional Complaints

When you aren't feeling yourself, suffer from the blues or the blahs, can't get yourself together to face the day, are slightly depressed, down on yourself, convinced that life should offer more, have a vague sense that nothing really matters very much, that there is little you can do about your circumstances, that you are out of sync with your work, your loved ones, the world, or otherwise are on the low side of your emotional spectrum, you may require some quick self-psyching attention.

These complaints may be the first signs of the development of serious depression. They can reduce your effectiveness and your joy in living to a sufficient degree that you may experience the familiar snowballing effect that leads to greater emotional, social, and even physical problems. Don't start the ball rolling — catch it while you can.

Everyone goes through low periods, but regular use of some of the following techniques may reduce their frequency and their impact.

Consistent use of Relaxation or Meditation seems to give greater tolerance for the pressures that cause minor emotional upsets. And employment of either when you feel down can usually bring you up.

Incompatible Behavior is specifically intended to counter emotional lows and guide you in restoring your optimism and vigor. And understanding Biorhythms can help you determine your normal pattern of emotional highs and lows, while fairly strenuous Exercise can elevate your mood by stimulating you physically.

See also:
Depression

Techniques to try:
Relaxation
Meditation
Incompatible Behavior
Biorhythms
Exercise

TECHNIQUE

Modeling

Particularly useful in dealing with such problems as Fears and Phobias, Shyness and Inhibitions, Disagreeable Tasks and Encounters, Frustrations, Conflict Avoidance, Standing Up for Your Rights, Marital Problems.

Also of use in improving Work and Study Habits and handling Anxiety.

Supplementary or alternative techniques: Behavior Rehearsal, Desensitization, Assertiveness Training, Stimulus Control, Rewards.

WHAT MODELING IS

We learn not only by doing but also by watching what others do. Modeling can help us alter our feelings, attitudes, and behavior through a process known as vicarious learning. We observe — or imagine we observe — someone else doing what we find difficult or distressing, picture ourselves behaving likewise and achieving similar success, and finally emulate our model in real-life situations.

Modeling is literally as old as "monkey see, monkey do." All primates learn by imitating their own kind. Most can master terribly complex tasks or patterns of interaction just by watching how others perform. Children gain most of their basic skills in this manner. Modeling seems to be a natural process, a particularly important means of learning, given that primates, especially humans, have relatively few instinctive drives to guide their behavior. As a self-psyching technique, Modeling allows you to consciously control this natural process for the purpose of overcoming emotional and behavioral problems.

Even though you may not be aware of it, much of your behavior has been and is being shaped, to some degree, by Modeling. The clothes you wear, the car you drive, the college you choose to attend, the cocktail you drink, almost every facet of your social behavior can be influenced by your efforts to emulate individuals you envy or respect. Your thoughts, behavior, and appearance are modified by your desire to be more like peers, mentors, and heroes and to earn their affection and respect.

Your models may not be people you know personally. We are influenced by the way public personalities look and act. The Beatles revolutionized men's hair styles. Steve McQueen has only to appear once in a jumpsuit and thousands line up to buy such a garment. Billie Jean King switches to large, wire-rim glasses and battalions of her admirers switch with her. Johnny Carson wore a Nehru jacket on the *Tonight Show* a few times and stores sold out of them. And when Carson gave up the style soon after, most men also left their newly purchased coats hanging in the backs of their closets.

Even historical figures and fictional characters serve as models for people who admire them. Much of the lasting influence exerted by Christ, Buddha, Gandhi, Lincoln, and others is attributable to the fact that thousands of less distinguished people have tried to pattern their lives on the behavior of such heroes. Characters in the Horatio Alger stories inspired a generation to hope that their own hard work, fidelity, and good luck would bring them success and fortune. More recently, the black heroes of *Roots* have given black people models of courage and perseverance in the face of oppression and injustice.

Because Modeling is so common and natural a process, as a self-psyching technique it is easily learned and readily applied to numerous common problems in living. Uncontrolled Modeling influences much of our behavior without our knowledge; we can learn to control it and make it work for us.

HISTORICAL DEVELOPMENT

Within the last two decades there has been carefully documented research on Modeling and its effects. Albert Bandura has done extensive research demonstrating the effects models have on the behavior of children. A group of children had watched another small child play with a dog, get closer and closer to it, provoke it to play more and more roughly. The child modeled fearless behavior. Afterwards, these children and children who had not previously watched the model were exposed to large dogs. The children who had seen the model were less afraid to approach the dogs. Apparently, the model had encouraged the children to overcome most of their own fears.

Similar experiments, by Bandura and others, have shown Modeling to be highly effective in modifying people's actions, outlook, emotional responses, and self-esteem.

BASIC ELEMENTS OF MODELING

Identifying the problem (see Introduction)
Setting goals (see Introduction)
Choosing a model
Observing your model's behavior
Checking every detail of your model's behavior
Mentally rehearsing your own behavior
Trying your modeled behavior in the real world
Looking for changes in your behavior (see Introduction)
Repeating the technique with other problems

HOW TO USE MODELING

Identify the problem. Your first attempt to use this technique should involve a relatively simple, clear-cut difficulty — such as an inability to make effective contact with members of the opposite sex. As a guide to selecting a target problem, consider situations that you know others handle better than you do. Whatever the specific problem, the modeling procedure is much the same. If you are trying to improve your work or study habits or overcome the fear of flying, you will use the same basic approach you would use to improve your social life.

Set goals. How much Modeling can help you and how soon you can expect to see results depend on the seriousness of your problems. Minor difficulties — such as an inability to ask for raises at work — should respond to Modeling in a very short time. There should be some progress in a week or so. Major problems — such as phobias or fighting with your wife or husband — take longer.

Overcoming your problem is, of course, your ultimate goal. But the most important initial goal in Modeling is to single out everything your model does in dealing with your problem that you do not. Don't concentrate only on the fact that your model gets the results you are after — gets the dates, wins promotions, studies longer and to greater effect. Pay scrupulous attention to *all* the stages and steps taken to achieve the results.

Choose a model. Your model can be a person you know and can watch or a person you are sufficiently familiar with to imagine at every step of a given activity. You can use noted people or fictional characters whose style you respect and whose behavior you can imagine and imitate. It is important that you feel confident that you actually know how your model would handle the problem you are working on.

If you choose a model you know personally, someone you like and respect, that person's behavior will provide you with numerous concrete examples you can readily observe. Choosing models you know personally can also present some options. You can pick someone who is more or less like you but who handles problems better, or you can choose someone you know who is quite unlike you. It can be tempting to select a model who has many of your characteristics — who is, for instance, basically introverted or studious — but seems to have learned to live more successfully. Such a model offers the example of what you'll be like if you can modify your behavior. But there is more room for change and probably greater inspiration in choosing as a model a person very little like you in personality but whom you genuinely respect and would like to emulate. Working with such a model in your self-psyching can initially be a bit frustrating as you observe the gap between your actions and attitudes and those of your model. But the more you progress, taking advantage of every opportunity to observe and gain more information on how your model acts, the closer you will move to your goal of improved behavior and more successful living.

Using famous or fictional figures requires more imagination, but such larger-than-life individuals may serve to motivate you more and give you a higher standard to reach for. Fictional characters, who are sufficiently described so that you can predict how they would act in various situations, can be effective models, especially if you go back to the works in which they appear and refresh your knowledge of their "moral fiber."

Perhaps the best models among people not known to you personally are film heroes and the actors who play them. The visual and emotional impact of characters in a film is so great that many people find it easy to identify with such figures and make them effective models. Most of us have a pretty clear idea of how John Wayne, Humphrey Bogart, Jane Fonda, or Katherine Hepburn would handle a problem. Most of us have favorite characters—James Bond, Cool Hand Luke, or Mame — whose idiosyncrasies and methods of coping define them for us. Models made up of the combination of the fictional movie character and the film actor may fill your bill.

Observe your model's behavior. If your model is a person you know, watch what he or she does. If you don't know your model personally, imagine what he or she would do if faced with your problem. Consider how your model handles the task from start to finish. You will not only learn how to improve your overall approach, but you will also see fine points you may have been missing that were critical in keeping you from succeeding.

Check every detail of your model's behavior. This is where you learn exactly what you hadn't been doing and what you probably must try to do if you are to match your model's success.

Say you're trying to increase your opportunities for meeting members of the opposite sex. Pay close attention to all the occasions your model finds to be with potential dates: at meetings, around the coffee machine or duplicator, among large groups at lunch, the college lounge or company cafeteria. Watch your model's actions: Does he or she look people in the eye while you tend to stare off into space or gaze at the ground? Does she respond enthusiastically to the comments and attention of others while you usually say or do nothing? Is he friendly, and even a bit forward? Does your model take some chances of being rejected? Does she touch a man's arm to establish more intimate contact?

It might take considerable effort for you to duplicate the moods and attitudes of your model, to learn and eventually repeat the actions that bring your model success. But the positive responses of other people will make what at first are imitated and possibly insincere postures natural and genuine for you. For this to happen you must begin your Modeling with careful and conscientious observation.

If you are imagining, rather than watching, your model, don't worry about being perfectly accurate, being true to your actor's life. The idea is to be complete in your own re-creation of a series of actions. If you fill in all the details, you are likely to add many of the fine points you have been leaving out of your own performance. The miraculous powers of the human imagination can permit you to take mental note of the way Clark Gable or Rhett Butler, Robert Redford or Romeo, Farrah Fawcett or Bella Abzug would handle a situation or challenge you've always had trouble handling.

Whether your model is a real person you know and respect (and perhaps envy not a little), a famous person such as a movie star, or a fictional character, just be sure to take into account every detail of his or her behavior in specific settings.

Mentally rehearse your own behavior. In your mind, create a scene in which you run through all the moves your model demonstrated. These are the parts of a successful sequence.

Begin your attempt to implement modeled behavior by imagining yourself acting in the target situation as your model would. Be sure to include all the details — actions, attitudes, expressions, postures, even what you think your model would say. This is where Modeling and Behavior Rehearsal overlap: Both techniques have you make dry runs without the possibility of a discouraging failure. In a quiet place, free of distractions, go through several rehearsals over a period of a few days, or until you feel fairly comfortable in the role created by your model and directed and acted by you. You should now be ready to attempt a real encounter.

Try your modeled behavior in the real world. Do not feel self-conscious. Have confidence that you can duplicate the desirable aspects of your model's performance — while remaining basically yourself.

When you employ modeled behavior in real situations you are not deceiving yourself. You are not trying to become someone else; you are using another person's successful behavior to teach you how to be successful in your own way. Modeling can free your own best instincts, getting you started on being successful in formerly troublesome situations — without robbing you of your individuality. Modeling can't turn Woody Allen into Humphrey Bogart but it can help Woody break out of his shell and be all that he really is.

As you practice modeled behavior in a real situation, be sure to run through all the steps, make all the moves your model showed you that led to success and that you rehearsed. If the circumstances and the rush of real events make it impossible to get all the details of your performance in, improvise as best you can by at least keeping the sequence of actions intact and by maintaining your model's general outlook. And whatever success you attain will prompt you to stay with your efforts and try to give a better performance next time. Success will lead to more success and more confidence, both in the Modeling procedure and in yourself.

Look for changes in your behavior. Has Modeling helped you learn that the best student in your class always studies in the usually quiet Classics Library instead of in the always crowded Main Reading Room? Where do *you* study now? Has your model's habit of making pleasant physical contact with others prompted you to duplicate that behavior? Has doing so increased your rapport with the opposite sex? Any such signs of Modeling's success should encourage you to try the technique on various problems you have not yet attacked.

Repeat the technique with other problems. Apply the technique to one problem at a time. Give each problem sufficient time and practice to show results, then go on to another difficulty. It's best to work your way up from simpler problems, like poor work or study habits or standing up for your rights, to learning to avoid conflict with loved ones, or even trying to overcome some great fear or phobia.

PRECAUTIONS

The only serious problems that may arise while using Modeling stem from efforts to do things totally alien to you or from efforts to model yourself on someone you don't truly respect and like. The purpose of Modeling is not to make you a new person but to help you overcome inhibitions and learn new ways to do what you are actually capable of doing and succeed in situations you previously approached with fear. Modeling is a method for heightening your awareness of critical patterns of behavior of which you may have been ignorant, not a means of personality transformation. Never pick a model so unlike you that you don't really want to emulate him or her. If the office beauty gets lots of dates but you detest her she's a useless model for you. If the boss's favorite is a pushy, obnoxious hustler or a self-serving sycophant, find a model closer to your own approximation of what you would like to be.

Whatever you do, don't attempt things entirely outside your range of competence. Use sky diving, hang gliding, or mountain climbing as model activities to augment your social life only if you are sure you won't have a rotten time or even do yourself a serious injury. Modeling will fail if you try activities you are likely to fail at — and you will give up further attempts even with simpler modeled behavior. So don't make your first attempt at imitating James Bond with your boss — practice on your best friend. Be confident, not foolhardy. Start slowly and work your way up by easy steps to harder situations. Try to improve your life by altering your behavior gradually — not radically and suddenly.

Finally, if Modeling doesn't seem to work for you, give it up and attack each of your problems with other techniques you feel more comfortable with. Desensitization, Behavior Rehearsal, Stimulus Control, Assertiveness Training, or Rewards may be better for those who want more structured guidelines. Modeling isn't for everyone. But it can be fun and does work. Give it a fair chance.

Sources of further information:

Bandura, Albert, Ed.*Principles of Behavior Modification.* New York: Holt, Rinehart and Winston, 1969.

Bandura, Albert. *Psychological Modeling: Conflict Theories.* Chicago: Aldine-Atherton, 1971.

Goffman, Erving. *The Presentation of Self in Everyday Life.* Garden City, N.Y.: Doubleday, 1959.

Miller, N. E., and Dollard, J. *Social Learning and Imitation.* New Haven: Yale University Press, 1941.

Nail Biting

This is probably the archetypal nervous habit, causing millions of persons pain and embarrassment. The article on Nervous Habits goes into some detail on what people have gone through in the past to break the habit and suggests some effective modern techniques.

See also:
Nervous Habits

Negative Practice

Particularly useful in dealing with Nervous Habits.
Supplementary or alternative techniques: Incompatible Behavior, Thought-Stopping.

WHAT NEGATIVE PRACTICE IS

This self-psyching technique involves consciously performing a problem behavior that you often unconsciously engage in. You isolate its components by concentrating on what customarily happens when you unthinkingly do such things as bite your nails, gnash your teeth, or pick at yourself. This removes the problem behavior from the purely reflexive realm because your concentration on it gives you a new degree of conscious control. Furthermore, Negative Practice (also known as Massed Practice) appears to exhaust the impulse to perform a nervous habit by having you engage in your habit vigorously, but in a controlled manner.

HISTORICAL DEVELOPMENT

The technique was developed in the 1930s by K. Dunlap, who employed it successfully with people who stuttered, had annoying tics, or did such things as repeat typing errors to the point of painful frustration. It is currently being applied in clinical settings mainly to help those with tics. But it has also proven effective for people with nervous habits like nail biting and uncontrollable scratching, especially if the habit is engaged in unconsciously or during sleep.

One woman was freed of a long-standing habit of gnashing her teeth while she slept. Each day she took time to practice teeth gnashing. She would grind her teeth for one minute, then rest for a minute. The procedure was repeated five times each session for six sessions a day. After about two and a half weeks her involuntary nocturnal teeth-grinding habit was eliminated — permanently.

The precise mechanism that makes Negative Practice work is unknown. However, it is theorized that repeated practice of a habit that involves the body's motor responses can fatigue those responses and weaken the reflexiveness of the habit. Conscious practice of a habit also makes it less of a habit. You can see this if you attempt to change some habitual movement you've been making in a sport, such as your golf swing. You will have to stop and think before you follow through. Try to control your walking by consciously commanding each step you take. You will falter and maybe stumble because such willful and conscious control disrupts habit patterns. Negative Practice seems to weaken and confuse the impulse to gnash, scratch, bite, or whatever.

BASIC ELEMENTS OF NEGATIVE PRACTICE

Identifying the problem (see Introduction)
Setting a goal (see Introduction)
Establishing a program of Negative Practice
Employing Negative Practice
Monitoring your behavior to determine if the technique is working (see Introduction)
Employing the technique with other problems

HOW TO USE NEGATIVE PRACTICE

Identify the problem. You probably already have a good idea of any nervous habits you'd like to attack. If you gnash your teeth while you sleep or scratch at yourself unthinkingly and uncontrollably, you should know it. Waking up with tight, sore jaw muscles is a clue; having your bedmate tell you of your habit is proof positive.

Set a goal. Having chosen one problem to deal with first, decide to work on it daily for at least two weeks. You should experience appreciable reduction of the habit in that time, though total elimination of the problem may take one or s longer.

Establish a program of Negative Practice. At the very least, allow for one session each day. As many as half a dozen sessions of five to ten minutes each, however, should certainly produce better results, and faster. The number of daily sessions depends on the severity of the problem and on your ability to fit the program into your normal schedule.

Employ Negative Practice. Say your problem is scratching at yourself while you sleep. Repeat the unwanted habit — consciously — to the point of exhaustion. Just before you go to bed, spend several minutes scratching those areas (perhaps your elbows) you usually attack while asleep. Concentrate on the process; build an awareness of what you are doing and how it feels. Don't scratch yourself so hard that you break the skin, but keep it up with full concentration until you have exhausted your interest in and tolerance for the activity. This shouldn't take more than ten minutes, including one-minute rest periods every minute or so.

Repeat the technique every night for two weeks. If you can add one or more practice sessions at other times in the day, only a week or so may be required before you find that you have measurably diminished your nocturnal, unconscious scratching.

Monitor your behavior to determine if the technique is working. For totally unconscious habits, like nocturnal teeth gnashing, you may need the observations of another person to evaluate improvement. But, usually, you will recognize that you feel better (your teeth and jaws no longer ache, you no longer wake up all scratched) and that while awake you no longer have an impulse to engage in your target behavior.

Employ the technique with other problems. After one success, try the technique on other complaints. If you are one of the considerable number of people who engage in more than one nervous habit, Negative Practice was made for you. Use it faithfully on each problem in turn.

PRECAUTIONS

Be sure to follow the procedure regularly, long enough, and with sufficient concentration. Otherwise, you may just make things worse by reinforcing your body's habituation. Unless you exhaust the habitual drive by proper Negative Practice, the sessions can actually help your body become more used to the very behavior you've been trying to extinguish. In your practice sessions, keep going until you truly feel that you can't stand any more. Carefully check to see that your habit is breaking down over the course of your practice.

Before you try this technique with tics or stuttering, consult a physician to discover if there are any underlying physiological causes requiring medical attention.

Sources of further information:

Dunlap, K. *Habits: Their Making and Unmaking*. New York: Liveright, 1932.

Eysenck, H. J., Ed. *Behaviour Therapy and The Neuroses*. London: Pergamon Press, 1960.

Wolpe, Joseph, and Lazarus, A. A. *Behavior Therapy Techniques: A Guide to the Treatment of Neuroses*. New York: Pergamon Press, 1966.

PROBLEM

Nervous Habits

Nail biting; scratching; picking; knuckle cracking; teeth gnashing; hair pulling; putting pencils, pens, matches, or paper clips into your mouth; and even smoking are some of the many nervous habits that afflict great numbers of people. Such behavior is learned: People train themselves to engage in these pursuits in response to anxiety, as a way to comfort and distract themselves while engaging in or contemplating stressful encounters. Once learned, the habits are self-perpetuating. They become a regular part of our normal activities. But they can also be unlearned. You can recondition the responses that stimulate your nervous system and perpetuate your habit, and thereby learn to function without the habit.

Before behavioral scientists developed methods for breaking habits by reconditioning, all sorts of harsh and humiliating means were employed. Children — often adolescents — usually suffered under these methods. They had their fingers painted with horrid-tasting compounds to stop thumb sucking and nail biting. They had to wear gloves to bed or even had their hands tied behind their backs. Ridicule was most commonly employed — a measure that probably reinforced the victim's need for the comfort of the habit. Few of these methods had the desired effect. People did stop their nail biting — but usually for reasons other than the so-called cures.

Today the prospects are much brighter. If you have a nervous habit that embarrasses you, that is your typical response to stress or anxiety, that may be damaging you physically, there are a number of relatively simple procedures for altering even long-standing patterns of behavior.

Negative Practice is a proven method for overcoming deeply ingrained, chronic, virtually automatic and unconscious habits that you may even carry on while you sleep. Incompatible Behavior will make it more difficult for you to act habitually. Thought-Stopping, by directly attacking compulsiveness, has proved to be highly effective in extinguishing even nervous habits that you have engaged in for decades.

You can alter the stimuli that inspire your habit through Stimulus Control. You can employ Rewards and Punishments to reinforce your habit-breaking efforts. By Changing the Sequence of Events, you can rearrange the pattern of actions that customarily result in your engaging in the habit. And Covert Sensitization can force you to face, in your imagination, the worst possible consequences of continuing such resistant habits as smoking. Each of these methods has something to recommend it and practice of one or more will soon tell you whether your particular problem is responding.

Regular practice of Relaxation and Meditation may undermine your predisposition toward your habit. Learning to relax or experiencing the mind- and body-altering effects of Meditation might reduce your anxiety level to the point that you no longer need your nervous habit. And Self-Hypnosis lets you relax and follow your own suggestions for breaking habits.

If you find your nervous habits truly pleasurable, if they provide some sort of needed release, go right on practicing them. It's your life. But if they trouble you and you want to get rid of them, start right now to learn to live without them.

See also:
Compulsiveness
Smoking

Techniques to try:
Negative Practice
Incompatible Behavior
Thought-Stopping
Stimulus Control
Rewards
Punishments
Changing the Sequence of Events
Covert Sensitization
Relaxation
Meditation
Self-Hypnosis

PROBLEM

Nightmares

Nightmares are a problem insofar as they disturb sleep and increase your normal load of anxiety. But the creative use of Fantasy techniques, especially the Senoi dream method (see article on Fantasy), can turn them into occasions for gaining power over your subconscious. And by carefully recording the content of bad dreams, you can employ Desensitization to reduce the anxiety they arouse. Some people have even found that Stimulus Control, by altering the environmental and emotional stimuli that impinge upon them during the day and especially just prior to sleep, can be used to combat recurrent nightmares. And regular Exercise before retiring can promote deeper sleep, free of nightmare-provoking physical stimuli.

See also:
Insomnia
Sleep

Techniques to try:
Fantasy
Desensitization
Stimulus Control
Exercise

Obsessions

Obsessions are intimately related to compulsions, the latter involving uncontrollable impulses to perform specific actions, the former involving uncontrollable thoughts about certain things. Severe obsessions require professional help. Anyone so troubled by recurring thoughts that nothing else can be contemplated, a person who finds it impossible to think because the mind is filled with progressions of numbers, repeated phrases, or, worse, commands from disembodied voices, cannot be aided by a book.

But it is common, and surely not pathological, to be troubled periodically by an inability to get your mind off some problem. Worries about work, health, or love can distract you from dealing with anything else. For example, many people who are involved in a big romance (perhaps their first) may come to the conclusion that they must truly be in love, because they can't stop thinking about the object of their affection. Such preoccupation can be exciting, but it can also be wrong-headed and incapacitating and keep you from making an adequate appraisal of your situation so that you can get on with your day-to-day living. Some of the following techniques could help you cope with this problem.

Thought-Stopping was designed to teach people to shut off unwanted floods of thought, to stop aimless rumination, to give relief to chronic worriers. It is the method to try first.

Flooding can exhaust your impulses to think obsessively. Covert Sensitization can undermine your concern with obsession themes. And Modeling teaches you to imitate the more orderly thinking habits of others.

Obsessive thoughts are not usually a sign of impending mental collapse. We all have a lot on our minds at times and most of us worry too much to too little effect. The above self-psyching techniques teach you to shut off unwanted and profitless thoughts and to focus your attention and mental energies more selectively, in a more controlled manner. You can control your thinking; and you can employ Desensitization to control your emotions when your racing mind makes you feel that you are coming apart at the seams.

Use these techniques to cope with worry, with the tendency to examine and reexamine what you have done or plan to do, with the very common problem of having mental motors so revved up that it is hard to get them back to idle.

See also:
    Compulsiveness
    Floods of Unwanted Thoughts

Techniques to try:
    Thought-Stopping
    Flooding
    Covert Sensitization
    Modeling
    Desensitization

PROBLEM

Overeating

Overeating and consequent obesity trouble millions of Americans. Those with the most serious problems — compulsive eaters who may be twenty, thirty, or even fifty or more pounds overweight — probably require the assistance of trained professionals, therapy sessions at one of the many clinics in operation for such people, strict medical supervision, and perhaps even hospitalization, or at the very least, consultation with a physician. But for the vast majority of overeaters who are only ten or fifteen pounds overweight, some self-psyching may turn the tide and keep them from sinking further into their problem behavior.

The first step in self-controlled modification of eating habits is to compile an accurate record of your current eating behavior. For one or two weeks at least, without trying to change the way you eat, keep a record of how, when, what, with whom, and under what circumstances you eat. A sample page from a typical eating log or diary is supplied below to give you some idea of how such record keeping works.

Sample Page From Eating Log

Food Item(s)	Calorie Count	Type of Food	Time	Place	With Whom	Other Activities	Eating Rate	Mood Before and During
½ cup tomato juice; 1 slice toast; 2 eggs	25 150+	carbohydrate & protein	7:00 a.m.	kitchen	alone	watching TV	slow	anxious & tired; then less so; then uplifted
2 doughnuts; black coffee	200 0	carbohydrate	9:20 a.m. to 9:25 a.m.	office	alone	working	very fast	stressed, then less stressed
4 pieces of fudge	400+	carbohydrate	11:00 a.m.	water cooler	secretary who made fudge	conversing with several people	quite fast	stressed, then elated
½ ham salad sandwich; 2 beers	200 400+	protein, fat carbohydrate	12:30 p.m.	bar	two colleagues	talking	slow	run down; no change; maybe a bit sluggish
peanuts	150-260	fat, protein	3:00 p.m. to 4:00 p.m.	office	alone	working, musing	fast	anxious about afternoon meetings, then more relaxed
2 candy bars, with nuts	300+	carbohydrate & fat	5:30 p.m.	car	alone	driving	very fast	depressed, then less so
glass of wine, spaghetti & meat sauce	200 300+	carbohydrate	7:10 p.m.	dining room	wife	arguing, trying to read paper	fairly slow	depressed, then guilty, then angry
2 beers; 12 cookies	400+ 600	carbohydrate	10:30 p.m.	living room & bedroom	wife	arguing	steady	depressed, then less so

Note that there are boxes for indicating what you ate — the food item, calorie count, and whether it was largely protein, fat, or carbohydrate — when, where, with whom — if anyone — what you were doing besides eating, how fast or slowly you ate, and what your mood was before and during eating.

Using your eating log, you should be able to determine your current eating pattern and establish targets for behavior change. You might want to employ Stimulus Control to alter the environmental stimuli such as certain places, people, or accompanying activities that most often seem to appear in your log and may be encouraging you to eat too much or too often. Changing the Sequence of Events could help you modify your habit of eating too much or too rapidly. And you can use the Rewards technique and Punishments to supply an incentive to eat less or to eat less-fattening foods.

If your eating diary informs you that your mood improves during meals, you may be eating to overcome anxiety or depression. Relaxation and Desensitization can diminish these problems and may consequently reduce your compensatory need to eat too much.

If you discover that you do most of your eating while you read or watch TV, you can try to change your habit with Stimulus Control or even Thought-Stopping. And if you always seem to eat most when with certain people, Assertiveness Training can give you the confidence to tell those individuals that you'd rather eat alone.

Noting that your eating log shows an unusually high intake of calories, you may be able to use the information to design a more reasonable diet that is lower in calories and higher in protein. And if you engage in a regular program of Exercise you will burn up even more of these excess calories while keeping yourself more fit.

While compiling your log and employing the various self-psyching techniques, your goal should be to identify any factors contributing to overeating and to apply the methods that can reduce the influence of such factors. You don't have to try to become an entirely different person, you merely want to modify the forces that have in the past encouraged you to eat too much of the wrong foods too often, too fast, in inappropriate places, and as an inappropriate antidote to anxiety, depression, or just boredom. Eating should be a physiological, not a psychological, necessity.

See also:
  Compulsiveness
  Nervous Habits

Techniques to try:
  Stimulus Control
  Changing the Sequence of Events
  Rewards
  Punishments
  Relaxation
  Desensitization
  Thought-Stopping
  Assertiveness Training
  Exercise

Sources of further information:
Fanburg, Walter H. *How To Be a Winner at the Weight Loss Game.* New York: Simon and Schuster, 1975.

Mahoney, Michael J., and Mahoney, Katheryn. *Permanent Weight Control: A Total Solution to the Dieter's Dilemma.* New York: W. W. Norton, 1976.

Stuart, R. B., and Davis, B. *Slim Chance in a Fat World: Behavioral Control of Obesity.* Champaign, Ill.: Research Press, 1972.

Stunkard, Albert J. *The Pain of Obesity.* Palo Alto, Calif.: Bull Publishing, 1976.

PROBLEM

Overworking

Working too much, too long, or unproductively can result in psychological and physical exhaustion. Sleep is an obvious answer. Improving your work habits is another. The chronic overworker may be a low-grade compulsive who needs to work on that problem. And heart disease researchers have found that habitual overachievers who stress themselves continually are "type-A personalities" — people inordinately prone to heart trouble and early death.

Many people are sadly aware that they have an overwork problem; others are not. There are several clues to warn you that you may be pushing yourself too hard and to ill effect. Overworkers tend to move and speak too rapidly, try to think about several things at once, are usually impatient, feel guilty about relaxing or taking time off, seem to be unaware or uninterested in anything but their work — provoking complaints from loved ones that they bring their work home, never take the trouble to spend time or energy on their children and spouse, have no hobbies, and so on — try to schedule more activities than they can possibly handle, and see life as a constant struggle requiring endless effort.

The following articles should help you see more clearly if overworking is truly a problem for you. They suggest useful techniques for handling this potentially damaging difficulty.

See also:
Compulsiveness
Work and Study Habits
Fatigue and Lethargy
Sleep

Pain

Injuries or illnesses that cause pain are the concern of a physician. Pain with no apparent physical cause may be no less troublesome and may hurt just as much. Let your doctor dispose of organic pain, then, if you find you have a psychogenic, emotionally caused hurt, consider trying to get some relief from the methods listed in the article on Psychosomatic Complaints and Pains.

See also:
Psychosomatic Complaints and Pains

Perfectionism

See:
Procrastination
Compulsiveness

Pessimism

See:
Depression

Picking

Monkeys, apes, and humans — marvelously equipped with dextrous fingers and accustomed to grooming themselves and each other — commonly probe at their own noses, eyes, ears, and other parts to make themselves more comfortable. Self-touching is a natural animal instinct, especially characteristic of primates.

People touch themselves to enhance their appearance — smoothing their hair, for example. They often do so reflexively, as a means to gain reassurance in the face of anxiety. They even touch other things, like portions of their clothing, objects near at hand, or touchstones or lucky pieces they carry for just that purpose. Such touching is fine, but picking that becomes an uncontrollable nervous habit is far from gratifying. It can destroy confidence, make one self-conscious, and cause infection at the sites thoughtlessly assaulted.

Highly effective self-psyching techniques — especially Negative Practice and Incompatible Behavior — can free you of a picking habit that you find distressing or embarrassing.

See also:
Nervous Habits

Techniques to try:
Negative Practice
Incompatible Behavior

TECHNIQUE

Prayer

The theological reason for praying and the results obtained are matters outside the scope of this book. However, above and beyond the value of maintaining contact with one's God through devotional exercises, there is evidence that Prayer, like Meditation, can provide the psychobiological benefits of stress reduction.

Prayer is perhaps the most ancient means of increasing self-awareness by encouraging you to express your deepest desires. And it can play a role in self-psyching by helping you identify problems, set goals, and thus encourage you to begin answering your own prayers.

Because Prayer should involve concentration and focused contemplation, it can heighten one's awareness, block out disruptive and anxiety-provoking distractions, provide respite from the cares and trials of daily life. Prayer can produce some of the same relaxing and spiritual benefits as Meditation and formal Relaxation exercises because it is best carried out in solitude or in the conducive surroundings of a house of worship, and perhaps with the rhythmic chanting of some meditative methods.

If you pray, keep it up. If you are a believer but haven't prayed recently, you may want to go back to this practice, if for no other reason than that the spiritual gains to be realized are supplemented by emotional benefits verified by scientific research into stress, meditation, and altered states of consciousness.

See also:
Meditation
Relaxation

PROBLEM

Problem Drinking

A severe addiction to alcohol is unlikely to respond to self-psyching. But you may be one of the millions of people who want to reduce how much and how often you drink. Your problem is relatively small-scale: A couple of drinks at lunch, a few before dinner may be slowing down your reflexes, dulling your ability to concentrate, keeping you from performing adequately on your job and elsewhere. There are self-psyching techniques to help you gain greater control over your impulse to drink more than you feel you should.

The articles on Smoking, Overeating, Nervous Habits, and Compulsiveness suggest several techniques that you can use to deal with drinking. Read them.

Thought-Stopping should be considered as a simple measure for altering your reflexive impulse to order that additional drink you may not really want. Incompatible Behavior gives guidance in replacing your drinking with other actions less likely to cause you trouble. And Covert Sensitization has even worked with serious alcoholics — you might learn something from it and lose some of your fascination with drinking.

Assertiveness Training may play a role in your efforts to cut down on your drinking; some researchers contend that drinking is sometimes a substitution for assertive behavior. And Relaxation is worth trying because this technique permits you to reduce anxiety and stave off depression without recourse to the dulling effects of liquor. Some people have found regular Meditation to have the same effect.

Only you know how serious or insignificant your drinking is. It is a problem if it intrudes upon your otherwise normal functioning. And if it has become that much of a problem that you need to act on it, self-psyching can help.

See also:
  Smoking
  Overeating
  Nervous Habits
  Compulsiveness

Techniques to try:
  Thought-Stopping
  Incompatible Behavior
  Covert Sensitization
  Assertiveness Training
  Relaxation
  Meditation

PROBLEM

Procrastination

Only half-jokingly, I told my publisher that I would have finished writing this article sooner but couldn't seem to get around to it. Procrastination, putting things off until the last minute, is a tendency many people have, and is quite common among students, homemakers, and especially creative individuals. The fear of failure or of being wrong, periods of mild depression during which they cannot function well, disorganized thinking, and unnecessary perfectionism can outweigh such people's ordinary good work habits and high motivation.

If you are troubled by procrastination, some of the following techniques could serve to release you from a pattern of missing deadlines, feeling guilty, promising to meet even more unrealistic deadlines to make up for missing the earlier ones, and then finding yourself once more a victim of your own procrastination.

Rewards and Stimulus Control can help you reorganize your work or study habits and provide effective incentives for getting things done on time. Behavior Rehearsal can allow you to preview your work before you make completion commitments. Assertiveness Training will make it easier for you to demand reasonable deadlines. And studying your Biorhythms can help you coordinate your efforts to your most productive periods.

Desensitization shows you how to divide every major task into smaller, more manageable parts. By doing this and then learning to tackle the easiest part first, you can accustom yourself to getting into a task with a minimum of hesitation and anxiety. If you approach a job as a whole, you may find yourself procrastinating because you are intimidated by the work that lies ahead: You don't know where to begin. Using Desensitization, you can atomize each job and finish one small part after another until you've done it all.

See also:
Work and Study Habits
Fear of Failure
Depression

Techniques to try:
Rewards
Stimulus Control
Behavior Rehearsal
Assertiveness Training
Biorhythms
Desensitization

PROBLEM

Productivity

See:
Work and Study Habits
Procrastination

TECHNIQUE

Psychodrama

This formal, supervised therapy is usually carried out in groups and is therefore not suitable for self-psyching. But some elements of it are employed in various techniques dealt with in this book, and a description of its origins and purposes is in the article on Behavior Rehearsal.

See also:
Behavior Rehearsal
Modeling
Role Playing
Fantasy

<hr>

PROBLEM

Psychosomatic Complaints and Pains

"You're not sick, it's just psychosomatic." This statement is *not* true. Psychosomatic, psychogenic, or psychophysiologic illnesses make one just as sick as those caused by germs and viruses. The disorders are just as real, the suffering as genuine, the pain hurts as much.

Emotional disturbances — undue stress, too much anxiety — can produce physical disturbances that show up as ulcers, skin disorders, circulatory problems, asthma, arthritis, colitis, diarrhea, headaches, and other ailments. When swayed by such emotions the sufferer is also accident prone.

We seldom want to admit that our complaints are psychosomatic. We suffer pains in the abdomen, belch, get the runs, maybe even vomit. Many of us say, "It's something I ate." Very often it is really something that is eating you. Symptoms such as these can eventually turn into outright illness that will require medical intervention. Knowing this, knowing that many of us are prone to illnesses inspired by emotional disturbances, it is only common sense to admit and deal with the problem.

But the first thing to do about any pain or illness is to consult a physician for a full examination and requisite tests to rule out physical causes. Once biological disorders are eliminated you can turn to self-psyching to reduce your distress.

Because most psychosomatic complaints are traceable to stress, tension, and anxiety, techniques for dealing with these problems are useful: regular Relaxation sessions, Meditation, Biofeedback, Desensitization, Autogenic Training, Self-Hypnosis, and involvement in restful and restorative hobbies, sports, or pastimes. These techniques will not only reduce your chances of getting psychosomatic illnesses but also increase your general health and well-being. And you will certainly find that you look better, sleep better, get along better with others, perform up to par more consistently, and approach that state called happiness more often.

See also:
  Anxiety

Techniques to try:
  Relaxation
  Meditation
  Biofeedback
  Desensitization
  Autogenic Training
  Self-Hypnosis
  Fantasy

PROBLEM

Public Speaking

Psychologist Manuel J. Smith, author of *Kicking the Fear Habit*, holds that more people fear speaking in public than anything else — even illness or death. You may not have a phobic aversion to the prospect of talking in front of an audience, but you may prefer to avoid such encounters. Yet when you do speak publicly, you may experience some of the symptoms of anxiety: rapid pulse, shortness of breath, dryness in the mouth. And if your professional or social life requires you to speak before groups of people, it would be helpful to be able to do so without feeling anxious and with an increased degree of confidence.

The following articles, particularly the one on Disagreeable Tasks and Encounters, offer a wide range of self-psyching techniques that can help you with this problem.

See also:
  Disagreeable Tasks and Encounters
  Fears and Phobias
  Shyness and Inhibitions

PROBLEM

Punctuality

Most people's problems with punctuality involve an inability to perform: They just can't do things on time. If you have this difficulty, see the articles on Procrastination, Tardiness, and Fear of Failure for reference to useful self-psyching techniques.

But if you find that you always seem to be waiting because you arrive too early or that you drive yourself unreasonably to get tasks completed far ahead of schedule, you are probably compulsive about punctuality. This compulsion assumes a problematic aspect only if it causes you to make unnecessary demands on yourself. Such compulsive punctuality can be handled as you would any compulsion.

See also:
Procrastination
Tardiness
Fear of Failure
Compulsiveness

TECHNIQUE

Punishments

Useful in dealing with such problems as some Nervous Habits, minor Compulsions, certain Inhibitions.

Best when employed in support of a Rewards program.

WHAT PUNISHMENTS IS

The first image that comes to many people's minds when behavior change or behavior modification is mentioned is that of a psychologist applying a device to shock helpless experimental animals or strapped-down patients who are being "taught" to quit smoking. After all, a universally recognized consequence of doing something you shouldn't is punishment — whether a spanking for getting into the cookie jar or twenty years in jail for getting into the First National Bank. Punishment is supposed to keep people from doing the same thing again.

Prison terms and even the threat of the death penalty have not been found to decrease the incidence of crimes. Recidivism is high for a number of reasons, among them the fact that prisons neither rehabilitate nor work as the type of punishment that discourages repetition of criminal activities. If people want to do something, they will find a reason and a way to do it — punishment or not.

For self-psyching, punishment is best thought of as something that, when removed or reduced, can reinforce desirable behavior or can amplify or remind you to use more positive techniques.

HISTORICAL DEVELOPMENT

Punishment does work in some therapeutic situations; punishment (aversive stimulus) has been used by experts to condition people to associate unpleasant elements with formerly preferred behavior. But it is different to punish yourself. A natural human and animal reaction is to try to get away from painful, distasteful stimuli. This natural reaction can be countered when you lay out a great deal of money to a clinic using aversive techniques. Having paid your money, you will stick around to get your money's worth, even if it means experiencing pain or discomfort.

The behavioral therapists who have had success with punishment techniques worked in settings that gave them almost total control over patients to prevent them from escaping treatment. Clinicians have helped people with sex problems, heavy smokers, alcoholics, and others with serious difficulties. But the escape instinct, or avoidance behavior, can make it difficult for most people to use self-administered punishment to much purpose for long.

Some experimenters in self-directed behavior modification have had a measure of success in getting people to punish themselves in order to modify various habits and behaviors — smoking, drinking, overeating, swearing, compulsiveness, and obsessiveness, for example. Researchers are not convinced of the effectiveness of self-punishment approaches that call for people to hurt or stress themselves. But positive self-punishment — the withdrawal of something pleasant or desirable — is suggested, especially for such common problems as smoking or nervous habits like nail biting.

Among many encouraging cases of successful Punishments is the following: A woman agreed to tear up a dollar bill for every cigarette she smoked over a predetermined daily limit. The limit was decreased by one cigarette every five days until she had stopped smoking entirely. When a follow-up study was conducted two years later, she was still a nonsmoker.

The withholding from yourself of what you enjoy, want, or need is the approach recommended for self-psyching. The Punishments technique is thus an auxiliary to a Rewards program.

BASIC ELEMENTS OF PUNISHMENTS

Undertaking a Rewards program
Incorporating Punishments into the Rewards program
Applying Punishments without rewards

HOW TO USE PUNISHMENTS

Undertake a Rewards program. Read the article on Rewards and determine what problem you wish to attack and what Rewards you will employ.

Incorporate Punishments into the Rewards program. Use Punishments by deciding to take away an appropriate number of tokens that earn you rewards or try to deny yourself rewards if you fail to accomplish the behavioral goals set in your Rewards program. The Punishments technique can add to the incentives of the Rewards approach by encouraging you to work harder to get your rewards or tokens, to pay more attention to meeting your behavioral goals. Not getting something you want can be a strong inducement to changing your behavior, often stronger than promising yourself even more rewards.

Apply Punishments without rewards. To use Punishments independent of a Rewards program, you must be careful to pick punishments that are not so aversive that they discourage you more than they motivate you to change. Examples of nonphysical punishments include agreeing to do things you normally would not do, such as spending time with people you usually avoid, and tearing up money or contributing money to causes you don't really support. Some people find the threat of having to engage in such distasteful activities an effective deterrent to problem behavior.

The technique is useless if you cannot bring yourself to apply it. Merely wearing a rubber band around your wrist and snapping it to remind you of your failure to perform up to your standards has some merit. But the approach further requires you to establish a set of specific behavioral goals, by first breaking your problem into distinguishable parts (see the Introduction) and then to regularly apply Punishments to consistently reinforce responses and condition you out of old habits and into new ones.

PRECAUTIONS

Totally self-directed behavior change is enormously difficult when it relies too much on self-punishment. For self-psyching to work it must involve techniques people willingly, even eagerly, pursue. Punishment seldom fits that description and so is best considered a supplement to Rewards and other methods.

Sources of further information:
Azrin, N. H., and Holz, W. C. "Punishment." In *Operant Behavior: Areas of Research and Application*. W. K. Honig, Ed. New York: Appleton-Century-Crofts, 1966.

Krasner, L., and Ullman, L. P., Eds. *Research in Behavior Modification*, New York: Holt, Rinehart and Winston, 1965.

Rachman, S., and Teasdale, J. *Aversion Therapy and Behavior Disorders*. Coral Gables, Fla.: University of Miami Press, 1969.

Sansweet, S. J. *The Punishment Cure*. New York: Mason/Charter, 1976.

Relaxation

Specifically intended to counteract Anxiety.

May also be useful in dealing with such problems as Nervous Habits, Insomnia, preparing for Disagreeable Tasks and Encounters.

Regular practice of Relaxation can increase energy levels; provide new sources of strength; lessen the impact of Psychosomatic and Minor Emotional Complaints; and generally improve your capacity for coping with everyday demands, for breaking habits like Smoking and Overeating, and for performing better while working, studying, or playing.

It is necessary to master some form of Relaxation if you are to make successful use of Desensitization.

Supplementary or alternative techniques: Autogenic Training, Meditation, The Relaxation Response, Biofeedback, Exercise, Fantasy, Prayer.

WHAT RELAXATION IS

Relaxation is the opposite of tension. Being alive means experiencing both: With each heartbeat we are sustained by the blood pumped through our bodies as the heart muscles tense, then relax. We are able to walk, talk, smile, manipulate objects because opposing sets of muscles can be made to tense or relax. Total relaxation or total tension is impossible in a living being.

The balance between tension and relaxation is controlled more or less automatically, by the normal functioning of our bodies. Because the system requires the operation of both tensing and relaxing mechanisms, there is a natural tendency to restore equilibrium.

But the system can get out of balance. Meeting the demands of a stressful world can cause tension to build up, creating physical discomfort and anxiety (see the article on Anxiety for a discussion of the signs and symptoms of stress-caused anxiety). However, while outside pressures may lead to increased tension, the tension/relaxation system is an internal one over which we can achieve a degree of control. By learning techniques for consciously inducing relaxation, you can reduce your load of residual tension and moderate its impact.

The techniques involve learning to employ the natural capacities of your mind and body to recognize the differences between tension and relaxation and to take practical steps to minimize harmful tension while maximizing beneficial relaxation.

HISTORICAL DEVELOPMENT

You don't have to be a scientist to recognize that relaxation is a natural process: Get tired enough and you will yawn, stretch, or shake in an automatic release of tension and yearning for rest.

Animals vividly demonstrate the relaxation process. Watch a dog or cat get ready to sleep — it will yawn, stretch its body from muzzle to tail, and then let go in complete release. Animals know how to relax and seldom get unduly tense because, unlike their masters, they lack the human tendency to drive themselves beyond reasonable limits. Lacking reason, animals must rely on instinct to tell them when they need rest. Their instincts protect them from the damage that tension and anxiety cause in humans. Most human infants exhibit this instinctual knowledge but lose it as they face the pressures of growing up and, as adults, must relearn it.

People have employed formal methods of relaxation for thousands of years. Meditation, yoga, religious and spiritual exercises have been used to increase self-awareness and well-being by relaxing the mind and body. These techniques, like more recently developed scientific ones, work by relaxing the body as a means of relaxing the mind or by relaxing the mind to relax the body. The Relaxation techniques described in this book involve one or both of these approaches.

One of the most widely used scientific Relaxation techniques is the so-called Progressive Relaxation method, developed by Edmund Jacobson more than forty years ago. It is a body-relaxing approach that then serves to relax the mind and emotions in turn. The core of this method is the identification of points of tension through tensing then relaxing various groups of muscles. The exercise allows you to compare muscle tension with muscle relaxation. And, because of the intricate feedback system connecting mind and body, the physical relaxation produced results in a corresponding reduction of mental and emotional tension.

Because Progressive Relaxation is relatively easy to learn and because it is especially recommended for use with such self-psyching methods as Desensitization, it is an ideal approach with which to begin your efforts to master Relaxation. This approach will give you a firm foundation for attempting the more sophisticated variations that researchers and clinicians have devised, the most readily employed elements of which have been incorporated into the technique descriptions below.

BASIC ELEMENTS OF RELAXATION

Learning the differences between tension and relaxation — Progressive Relaxation
Employing verbal cues to relax
Adding breath control to your relaxation routine
Relaxing while you are active — Differential Relaxation
Monitoring your progress

HOW TO RELAX

Learn the differences between tension and relaxation — Progressive Relaxation. Begin by lying on your back on the floor. Close your eyes and get comfortable. The point of the exercise is to compare tension you will produce in various parts of your body with what you will feel in other, relaxed parts of your body and in the tensed muscles after you have relaxed them.

First, simply clench your right fist as tightly as you can. Hold it that way for a half a minute or so. Notice the way the hand and wrist feel, how tight and hard they are. Feel the duller but recognizable tension in your arm and shoulder. Pay close attention to the differences between the feelings in your tensed right hand and arm and in your more relaxed left hand and arm.

Unclench your right fist and carefully notice the differences between how it now feels and how it felt while being tensed.

Repeat the procedure with the other arm, then with other

groups of muscles. As you practice this identification procedure with your jaws and facial muscles, with your legs, feet, back, and buttocks, be sure to hold the tension long enough to feel it and measure the differences between muscles that are relaxed and those that are tense. When you release any tense muscles, be sure you don't try to *make* them relax, that you don't try to force relaxation. Just let go.

The procedure shouldn't take more than ten or fifteen minutes, which may be enough for your first session. Either go directly to the next step or wait until later in the day or until the next day.

Again lying on the floor, raise your right arm about a foot off the floor and clench your fist. This time clench it very slowly, taking as much as thirty seconds to make the muscles as tight as possible. Then reverse the process and *slowly*, progressively release the tension until you feel it completely gone. Then let your arm drop to the floor. At this point your arm should feel almost totally relaxed.

Your previous practice in identifying the differences between tense and relaxed muscles should make it easy for you to recognize when this progressive tensing reaches the maximum and when the progressive relaxation produces the ultimate release.

Repeat progressive tensing and relaxing with your other arm, then with each of your legs. Next tense and relax your chest; notice that your breathing becomes less forced. Work on your jaws, your facial muscles — progressively clench and release your teeth, grimace then relax. Apply the technique to your neck, which can be very tense without your knowing it. Finally arch your back and try to progressively tense your entire body — then let it go limp.

Practice this Progressive Relaxation technique daily for several days until you have definite knowledge of the differences between tension and relaxation. By the end of this initial practice you should find the method producing measurable effects. You should find it easier to recognize and release tensions you haven't deliberately caused.

Daily practice offers you a chance to avoid the psychosomatic complaints that have been attributed to physical stress and anxiety. Practicing the method before bedtime can prevent or alleviate insomnia. A session in the morning may get you in shape for the day's activities. Experiment to determine the best time for you.

As you become more proficient with this method, it won't

be necessary for you to relax each part of your body during every session. You should be able to recognize which parts of your body are most tense and work hardest at relaxing them.

The better you get at the technique the less time it will take you to identify which portions of your body are tense and the less time it will take to induce identifiable relaxation. In fact, you may soon be able to identify target muscles and literally tell them to relax — and they will.

Employ verbal cues to relax. Once you have mastered the elements of Progressive Relaxation, you can begin practicing it in conjunction with verbal cues. The idea is to have the mind relax the body by associating the sensation of relaxation with a word such as "relax" or "calm."

In your formal Relaxation sessions use such a word to cue relaxation. You will soon find that just saying or subvocalizing the word will produce almost the same degree of relaxation that you achieved with the full program of tension and muscle release. This is because your body becomes conditioned to respond automatically, through visceral learning that associates the cue with the sensation of relaxation. Once the verbal cues begin working for you, you can employ them in a wide variety of situations where full, formal relaxation practice is impossible. This approach is ideal when you are at school or work, when you are engaging in a sport, or when you are involved in a social function in which you want to derive the benefits of Relaxation quickly and covertly.

Use of verbal cues with a shortened relaxation routine, targeting on particularly tense muscle groups, is helpful in preparing yourself for difficult encounters or demanding tasks in which anxiety and tension are expected. This approach, which can be employed moments before the stressful situation, facilitates better concentration by reducing the distractions of stress. As a result, you will be able to perform at full capacity at work, study, or play.

Another Relaxation method employing verbal cues is amazingly simple. C. A. Bugg devised a three-step technique to employ in tense situations or any time you feel anxiety creeping up on you. First, breathe in deeply and let the air out suddenly. Next, give yourself one of the verbal cues to relax. Finally, concentrate on something pleasant, on thoughts or images that make you happy. Bugg has found that the method produces sufficient, though very brief, relaxation to disrupt the anxiety-development process. And one or two easy repetitions seem to hold off the anxiety even more forcefully. The approach is recommended for stressful situations in which there is no chance to use a more elaborate relaxation routine.

Bugg's method employs not only verbal cues but breath control and fantasy (see Fantasy article), both of which can contribute significantly to achieving relaxation.

Add breath control to your relaxation routine. Taking a deep breath, perhaps counting to ten, is an old, commonsensical approach to coping with stress. In fact, just yawning is a natural, reflexive response to tension and to the release of adrenalin into the blood stream in the face of stress. The conscious control of your pattern of breathing — either alone or in conjunction with Progressive Relaxation and verbal cues — can contribute to achieving relaxation.

As a formal exercise at a time of your choosing, or immediately preceding stressful encounters, practice breath control. There are many forms of this technique (and you may develop your own variation), but the following is a simple, basic method worth starting with.

Take three deep breaths through your nose. Make each breath deeper than the last. Hold the third, deepest breath for several seconds without forcing or distressing yourself. Try to fill yourself with air; feel the air reach all the way down into your lower abdomen, perhaps even causing a tingling sensation above your genitals. Continue this deepest breathing for several minutes or until you feel yourself begin to relax. Be sure to breathe in through your nose as slowly and deeply as possible and out through your nose as slowly as you can without discomfort.

Some people intensify the effect by breathing through each nostril alternatively. They hold the right nostril closed and breathe in, then out, through the left. Then they hold the left nostril closed, inhaling and exhaling slowly through the right. Try this variation a few times to see if it adds anything to your efforts at relaxation.

You should find that slow, controlled deep breathing is pleasantly relaxing. It is particularly helpful right before you fall asleep and may, in fact, be used to induce sleep. It may also intensify the relaxation you achieve with Progressive Relaxation if you breathe this way during your sessions.

Remember to breathe slowly and through your nose. Short, rapid, shallow breaths through the mouth increase tension and can produce hyperventilation. In fact, one sign of anxiety is rapid, shallow breathing. Deep breathing produces countervailing effects, feelings of well-being that can be experienced only if the breathing is truly deep, slow, and controlled.

Relax while you are active — Differential Relaxation. Very few activities require you to tense all of your muscles. Weight lifters, pole vaulters and high jumpers, mountain climbers at certain moments in their climb must place stress on most of their muscles. But most of what we do each day demands tension in only some of our muscles at any given moment. Differential Relaxation is a method for identifying muscles that are unnecessarily tense and allowing them to relax while the muscles actually doing the work operate.

Like Progressive Relaxation, this approach requires you to pay close attention to how various muscle groups feel. Say you are driving a car. Your arms and hands will be occupied with steering, your right leg with manipulating the accelerator. Some of your trunk muscles will be helping you to sit erect, but few of your other muscles will have to be tight and stressed. Slowly take an inventory of your entire body, thinking about how each group of muscles feels and what it is doing. As you locate muscles that you know are not being employed directly and yet feel tight, relax them — using Progressive Relaxation, verbal cues, breath control, or whatever method you find works best for you.

The trick is to distinguish between usefully tense muscles and those that are knotted from residual tensions that you can work out. Get rid of such unnecessary tension and you'll feel better all over and have more stamina for what you are doing.

Differential Relaxation can be employed while you are reading, watching TV, standing in a long line, doing housework, or busy at a desk or work bench. With practice you can learn to tell which muscles are really needed for a task and which ones can be safely relaxed.

Monitor your progress. Proof that Relaxation methods are working for you comes in stages. First, you will gain the ability to tell the difference between tension and relaxation, even be able to identify subtle residual muscle tensions. Then you will find an increase in your ability to relax target muscle groups. Within a couple of weeks, if you have practiced daily, you should begin feeling better and noticeably less tense. This reduction of physical tension should be reflected in a steadily diminishing level of general anxiety.

You should be able to get to sleep more easily — especially if you practice Relaxation right before retiring. By practicing Relaxation regularly you may find that nervous habits like nail biting or teeth clenching don't seem to trouble you as much or as frequently. Relaxation replaces the anxiety that nurtures such habits with a sense of well-being that makes the habits unnecessary. Relaxation may even help in the breaking of such deeply ingrained habits as smoking and overeating. A relaxed person has less need than a person under stress does to reach for candy or a cigarette.

And if you become an accomplished student of Relaxation, encounters that were previously anxiety provoking should be easier to face and disagreeable tasks easier to undertake. By becoming a more relaxed person you should become a more competent and effective person in your work and play.

PRECAUTIONS

To enjoy the benefits of Relaxation, you must master at least one technique and practice it regularly — daily or more often. Which technique or combination of techniques you choose will depend on the results you achieve after experimenting. Be sure to try each one regularly for a week or so, which should be long enough to get results or to demonstrate that it simply isn't right for you. And consider the alternative methods listed at the beginning of this article. Whichever technique you eventually settle on, make it a permanent part of your self-psyching routine, something to look forward to — both in the doing and for the benefits it supplies.

As you learn to relax and as long as you use a Relaxation technique, concentrate on your feelings. Your body will tell you what its state of tension is — listen to it. You cannot lessen physical or mental stress unless you know where and to what degree you are experiencing tension. And you cannot be sure Relaxation is working unless you pay close attention to the often subtle changes that your efforts can produce in your muscle tension and level of anxiety.

Remember the mind-body connection. Either your mind or your body can relax or cause tension in the other. Applying Relaxation techniques to one will affect the other. Conversely, if you let your body tense up too much, your emotions will respond with signs of anxiety, and allowing yourself to get anxious can undermine your efforts to relax your body. The regular practice of controlled Relaxation can maintain the proper mind-body balance.

Sources of further information:
Bernstein, D., and Borkovec, T. *Progressive Relaxation Training*. Champaign, Ill.: Research Press, 1973.
Geba, Bruno H. *Breathe Away Your Tension*. New York: Random House, 1973.
Jacobson, Edmund. *You Must Relax*. 4th ed. New York: McGraw-Hill, 1957.
Jacobson, Edmund. *Anxiety and Tension Control*. Philadelphia: J. B. Lippincott, 1964.
Walker, Eugene C. *Learn to Relax*. Englewood Cliffs, N. J.: Prentice-Hall, 1975.

TECHNIQUE

The Relaxation Response

Particularly useful in dealing with such problems as Anxiety, Tension, Frustration, Disagreeable Tasks and Encounters, Fatigue and Lethargy and Insomnia.

Supplementary or alternative techniques: Relaxation, Autogenic Training, Biofeedback, Meditation.

WHAT THE RELAXATION RESPONSE IS
This is a stripped down, simplified, nonmystical version of Meditation that seems to provide similar emotional and physical benefits (see article on Meditation). It requires no involvement with a group or movement, no leader or guru. It merely calls for the regular practice of a program of mental and physical relaxation exercises that reduce stress by countering the fight-or-flight response.

HISTORICAL DEVELOPMENT
Herbert Benson conducted laboratory studies of the physiological and psychological effects of Meditation. An outgrowth of his research was a technique called The Relaxation Response, which he discovered had the power to slow the heart rate and respiration, lower metabolism, and alter other signs of stress and anxiety (see article on Anxiety).

BASIC ELEMENTS OF THE RELAXATION RESPONSE
Scheduling your practice
Achieving The Relaxation Response

HOW TO USE THE RELAXATION RESPONSE

Schedule your practice. Most who use this technique find that twice a day — once in the morning and again in the evening — for ten to twenty minutes each session works best. Because of the conflicting demands of the digestive system, practicing the method within two hours of eating can undermine its effectiveness, but your own experience will be your best guide.

Achieve The Relaxation Response. Once you have mastered the technique, usually after several weeks of regular practice, you may replace or supplement your practice sessions with sessions timed to meet your particular needs for relaxation and anxiety prevention. Every session should involve these basic elements:

1. An appropriate (usually quiet) place
2. A comfortable position
3. Eyes closed or directed toward a single object
4. Concentration on your breathing
5. Maintenance of a passive attitude

A typical session might go this way: In a place of your choosing, sit or recline comfortably, clothing and shoes loosened if necessary. At first find a quiet spot, though later, like many who have adopted this method, you may be able to practice even in the noisiest environment.

Close your eyes or, if you find it more relaxing, gaze steadily at something — like a spot on the wall, a door knob, a pattern in the rug, the diffused light of a shaded lamp.

Try to relax your muscles, working with little effort or insistence, from your toes to your face. (Knowledge of the techniques discussed in the Relaxation article may be helpful.)

Breathe normally, concentrating on your breathing. And as you breathe in and out through your nose, silently say the word "one" to yourself on each exhalation. Continue this for about twenty minutes.

Throughout, maintain a passive attitude. That is, whenever distracting thoughts or feelings intrude, ignore them, focusing on your breathing and on your subvocalization of the word "one." This should permit you to maintain your concentration and your relaxed state. Don't fight intruding sounds or sensations but accept them passively and use your calm concentration to ignore them.

For a few minutes at the end of each session, continue to sit or recline quietly, your eyes still closed or gazing. Then open your eyes or let your gaze begin to wander, but remain in your peaceful position as you take a few moments more to come out of your relaxing interlude.

That's all there is to it. Give it a try and judge for yourself whether or not it should have a place in your self-psyching program. You can use the technique regularly to increase your general well-being and resistance to anxiety or, once you have mastered it, to prepare yourself to face particularly stressful tasks or situations.

PRECAUTIONS

There is nothing dangerous or harmful in this technique. If you practice it while in bed, there is a chance that you might fall asleep and not get in a complete practice session, so this isn't advisable unless you are using the technique to fight insomnia.

The method recommends itself for its simplicity and ease of use. Your only concern should be to make certain that you are in fact getting positive results. While most people report considerable success, if after several weeks of practice you don't notice a lessening of tension and anxiety, you may be performing the technique incorrectly or it may just not be right for you. Before abandoning the technique, review the instructions and try it again. If you still experience no results, it could be a lost cause as a self-psyching technique for you and you should consider a more formal, structured form of Meditation or Relaxation.

Sources of further information:

Benson, Herbert. *The Relaxation Response*. New York: William Morrow, 1975.

Ebon, Martin. *The Relaxation Controversy*. New York: Signet, 1976.

Rewards

Particularly useful in dealing with such problems as Habits, Shyness and Inhibitions, Fears and Phobias, Disagreeable Tasks and Encounters, Marital Problems.

May also play a role in handling Indecisiveness, Procrastination, Tardiness, Compulsiveness, Overeating, Smoking, Problem Drinking.

Supplementary or alternative techniques: Stimulus Control, Changing the Sequence of Events, Modeling, Behavior Rehearsal, Punishments.

WHAT REWARDS IS

Rewards are not just prizes you award yourself for accomplishing some change in your behavior or feelings. They are devices that can be employed systematically to alter how you act and feel. Behavioral scientists call them *reinforcers*. Any consequence of a behavior that increases the likelihood of the recurrence of that behavior is a reinforcer. Thus, reinforcers may perpetuate both good and bad habits or feelings. So think of rewards both as additions to your life that encourage desirable behavior patterns or emotions and as reinforcements that you remove or replace to break habits they sustain.

The specific rewards that will serve you best in altering your own behavior must be yours to decide as you begin using this technique. Different people find different things rewarding. In the instructions for using this method you will learn how to choose rewards appropriate to your needs.

HISTORICAL DEVELOPMENT

The use of rewards, or reinforcers, is a basic element of behaviorism. In fact, research on the role of reinforcement in controlling behavior opened the way for many of the most successful clinical applications of behavior modification. The underlying principle is that people's actions are naturally controlled by reinforcers, and that it might therefore be possible to shape new behavior by the deliberate manipulation of reinforcers.

Experiments and numerous clinical studies by B. F. Skinner, Albert Bandura, and dozens of other psychologists have confirmed the validity of the theory and the efficacy of the

Rewards approach to behavior modification. By controlling reinforcement, researchers have trained thousands of mice to run through complex mazes or taught pigeons to play a sort of Ping-Pong. Introductory psychology students in most universities repeat some of the basic experiments in their courses. They discover that they can make a white rat act in predetermined ways by consistently rewarding its correct responses.

Reinforcement control — the bestowal of rewards for the successful performance of a specified behavior or the removal of a painful or distressing stimulus as the result of appropriate action — is the foundation of widely used behavior therapies.

The scientific studies add expert testimony to what most of us know from common sense and everyday experience. Every time you promise yourself a reward for doing something such as finishing a task or facing some tough encounter you are using this technique in an unstructured manner. And when a parent tells a child that he or she will receive a prize or privilege for completing homework or chores or behaving properly, the parent is using a Rewards approach. When you gamble, knowing that most of the time you will lose, but go on because you expect to win sometime (to get a reward sometime), this technique is at work. It is at work when, after you receive a compliment, you tend to repeat the behavior that resulted in the compliment. The instructions below can help you apply this natural method more systematically, predictably, and effectively.

BASIC ELEMENTS OF REWARDS

Monitoring your behavior to identify problems (see Introduction)

Choosing the rewards you will use

Establishing a Rewards program

Practicing regularly

Employing a Rewards Program with other self-psyching techniques

Monitoring your behavior to evaluate improvement (see Introduction)

HOW TO USE REWARDS

Monitor your behavior to identify problems. Following the instructions in the Introduction, spend a week or two keeping a record of your normal behavior with the goal of identifying specific problem areas. Compile a list of problems that might include habits, tardiness, or compulsiveness. Plan to attack one such problem at a time — for example, the habit of being late for work or school.

Choose the rewards you will use. A reward is not a reward to all people. You must decide what objects, activities, people, or situations are most gratifying or desirable to you. Make a list, concentrating on rewards that are truly rewarding. Otherwise you'll just avoid the whole program and fail to change your target behavior. Desirability, accessibility, and controllability are what you should look for in compiling your list of possible rewards. Do not include unreasonable or unattainable rewards; they will prevent you from making practical use of this technique even before you begin.

Your list may include certain foods, favorite activities like a night at the movies or on the town, the privilege of not working or studying for a certain period, a special gift to yourself, or something as simple as taking time to read, watch TV, or enjoy a beer.

For example, if playing tennis is something you enjoy and do as often as you can, you can make it a reinforcer by making your playing conditional on having first completed some target task — cleaning out the garage (a one-time target task), studying or working for a certain number of hours, practicing restraint and affection with your spouse who has been complaining that you are abrupt and thoughtless. (The theory behind this approach — known as the Premack Principle — is that you can increase the performance of a behavior by making another more pleasurable behavior conditional on first doing the tougher target task.)

Another key to choosing suitable rewards is to examine your motivations, to think about what incentives propel you through life. Does praise inspire you? If so, enlist a friend or loved one to serve as cotherapist, supplying the praise you desire — but doing so only after you demonstrate your success in meeting the behavior change goals you have set. When you work, do you work merely for money? Does the thought of ending the work day and having a chance to relax and enjoy yourself play a big part in getting you through the day? Consider such things while making your list.

Establish a Rewards program. Such a program begins with clearly delineated goals. General goals, like being a better person or being happier, will not do. To make the Rewards approach work, you must have specific goals that reflect your specific problem. Break your problem into small parts and reward yourself for success with each part. The parts may be discrete behaviors or arbitrary time periods during which you perform a desired task or refrain from doing something you are trying to free yourself of.

For example, if tardiness is your problem, you can make responding to the call of your alarm clock a rewardable part of the program. Getting out of bed within a certain period after the alarm goes off merits another reward. Taking no more than, say, twenty minutes to get washed and dressed is another. Limiting breakfast to a fixed period, leaving for work or school by a specific time, and settling right down to work are similar parts of the tardiness problem you can attack.

Having broken your problem down, set specific rewards for success on each part. Needless to say, the rewards should be sensible. A trip to Europe is hardly a suitable reward for getting out of bed! But the purchase of a favorite magazine is. Don't buy the magazine unless you complete the problem segment for which the magazine is the reward. It may be best to make several days' success with a target behavior the prerequisite for the reward, but you can determine how to proceed as you get into the program and see how much prodding you really need.

Once you have spent several days with a Rewards program, you should find that it is no longer necessary—or even effective — to reward the initial behaviors in the chain leading to your overall goal. So you can concentrate on rewarding the areas you begin to see as most resistant to change — perhaps getting out of the bathroom in time to leave for work without being late.

Similarly, starting with a set time for getting to work — 9:00 A.M. — you can reward yourself for getting closer and closer to that goal. If you arrive at 9:25, a certain reward is payable; 9:20 earns more, and so on. But there is a catch. If you arrive at 9:20 one day and reward yourself, you get no reward for coming in at 9:25 the next day. And if you get in at 9:15 one day, you no longer get any rewards for later arrivals. Psychologists call this *shaping*. Successive approximations of a target behavior are rewarded, but rewards are denied for lesser approximations once higher levels are reached. As you see yourself getting closer to your goal, you will probably find it easier and easier to continue performing at the new, higher levels — ultimately without any rewards at all.

The timing of rewards is crucial. It is most desirable and

effective to reward yourself as soon as possible after each successful performance, after a set number of successes, or after a certain period of successful performance. But sometimes it is impossible to do so; you can hardly reward yourself for getting to work on time by immediately taking off for the nearest movie house. This is where tokens come in.

A token system allows you to build up points toward a total that may be exchanged for the reward you have set for yourself. Say going to the movies is your reward and worth ten points. You can establish ahead of time that each success with some segment of your problem is worth a point and that the achievement of your final goal — getting to work on time — is worth five points. You can modify the values as you get used to the system and evaluate your performance realistically.

The record of your tokens can be kept in writing or you may even carry a pocketful of toothpicks, match sticks, or paper clips and move the requisite number into a different pocket each time you earn points. Count up the points at the end of each day and see if you've earned your reward yet. The token system is convenient and effective, but you must remember to take your tokens as soon as possible after achieving a behavior change goal.

Practice regularly. You will not have to practice a Rewards program forever for any one problem. But if you are to lick that problem, you must practice until you see the desired changes in your behavior. Hit-or-miss practice is of no use because the failure to form new habits may make old ones harder to influence. Taking one problem at a time, breaking it down into parts, establishing proper rewards (perhaps with a token system), and sticking to the Rewards program will produce results for most people and for most problems within two or three weeks. Deeply ingrained, long-standing habits like smoking or overeating will be easier to handle if a Rewards program is incorporated into other techniques.

Many problem behaviors and emotions are perpetuated because not changing them is "rewarding." Trying to change seems too difficult and distressing. But rewarding each step toward change can have a great impact. Shyness, for instance, can be hard to overcome because shy people find it too difficult to achieve their ultimate goal — freedom from shyness. A Rewards program can supply incentives for the smaller steps taken to the ultimate goal of easy and uninhibited interaction. As rewards reinforce new behaviors, the forces perpetuating undesirable habits will be undermined.

Employ a Rewards program with other self-psyching techniques. You should find it easier to make progress with Stimulus Control, Changing the Sequence of Events, Modeling, Behavior Rehearsal, and Punishments if you also use a Rewards program. As you succeed with any segment of these methods, note your achievement by taking a reward. This will reinforce your desire to continue with the techniques you are using. Almost any self-psyching technique can benefit from supportive rewards, as long as the rewards are not in themselves objects or actions you're trying to do without or overcome. Obviously, you shouldn't reward yourself for becoming more punctual by allowing yourself a satisfying session of nail biting.

Monitor your behavior to evaluate improvement. By keeping a record of your progress with a Rewards program, you will soon detect both successes and soft spots. Begin attacking the areas where little progress is apparent. Break that segment of the problem into smaller parts, if possible, or try to find more appealing rewards to offer yourself. In time you should notice improvement. Your record should tell you in which areas you are coming along well enough so that you no longer need rewards. Conversely, if it shows that you have made little progress in a month of practice, other techniques may be needed to supplement or replace Rewards in dealing with the resistant problem.

PRECAUTIONS
Keep in mind that a Rewards program involves two factors: your genuine desire for the reward and your hope for the modification of some behavior. One factor influences the other. The rewards cannot be too important, too easy to obtain, or too irresistible, and you must not give yourself rewards without first accomplishing designated portions of behavior change. However, if you make it too hard to get the reward, if the reward is too grand or distant, or if the reward isn't truly important to you, you may not be willing to take the trouble to earn the reward or may find that the reward doesn't actually reinforce your new behavior. Therefore, you must choose rewards and set the value of tokens with the

same care with which you establish the goals of behavior change that trigger the payment of those rewards.

Use your head, be honest and reasonable, and you will benefit both by changing the way you act and feel and by getting the rewards you have chosen.

Sources of further information:

Ayllon, T., and Azrin, N. H. *The Token Economy: A Motivational System for Therapy and Rehabilitation.* New York: Appleton-Century-Crofts, 1968.

Kanfer, F. H., and Phillips, J. S. *Learning Foundations of Behavior Therapy.* New York: John Wiley & Sons, 1970.

Kazdin, Alan E. *The Token Economy: A Review and Evaluation.* New York: Plenum Press, 1977.

Skinner, B. F. *Science and Human Behavior.* The Macmillan Company, 1953.

Thoresen, C. E., and Mahoney, M. J. *Behavioral Self-Control.* New York: Holt, Rinehart and Winston, 1974.

PROBLEM

Ritual Behavior

See:

Compulsiveness

TECHNIQUE

Role Playing

Improving your ability to assume different roles can facilitate the successful use of such important techniques as Modeling and Behavior Rehearsal.

Extensive training or dramatic experience is unnecessary. Role Playing is a natural part of our daily lives. It is an inescapable result of belonging to a culture in which we must accept various responsibilities, perform numerous functions, deal with a variety of relationships, and occupy a wide range of positions in the social order. We are children, lovers, spouses, siblings. We are employees or employers, supervisors, subordinates. Even without consciously trying to model ourselves on others, we naturally and automatically play many roles simultaneously, altering our behavior to suit the roles we play, speaking to our mothers in a different way than we do to our children or the gardener. In fact, having to shift roles can cause us some anxiety, especially if new roles (father, husband, draftee, mother, widow, widower) are thrust upon us too suddenly. But for self-psyching purposes, controlled, deliberate Role Playing can be useful and therapeutic.

The principal benefit of Role Playing is that you learn to see things as another person sees them, as well as from your own perspective, in order to get a more complete picture of reality. When used with Modeling, for instance, by playing the role of people who handle problems more successfully than you do, you get insights into new strategies for coping. You can learn your models' tricks by playing their roles. And learning to play their roles is only a matter of carefully observing how they behave in situations that give you trouble.

If you want to reap some of the benefits of being more like someone else or of being as good as someone else at avoiding the behavioral and emotional pitfalls that trap you, just watch that person long enough to catch the subtleties of his or her actions. Then try mentally rehearsing these actions in situations appropriate to your own life. Finally, test your role playing in the real world. You can do this to some positive effect even without a formal program of Modeling or Behavior Rehearsal.

Role Playing has an added benefit. By assuming another person's role and point of view, you can get clues to what makes that person tick, to how that person may really feel about you, and even to how you appear in that person's eyes. It can be an illuminating exercise.

See also:
Modeling
Behavior Rehearsal

TECHNIQUE

Running and Jogging

See:
Exercise
Meditation

Sadness

Feeling sad, a bit down, unhappy? You should not allow these feelings to continue for too long without making efforts to counter your sadness. Allowed to persist, the mildest case of the blues could turn into a serious depression that requires professional help. There are several self-psyching techniques that provide simple and quite effective means for overcoming episodes of sadness that are so commonly experienced by most of us.

The Incompatible Behavior technique can work because it rightly assumes that you can't be sad and glad at the same time. And Relaxation and Exercise can make it difficult for tension to be present when your mind and body are relaxed and pleasantly stimulated.

See also:
Minor Emotional Complaints
Depression

Techniques to try:
Incompatible Behavior
Relaxation
Exercise

Sales Presentation Failures

See:
Fear of Failure
Disagreeable Tasks and Encounters
Shyness and Inhibitions

PROBLEM

Scratching

When the nerve ends in the skin become irritated, you feel them as an itch. The natural response is to scratch. But scratching may not stop the itching and can even make it worse.

And because self-touching is a pleasurable activity (a good scratch after removing one's clothing at the end of the day is often close to ecstasy) it is easy to fall into the habit of scratching even when there is no physical cause for the itch. When scratching becomes a nervous habit it can bring you embarrassment because it bespeaks a lack of self-control, can produce unsightly skin eruptions, and may even lead to infection.

If you find that you scratch at yourself reflexively, especially around others and in settings where your habit is a detriment to your social and professional standing, you probably want to break the habit. Identifying the situations that provoke nervous scratching may involve nothing more than thinking about the problem for a few days, checking your own behavior, checking your body for signs of scratching, or asking a close friend to play the role of confidential cotherapist and watch you.

See also:
Nervous Habits

Techniques to try:
Negative Practice
Incompatible Behavior

PROBLEM

Self-Consciousness

See:
Shyness and Inhibitions

PROBLEM

Self-Denial

See:
Shyness and Inhibitions
Standing Up for Your Rights

TECHNIQUE

Self-Hypnosis

Particularly useful in dealing with such problems as Anxiety, mild Depression, Psychosomatic Complaints and Pains, Nervous Habits, Insomnia.

Supplementary or alternative techniques: Autogenic Training, Meditation, Relaxation.

WHAT SELF-HYPNOSIS IS

This is a method for putting yourself into a light trance by concentration on some object, sound, or idea. You can train yourself to feel your eyelids growing heavier, your muscles relaxing, your breathing becoming slower and deeper as you pass into the state of altered awareness. Having achieved the mild trance state, you can give yourself suggestions to feel less anxious or less depressed, break certain habits, and sleep better.

HISTORICAL BACKGROUND

In the eighteenth and nineteenth centuries hypnosis was considered a magician's trick. By the end of the nineteenth century, scientists were examining its role in the relief of pathological states like hysteria and even experimenting with therapeutic applications. By the early twentieth century hypnosis had become a fairly common tool in psychoanalytic therapy. Only recently has it been recognized as a legitimate clinical technique. Trained physicians and therapists use hypnosis to alleviate pain, fears and phobias, and numerous other physical and psychological complaints. And Self-Hypnosis, or Autosuggestion, is only now gaining acceptance as a viable self-help tool in dealing with emotional and behavioral problems.

BASIC ELEMENTS OF SELF-HYPNOSIS

Learning to employ Autosuggestion
Giving yourself posthypnotic suggestions
Coming out of the trance
Repeating the procedure regularly until your problem diminishes

HOW TO USE SELF-HYPNOSIS
Learn to employ Autosuggestion. In a comfortable place where you will be free of distractions for about half an hour, relax and concentrate on a single object, sound, or idea. A candle flame will do nicely, though you may want to use the ticking of a clock, the movements of a metronome, or a mental image such as that of a field of black velvet.

Now tell yourself that your eyelids are getting heavy, you are feeling more and more relaxed, more sleepy, drowsy. Use key words like "relax," "deeper," "heavier." Keep concentrating on the focus of your attention — without staring directly into the flame — if you are using a candle — to insure that you will not be distracted and that the trance will steadily deepen.

When you start feeling drowsy and fully relaxed, when you begin to experience the floating, almost ethereal sensation of the mild trance state, you are ready to begin using Self-Hypnosis to attack your problems.

Give yourself posthypnotic suggestions. In your restful and relaxed trance state, suggest to yourself whatever outcome you wish for your problem: You are not anxious now or will not be in certain situations; your pain has disappeared; you will not bite your nails; you will work or study more or more effectively. Continue this self-suggestion for several minutes until you begin to believe it. And in your hypnotized state you will be quite receptive to such suggestions and be ready to believe them with little resistance or doubt.

Come out of the trance. End the session by telling yourself that the trance will end and that you will feel better and follow the commands you have been giving yourself about your problem. The suggestions are "posthypnotic" because you will be influenced by them even after you come out of your trance. Counting slowly to ten is a sure means of ending the trance, which you will command to end on the count of ten.

Repeat the procedure regularly until your problem diminishes. Practice the method once a day. During any Self-Hypnosis session, you should attack only one problem at a time. After several days of working on a single problem, you should begin to see changes in your attitudes or behavior, changes reflecting positive responses to your posthypnotic suggestions. When such progress is significant enough so that the problem no longer concerns you very much, you are ready to apply the technique to the next problem.

PRECAUTIONS

You must maintain your concentration and belief in the technique or it won't work very well, or at all, for you. Don't distract yourself at any stage of Self-Hypnosis and don't let yourself get tense. Don't lose your confidence in the method.

You need not be concerned that you will enter such a deep trance that you may not come out of it at all. Hypnosis, especially Self-Hypnosis, is a self-limiting phenomenon. Even if you don't specifically command yourself to come out of it, you will do so within a few minutes after you initially planned to end the session.

You may find that Self-Hypnosis doesn't suit your needs for one reason or another. You may simply think of it as mumbo jumbo and unworthy of your involvement. You may try it and find that it doesn't help you very much. If so, several alternative methods are available, suggested at the opening of this article and in the articles on the particular problems. But even if Self-Hypnosis doesn't solve your problems it may be worth trying from time to time merely as a relaxing and restorative interlude.

Sources of further information:

Bernhardt, Roger and Martin, David. Self Mastery Through Self Hypnosis. New York: Bobbs-Merril, 1978.

Brooks, C. H. The Practice of Autosuggestion by the Method of Emile Coué. New York: Dodd, Mead, 1922.

Caprio, Frank S. and Berger, Joseph R. Helping Yourself with Self-Hypnosis. New York: Warner Paperback Library, 1975.

Duckworth, John. How to Use Auto-Suggestion Effectively. Hollywood, California: Wilshire Book Company, 1960.

LeCron, Leslie M. Self-Hypnosis: Its Technique and Its Use in Daily Living. New York: New American Library, 1964.

PROBLEM

Self-Punishment

When things go wrong; when you get down on yourself for failures; when you become dissatisfied, disheartened, disillusioned, or depressed, you may take it out on yourself in both subtle and obvious ways. Such self-punishment can take the form of physical self-attack through nervous habits like nail biting. You may be troubled by floods of unwanted thoughts characterized by self-accusation and harsh self-criticism. You may even speak aloud against yourself, calling yourself names.

Self-punishment tends to diminish your ability to cope with other problems, especially those that triggered the self-punishing behavior. To clear away this obstacle to your effective functioning, you should take steps to overcome such self-defeating responses to life's difficulties.

The numerous techniques discussed in the article on Nervous Habits can aid you in ending various types of physical self-punishment. Thought-Stopping works to cut off negative thinking that can incapacitate you. And Assertiveness Training gives guidance in strengthening your self-confidence and self-regard.

See also:
Nervous Habits

Techniques to try:
Thought-Stopping
Assertiveness Training

PROBLEM

Sexual Hang-ups

Sexual problems such as impotence and lack of orgasmic response have been treated quite effectively in clinics using the Masters and Johnson approach and other methods. And people with antisocial sexual hang-ups (exhibitionism, criminal voyeurism, and so on) are regularly treated by psychiatrists and psychologists.

While self-psyching techniques are not intended to tackle such deeply rooted problems, you may have other problems that are contributing to your sexual difficulties. Self-psyching may help you deal with these problems and thus remove some blocks and increase your ability to handle sexual encounters. If you have trouble relating to other people socially, if you don't feel very positive about yourself, if you can't assert yourself and express your needs and desires, you may understandably not be experiencing satisfying sexual contacts.

These underlying problems can be handled with self-psyching.

Behavior Rehearsal and Modeling can teach you to approach sexual encounters with more confidence that you will not say or do the wrong things. Desensitization can remove the anxiety that may be keeping you from fully enjoying sexual interludes and can reduce your fear of rejection. Stimulus Control, Rewards, and Changing the Sequence of Events teach you to maximize your chances for giving pleasure both to your partner and yourself.

Assertiveness Training is ideal for learning to communicate more openly, to make your feelings and preferences known to your bedmate. And by employing Fantasy you may be able to enrich your sexual experiences by creating images that arouse and encourage you and consequently inspire your partner to more sensual activity.

Your biggest hang-up may be no more than your inability to be yourself in sexual situations. The above techniques can help you liberate the real you — with all your erotic potential — so that sex can become an enjoyable act, not a dreadful prospect.

Techniques to try:
Behavior Rehearsal
Modeling
Desensitization
Stimulus Control
Rewards
Changing the Sequence of Events
Assertiveness Training
Fantasy

Sources of further information:
Kaplan, Helen S. *The New Sex Therapy.* New York: Quadrangle, 1974.
Masters, William H., and Johnson, Virginia E. *Human Sexual Inadequacy.* Boston: Little, Brown, 1970.

PROBLEM

Shyness and Inhibitions

Shyness is like a curtain blocking out the sunlight, a curtain behind which those who feel shy dwell in the shadows of uncertainty about themselves and what they have a right to expect from the world. Recent research has exploded the myth that shyness is a major problem only among children and adolescents. Great numbers of adults suffer from the emotional and behavioral problem of shyness. Some have learned to present a confident face to others but must keep the lid on feelings of insecurity and anxiety.

Do you have few real friends outside your immediate family? Do you avoid situations where you might make new acquaintances or do you fail to involve yourself in conversations with strangers who might become friends? Do you engage in self-defeating rationalizations such as "Parties (sports events, conventions, dating bars) are never any fun and there probably won't be anyone there worth meeting?" Assertiveness Training could make it easier for you to make rewarding contacts and release you from inertia that keeps you from going to places where you might make such contacts.

In job-related activities, do you always seem to give way to the ideas and opinions of others? Do you fail to express yourself even when you have what you know is a good idea? Are you likely to freeze up when called upon to make a report or give a speech? Behavior Rehearsal and Assertiveness Training may help you master such inhibitions. And Desensitization will enable you to break your shyness problem down into small parts, each of which you can handle successfully.

Do you refuse to let yourself go even among friends? Do you find it hard to try new dances, sing along, let others see you in a relaxed mood? Are you afraid to let your hair down and unhappy that you don't? Modeling, Assertiveness Training, and Stimulus Control can give you the confidence you lack, remove your inhibitions, lessen your anxiety about allowing others to see you as you really are — or want to be.

While the particular character of your problem will recommend one or another technique, many are of general utility and will work to some degree for most shy people. Or, as therapists have discovered, a combination of some (or even all) methods will produce the best results. For example, if your main complaint is anxiety in specific situations, combining Desensitization with Behavior Rehearsal will permit you to prepare for each encounter by reducing the stressful responses you usually make to each component of troublesome situations. Modeling can intensify the effect by giving you a strong example of how a person who isn't shy would handle problems that plague you.

If only certain people, thoughts, or events trigger your shyness, Stimulus Control and Changing the Sequence of Events may be called for: You learn to identify anxiety-provoking stimuli, teach yourself to face or extinguish them without feeling tense and shy, and even encourage the development of new stimuli that build your confidence.

Perhaps you need some identifiable incentive to break out of your shell. A Rewards program may supplement other techniques. Should you find, as you more closely examine the nature of your shyness, that much of your problem stems from your own habit of putting yourself down, Thought-Stopping can help you overcome this self-defeating behavior.

By doing nothing to overcome your shyness you may be psyching yourself out of many of life's pleasures and rewards. Try some of these techniques for psyching yourself into the action.

Techniques to try:
Assertiveness Training
Desensitization (with Relaxation)
Behavior Rehearsal
Thought-Stopping
Modeling
Stimulus Control
Changing the Sequence of Events
Rewards
Flooding

Sources of further information:
Zimbardo, Philip G. *Shyness: What it is, What to do about it.* Reading, Mass.: Addison-Wesley, 1977.

TECHNIQUE

Sleep

Scientists have found that sleep takes two main forms, both accomplishing basic kinds of physical and emotional restoration.

Nondreaming sleep helps the body recover from exertion and rebound from fatigue. It prevents lethargy and tiredness in later periods of activity. It can also give the body a chance to recuperate from sickness or injury. Moreover, it appears that important protein synthesis, especially the production of the basic RNA molecules, goes on during these dream-free periods of sleep.

Dreaming sleep is more vital for emotional stability and intellectual flexibility. Basic brain chemicals are regenerated and brought into proper balance. And scientists think that the electrochemical transformations and reformulations that embed new knowledge while you are dreaming cause the memory system to function properly.

Most important, dreaming permits the body to recover from anxiety, depression, and similar emotional strains by giving the mind a chance to function without the feedback that operates during waking hours.

Sleep is perhaps the easiest, most natural, and most ancient form of self-renewal practiced by humans. Self-psyching techniques such as Relaxation, Meditation, and Fantasy (see the section on Dreaming) can aid you in getting to sleep more easily, in preventing insomnia, and in making creative use of your dreams.

See also:
Insomnia

Techniques to try:
Relaxation
Meditation
Fantasy

Sources of further information:
Foulkes, David. *The Psychology of Sleep.* New York: Charles Scribner's Sons, 1966.
Hartmann, Ernest L. *The Functions of Sleep.* New Haven, Conn.: Yale University Press, 1973.

PROBLEM

Smoking

This habit, like overeating and problem drinking, can be highly resistant to change, especially by self-controlled behavior modification techniques. But there are self-psyching techniques that, while they may not teach you to stop smoking altogether, may contribute to moderating or reducing your smoking problem.

The article on Nervous Habits suggests several techniques that you can employ to deal with smoking. Stimulus Control, Rewards, Punishments, and Changing the Sequence of Events are particularly useful because they help you reorganize your habit patterns, provide new incentives for cutting down on cigarettes, and remove many of the emotional and environmental stimuli that you currently respond to by smoking.

Incompatible Behavior may serve you well by giving your hands alternatives to holding a cigarette most of the time. Covert Sensitization could work for you by teaching you to imagine and feel the worst consequences of your habit, which you may then find less attractive.

Thought-Stopping has been used to good effect with smokers who were taught to recondition their reflex to smoke in various situations. Practicing Relaxation serves to reduce the anxiety that you now alleviate by smoking. Modeling could help you shape your behavior to reflect that of nonsmokers you respect.

Because those who meditate regularly tend to be less anxious, have less trouble with nervous habits, and appear to be less prone to such compulsive behavior as long-standing cigarette smoking, Meditation recommends itself to heavy smokers.

Many smokers consider their habit dangerous and distressing, but many enjoy and rely upon it. If you feel that the advantages of smoking outweigh those of not smoking, using these techniques is not called for.

Many smokers are also becoming sensitive to the poor reception their smoking receives from nonsmokers. If you have been trying to quit but feel you aren't doing all you can to cut down on cigarettes, these methods may contribute to your efforts to smoke less and enjoy it more.

See also:
  Nervous Habits
  Overeating
  Compulsiveness

Techniques to try:
  Stimulus Control
  Rewards
  Punishments
  Changing the Sequence of Events

Incompatible Behavior
Covert Sensitization
Thought-Stopping
Relaxation
Modeling
Meditation

PROBLEM

Speaking Up

See:

Standing Up for Your Rights
Shyness and Inhibitions

PROBLEM

Standing Up
for Your Rights

You have a right to get what you pay for, yet how many times have you settled for shoddy workmanship or inferior service because someone psyched you out? Have you ever had a car repaired, your TV fixed, a garment altered, or an appliance installed, only to discover that the job hadn't been done right? Have you complained and then been told something like "All Dodges make that noise," or "You said you wanted three inches off the hem, not one," or "You have to expect a dishwasher to leak a little in the first few weeks"? Did you let the person conning you get away with it, not wanting to make a fuss, taking it upon yourself to live with the unsatisfactory situation rather than demand your rights? Or did you allow the offending person to charge you extra for finally providing the satisfactory results you paid for in the first place?

Have you ever ordered a bottle of wine that, to you, tasted terrible? You may, in fact, have gone through the mandatory ceremony of tasting the wine. Though you found it wanting, your nod of approval told the waiter to fill the glasses. Why didn't you speak up, why didn't you exercise your right to ask for another, better bottle?

Many of us are unable to cope with the manipulative behavior of others, especially if they have some authority over us, claim an expertise we lack, are close friends we fear offending, or are even total strangers who rely on us to be courteous and submissive even if they are not.

This is no small matter. Our lives are made up of those hundreds of encounters requiring a choice between standing up for our rights and being manipulated and psyched out by others. Our own happiness is reduced if at every turn we engage in self-denial, back down, acquiesce to others' demands, agree when we are criticized, remain silent rather than stick up for our beliefs.

Whenever you believe your rights are being violated, your privacy invaded, your needs or desires unjustly ignored, you owe it to yourself to object. You don't have to be rude or aggressive — only firm and confident.

Assertiveness Training is specifically intended to give you coping skills for standing up for your rights. The Modeling approach enables you to effectively pattern your behavior on that of real or imaginary persons who don't back down.

By starting slowly, with relatively easy encounters, you begin getting results right away. Your confidence will grow and you will find it increasingly easy to have things your way — or at least have them be fair and proper — more of the time.

Techniques to try:
Assertiveness Training
Modeling

<hr>

TECHNIQUE

Stimulus Control

Particularly useful in dealing with such problems as Nervous Habits, Disagreeable Tasks and Encounters, Work or Study Habits, Tardiness, Procrastination, Overeating, Smoking, Marital Problems.

May also aid in handling Compulsiveness and Obsessions, Shyness and Inhibitions, Fears and Phobias, Nightmares, Anxiety, Fear of Expressing Anger, and Sexual Hang-ups.

Supplementary or alternative techniques: Rewards, Changing the Sequence of Events, Relaxation, Desensitization, Meditation.

WHAT STIMULUS CONTROL IS

This technique deals with the stimuli (or cues) that prompt

behavior and inspire attitudes and feelings. It teaches you to identify the stimuli that trigger problem behavior and troublesome habits and emotions, and to alter or replace them in a conscious program of Stimulus Control.

HISTORICAL DEVELOPMENT

Stimulus Control is based on many decades of research into the role of conditioning in animal and human behavior. The studies of Ivan Pavlov, early in this century, identified the relationships between stimuli and responses and showed experimentally how natural responses could be conditioned to occur in the absence of natural stimuli. Pavlov laid the foundations of the role of Stimulus Control in behavioral science with his famous experiments, in which he first conditioned dogs to salivate when a bell rang and food was given them and then found that they salivated on merely hearing the bell. A little later John B. Watson examined the plasticity of behavior and demonstrated that originally pleasant stimuli could be made unpleasant and cause an alteration in behavior.

Behaviorists are now employing Stimulus Control both clinically and experimentally in an effort to improve human learning skills and modify problem behavior.

Therapists have even had promising results using Stimulus Control on such tough problems as smoking and overeating. An outline of the sort of therapeutic regimen involved in the clinical use of Stimulus Control can highlight the technique's features, revealing how its use by experts may relate to its role in self-psyching.

Say the target behavior is overeating. A complete record is made of the patients' eating patterns.

The patients say where they eat: in the kitchen, dining room, at their desks, in bed, in cars, at the movies, everywhere.

They indicate when they eat: only at mealtimes, between meals, late at night, before bed, all the time.

They tell what they do while eating: nothing else, read, watch TV, talk with other people.

They list what they tend to eat most: main courses, sweets, bread products, everything.

They recount how other people respond to their eating: pushing food on them, telling them to eat less, saying nothing.

The patients also attempt to identify their feelings when they are eating: happiness, sadness, boredom, stress, guilt.

Then they honestly examine the role of eating in their lives to discover the extent of the problem. They determine whether or not eating intrudes on other activities, if being overweight makes them feel unattractive, and if they spend too much time just thinking about food.

Having recorded this baseline data over a period of a few weeks, the patients are ready to isolate the stimuli that are components of their overeating problem. Most of them find that they don't eat because food or the thought of food stimulates their hunger. They don't even eat because they are hungry. They eat most and most often because they are cued to do so by stimuli that may have no meaningful connection to food except through the patients' own conditioned responses to those stimuli.

What are some of these powerful stimuli that can make people who may not even be hungry eat — or overeat? Feelings are such stimuli. People who grew up associating mealtimes with warm family interactions will probably get those warm feelings at the very thought of eating. And wanting to revive such feelings, they may eat more often than their hunger dictates, clinging to the warmth and safety of the eating experience as they might to a security blanket.

Conversely, bad feelings can stimulate eating, too. Because eating is a naturally pleasurable experience, people tend to use it to drown out feelings of failure, guilt, and disappointment. Didn't have a good day at work? Have a big meal and two slabs of pie. Your fiancé call off the wedding? Eat or drink yourself into a stupor.

Patients find that their baseline records of eating habits reveal times when feelings — rather than hunger — cue eating.

Environmental stimuli similarly trigger overeating. The places, circumstances, and people associated with eating — rather than hunger — can prompt eating. Just walking into a movie theater makes many people want to eat popcorn, candy, or ice cream. People have become conditioned to associate eating with movies (a fact that theater operators have exploited to the limit, often getting as much income from concessions as from admissions). Part of this eating impulse is the anxiety-reducing power of food. In the dark, assaulted by strong sensations (fear, excitement), eating counteracts some resultant anxiety.

Other environments produce such stimulation of the urge to eat. Make it a practice to snack in the car and you will soon train yourself to keep candy in the glove compartment. Eat while reading or watching TV and it may be that the pleasure you think you are getting from eating is really resulting from the reading or viewing. Stimulus Control helps patients discriminate what exactly is giving them the pleasure that they associate with eating.

The list of stimuli that clinicians have identified in their patients' behavioral repertoire is long and varied: the position of their bodies while eating, the nature of the room lighting, the time of day, the color of the tablecloth, the character of the table talk — almost anything goes. Treating such patients successfully often involves eliminating those stimuli (perhaps by changing the place eating is done), reversing or neutralizing their impact, or replacing them with stimuli that don't trigger overeating (maybe by filling customary eating times with other activities).

Once the stimuli have been identified, the therapist can suggest ways for controlling them, establishing a list of behavioral goals ranked from the easiest to the hardest. Thus patients can limit their overeating by trying to achieve the easiest goal first, succeeding, and going on to the next. For example, it would seem easy to give up eating in church. Next, patients may be encouraged to place their cars off limits, then the bedroom, moving along this way until only one place in the house — usually the kitchen or dining room — is designated for eating. (The dining room, a place where food is not stored in quantity, may be preferable to the kitchen.) A final goal may be to confine eating to a single place at the table, with a particular place mat of a certain color. Most eating should now be prompted only by hunger and the new, controlled stimuli.

Notice that the technique does not require patients to suddenly give up overeating. The trick in Stimulus Control is to permit the habit to continue but to begin limiting the places, times, and circumstances that permit eating.

Eliminating some stimuli is simple and obvious: Big jars filled with fresh cookies shouldn't be left on counters to tempt you. Luncheon dates with heavy eaters and trips to county fairs should be avoided. Reduce exposure to any places, things, or people that your baseline data indicate prompt your eating. When you have gone long enough without exposure to such stimuli, facing them again is not as likely to cue overeating. The power of such stimuli will have been reduced and your response will be less reflexive, more controlled.

The above clinical approach has been applied to a

number of problems: smoking; overfastidiousness; interpersonal difficulties involving family, friends, or colleagues; poor work and study habits; shyness and inhibitions; fears and phobias. Use it as a self-psyching technique on any problem that is attributable, at least in part, to stimuli you are not now controlling.

BASIC ELEMENTS OF STIMULUS CONTROL

Identifying the problem and establishing objectives (see Introduction)

Identifying the stimuli that trigger the problem (see Introduction)

Controlling problem stimuli

Employing new stimuli

Monitoring your behavior to detect improvement (see Introduction)

HOW TO USE STIMULUS CONTROL

Identify the problem and establish objectives. Say your problem involves your relationship with your spouse. Your objective may be to reduce minor disputes, to get your spouse to be more cooperative, more supportive. You will not be trying to control or manipulate that person but to identify and control the stimuli that you find have been causing problems between you. You should be willing to spend as much as several weeks working on each problem.

Identify the stimuli that trigger the problem. Using the information in the Introduction as a guide, keep a record for a week or two (longer, if necessary) to gather baseline data about the circumstances surrounding your problem with your spouse. Find out under what conditions you argue, yell at one another, sulk, or get along best and most affectionately.

Pinpoint the stimuli that seem to trigger fights. For example, you may find that you always seem to fight in the same room — usually the bedroom — about the same things: money, chores, sex. You may discover that such arguments almost never occur when you are out with other people. This is a valuable piece of information, because it can later be used in reorganizing your interactions to take advantage of times and places where conflict is rare.

Try to make your record as detailed as possible. Watch for triggering words or phrases that seem to be spoken prior to most arguments. Does your mention of bills, of the quality of the housekeeping, of the frequency of lovemaking, of the need for a night out on your own cue conflict? Do the words "love," "money," "care," "help," "selfish," or "need" start a fight — or at least seem to immediately precede one? Make a list of all such verbal cues and the settings in which they have potency and those in which they have none.

Figure out if any individuals stimulate conflict between you and your spouse. See if in-laws, friends, bosses, or subordinates are in any way associated with your problems with your spouse. If fights customarily break out soon after you spend time with your parents or in-laws, make note of it. If comments about the attributes or superior circumstances of friends stimulate arguments, you'll want to deal with that, too.

Control problem stimuli. If you have found specific places that cue conflicts with your spouse, try to reduce the time both of you spend in those places.

For example, if the bedroom is a target location, make it a point to limit that room's use to sleeping and affectionate exchanges. Don't talk about money or anything your recordkeeping has told you may start fights. With a list of what triggers fights in that room you can try eliminating the elements one at a time until all are gone. And if you have found that the same subjects elicit noncombative responses in other locales, confine such discussion to those settings.

Similarly, the time of day during which fights take place may be important. When both of you are tired and a bit edgy, perhaps late at night, don't begin discussions of finances or career plans. Arrange to bring such topics up when both of you are fresh. Better, only pursue such subjects when the other person initiates the conversation in a nonarousing setting.

Examine your list of cue words and loaded expressions and take some time and effort to systematically remove them from your vocabulary. Find other words that mean the same thing but may not be as "loaded" — say, "Could we spend tonight alone?" not, "Do we have to go to your mother's house again?" Work your way into a discussion of a target subject by degrees, allowing the topic to emerge slowly rather than jumping on it all at once. Whatever you do, don't open a conversation — on the phone or when you first speak in the morning or when you get together in the evening — with a target topic.

If other people seem associated with your interpersonal

conflicts, arrange to talk about such people only in neutral ways. Refuse to be drawn into a dispute over your in-laws' interference in your life or the neighbors' seemingly greater ability to acquire desirable objects. Do this by making a list of more neutral subjects associated with such people that you can easily talk about in conversations with your spouse.

Alter your environment to modify the stimuli. If fighting seems to break out in a brightly lit room, try to keep the lighting dim. If your failure to shave or put on make-up is a stimulus to conflict, change your ways. When the look, sound, feel, or smell of other objects or even yourself are stimuli for fighting, change them. Paint a wall, put on soft music, buy some soft pillows for the couch, shower before going to bed.

Employ a Rewards program to support your use of this technique. Every time you have some success with Stimulus Control, reward yourself as soon as possible to strengthen your new habit patterns. You should be aware that your fighting itself may, in some strange way, be rewarding. That is, you may discover that fighting has become the easiest way for you and your spouse to communicate. Make nonaggression more rewarding, more satisfying.

See if stimuli are linked, one inspiring another. The article on Changing the Sequence of Events will help you eliminate critical early links in the behavior chain to make it easier to solve the entire problem.

Employ new stimuli. If there are few cues in your environment that provoke friendly interactions, you must not only avoid old cues but find new ones as well. Many existing cues may be irrational and nonproductive. For example, it does no good to say: "You must bring home more money," "Why can't you keep this house cleaner?" or "You always look terrible." Such statements are bound to start fights. It isn't hard to replace them with, "Maybe we can find some way to make our money go farther," "Is there anything I can do to help with the housework," or "I'd sure like to see you in that blue sweater that looks so good on you." The regular use of complimentary phrases may soon push out the loaded trigger words that have started fights before. It is hard to fight with someone who is stimulating your ego by saying nice things about you or offering help, encouragement, or understanding.

At the hot core of an argument, when the stimuli have already started you off on a fight, it is still possible to use

Stimulus Control to stop or lessen the impact of conflict. You can introduce new stimuli even during a fight. For instance, you can teach yourself — by practicing this method in simple stages — to stop reacting aggressively or defensively. Merely find new stimuli to distract you from fighting. Such stimuli may involve memories of pleasant moment, objects, or events associated with your spouse. As he or she is yelling, crying, or pouting, think of the nice times you've had together; of how he or she looked on some memorable enchanted evening; of the sights, sounds, smells, and related sensations of some intimate interlude — no matter how long ago. Teach yourself to associate these good thoughts with your spouse; don't consider the sensations provoked during a fight as your typical responses to your loved one. Practice such pleasant visualization when you are alone, when you aren't fighting, and when you are with him or her but not saying anything.

The trick is to associate the elimination of problem behavior with new stimuli, with the goal of undermining the impact of old, conflict-causing stimuli. However this is done, and for whatever problem, the results will begin to show in a fairly short time. You are not locked into a fixed pattern of action and reaction. You can make things happen that never happened before and make yourself feel good even in the face of unpleasantness. You can change habits by making the stimuli supporting them ineffectual. All you have to do is identify those stimuli and take measures to control them.

Monitor your behavior to detect improvement. Once you have seen some sign of improvement, employ the technique even more energetically until your target problem is entirely under control. Keeping a record of your actions and feelings while using the technique and comparing it to your baseline data will tell you how well Stimulus Control works for you. If successful, go on to other problems, from fighting with your spouse to poor work or study habits, inability to get to work on time, shyness, fears, phobias, or compulsions.

PRECAUTIONS

The success of Stimulus Control is dependent on your having correctly identified problem stimuli and their relationship to the problem you wish to solve. It is not an easy task to isolate these stimuli; it involves careful record keeping, patience, and attention to even the smallest detail.

And Stimulus Control may not work for you. Your ability to

carry out the method may be insufficient or your problem too great. You may have to seek professional help with deeply ingrained problems. And even less severe problems may not respond to the technique. For example, you may not be able to extinguish flare-ups with your spouse because you don't really want to, because you may not actually like one another that much any more, and so forth. It is also possible that your target problem is in itself a solution to other problems. That is, some compulsion or form of interaction may be your way of handling anxiety and stress. Blowing off steam, getting back at the world by fighting with your spouse may be a pleasure and a protection for you. If stress and anxiety are at the root of such problems, Relaxation, Desensitization, or Meditation may be used instead of, or in conjunction with, Stimulus Control. Stimulus Control is an exercise in self-awareness as much as in self-control. So be ready to find out things about yourself that may not be entirely flattering. But by uncovering them you may open the way to alteration of behaviors and attitudes that have caused you pain.

Sources of further information:

Bach, George R., and Wyden, Peter. *The Intimate Enemy: How to Fight Fair in Love and Marriage.* New York: William Morrow, 1969.

Ulrich, R.; Stachnik, T.; and Mabry, J., Eds. *Control of Human Behavior.* 2 vols. Glenview, Ill.: Scott, Foresman, 1966-70.

Watson, David L., and Tharp, Roland E. *Self-Directed Behavior.* Monterey, Calif.: Brooks/Cole, 1972.

PROBLEM

Stress

As a natural and inescapable part of living, we all must experience and attempt to cope with many varieties of stress. The article on Anxiety points out the ways in which people's responses to the stresses of life create problems and offers techniques to alter these responses.

See also:

Anxiety

PROBLEM

Study Habits

See:

Work and Study Habits

Tardiness

No matter how we may dislike the fact, time is of the essence in today's world. We must keep appointments, get to work or school on time, and stay within our own schedules or those imposed on us. We can — and must — be more punctual.

To attack tardiness we begin by discovering the causes of our failure to be on time. The problem may be as simple as a lack of the proper equipment: Buying a good alarm clock or clock radio may be the solution. You may be failing to set reasonable deadlines for yourself and so find yourself working against impossible deadlines, missing them, and thus feeling guilty. A commonsense, realistic appraisal of your capacities and responsibilities will help enormously in such cases.

Procrastination is a common cause of tardiness. You may be late all the time because you don't want to go where you expect to experience anxiety, frustration, or failure. A Rewards program can help you overcome this problem by supplying the incentives for you to operate within schedules and face tough situations. Desensitization and Behavior Rehearsal can help you dissipate the anxiety that causes much of the procrastination that makes you late. And Stimulus Control can teach you to break old patterns of behavior that lead to your habitual tardiness and show you how to forge a chain of behavior with new habits of greater punctuality.

Your tardiness could indicate that you simply haven't learned how to organize your daily activities. Changing the Sequence of Events is a good technique for removing distracting influences that slow you down and keep you from doing things when they should be done.

If insomnia is a recurrent problem, getting up and out of the house on time can be a morning ordeal. The article on Insomnia provides several practical suggestions for overcoming this cause of tardiness.

You need not become so obsessed with being on time that, like Phineas Fogg in *Around the World in 80 Days*, you have to carry two watches. But you should examine your behavior closely enough to detect the patterns of your habits and the typical feelings that may be preventing you from living within reasonable schedules and profiting by doing so. Self-psyching can assist you in being more punctual with less, not more, stress.

See also:
  Procrastination
  Work and Study Habits
  Insomnia

Techniques to try:
  Rewards
  Desensitization
  Behavior Rehearsal
  Stimulus Control
  Changing the Sequence of Events

PROBLEM

Teeth Gnashing

Bruxism, the habitual gnashing, grinding, or clenching of the teeth, can be an uncomfortable and damaging nervous habit. Many people are plagued by bruxism for much of their lives, grinding their teeth unconsciously whenever they are under tension and often even while they are asleep. The results can include tension headaches and so much wearing down of the tooth enamel that extensive dental work may be required.

The human jaw is a powerful mechanism for chewing, eating, talking. Evolution has assigned large portions of the brain to controlling the movements of the mouth. Our almost automatic employment of the mouth and jaws is a natural survival instinct readily observed in infants as they begin nursing right after birth. The problem arises when the force of this powerful and important instinct is channeled into an unconscious and uncontrolled habit.

Negative Practice is highly effective in dealing with this

problem, and additional techniques mentioned in the article on Nervous Habits can be of help.

See also:
Nervous Habits

Technique to try:
Negative Practice

PROBLEM
Tension

See:
Anxiety

PROBLEM
Test Anxiety

Our years of schooling have marked most of us with some degree of test phobia. Long after school we may still look upon any confrontation that measures our knowledge or skill as a test. We feel once again as if we were children facing failure and rejection. This need not be the case. The article on Disagreeable Tasks and Encounters presents some valid self-psyching techniques that you can put to the test.

See also:
Disagreeable Tasks and Encounters

TECHNIQUE
Thought-Stopping

Particularly useful in dealing with such problems as Obsessions, Floods of Unwanted Thoughts, Shyness and Inhibitions, Compulsiveness, Self-Punishment, some forms of Insomnia.

Might be useful as an adjunct to a general program for coping with Anxiety, Nervous Habits.

Supplementary or alternative techniques: Relaxation, Meditation, Modeling, Flooding, Covert Sensitization, Desensitization.

WHAT THOUGHT-STOPPING IS

Sometimes the mind can become crowded with unwanted thoughts. One uncontrollable idea or impression inspires another, then another, until the brain reels. Concentration is all but impossible, getting to sleep is out of the question, and often the content of these thoughts is anxiety provoking. It is a distressing and rather common experience. Thought-Stopping provides a means for regaining control over your racing mind, for restoring your ability to concentrate, for reducing the attendant anxiety, for preventing the recurrence of such problems.

With this technique you systematically engage in the sort of rumination that usually comes to you unbidden. And you learn to startle yourself out of your thoughts, creating a new reflex you can call upon thereafter to disrupt unwanted and hitherto uncontrollable patterns of thinking.

HISTORICAL DEVELOPMENT

J. G. Taylor is credited with the development of Thought-Stopping as a technique in the 1950s. However, a similar method had been suggested more than twenty years earlier, by J. Alexander Bain, as a way to control thoughts to improve one's ability to cope with day-to-day problems.

The target of Taylor's method was obsessive-compulsive behavior. That is, he treated people with serious psychological problems involving uncontrollable thoughts and irresistible urges to repeat certain acts.

Taylor had some startling successes. One hapless individual had suffered for more than thirty years from the compulsive habit of eyebrow plucking and was cured by Taylor in just ten days! During treatment, Taylor shouted, "Stop!" each time the patient engaged in, or signaled him that she felt the urge to engage in, her habit. He then trained her first to shout and later merely to subvocalize the command to stop the habitual behavior. The method is surprisingly simple, but it does work.

Like aspirin, which also works, the exact nature of Thought-Stopping's therapeutic action is not known. It is theorized that the abrupt disruption of the thought processes and the incompatibility of the command and the uncontrolled thoughts are at the root of the method's effectiveness. Further, some researchers think that such strongly asserted commands have the power to undermine insistent but less imperative ruminations. The consensus is that the regular and repeated distraction from uncontrolled thinking can stop such forms of thought and weaken them so that, with succeeding applications of Thought-Stopping, they can be more easily tamed. Despite the method's simplicity and the lack of precise knowledge about how it works, it continues to be used because it continues to work.

The technique is still employed in clinical settings to treat obsessive-compulsives plagued by an inability to control their thoughts or actions. But Thought-Stopping may also be considered a self-psyching method for those who are occasionally troubled by floods of unwanted thoughts or impulses to perform undesirable acts. Its clinical success in helping people with similar, though chronic and serious, complaints validates its worth to relatively healthy individuals.

BASIC ELEMENTS OF THOUGHT-STOPPING

Identifying the problem (see Introduction)
Setting goals (see Introduction)
Practicing on your own
Employing the technique in real-life situations
Trying a variation on the method
Monitoring your behavior to detect changes (see Introduction)
Using the method for other problems

HOW TO USE THOUGHT-STOPPING

Identify the problem. Reviewing the instructions in the Introduction will assist you in pinpointing problems that may respond to this technique. You will want to try Thought-Stopping if you suffer from periodic interludes of obsessive thinking. Long stretches of brooding, worrying, ruminating, and being preoccupied with unwanted ideas can sap your intellectual powers, keep you from attending to problems you should be thinking about, or prevent you from resting your mind when you have no real reason to be thinking at all.

The kinds of thoughts that present problems seldom lead to useful action, usually have no basis in reality, and cause an unreasonable degree of anxiety. All of us have reasons to worry. But it is one thing to feel a pain or get a fever and quite another to spend hours worrying that we may be getting sick even though no symptoms have emerged. And in most cases, unreasonable health worries are not allayed by a doctor's reassurance.

Thought-Stopping is called for if baseless worries or aimless compulsions preoccupy you — when you are sitting in your office, driving your car, doing housework, playing a game, pacing around the school library, or even while you are attending a movie or play. They take the joy out of whatever you are engaged in, decrease your effectiveness, and can even endanger you, as when you compulsively recheck the contents of your briefcase while trying to drive to an appointment. Left alone with your thoughts, as we all are much of the time, it is possible to let worry push out more productive thoughts and to let compulsiveness consume energies required for purposeful action.

Thought-Stopping is also needed when your brooding keeps you from sleeping. Use it if you are very often kept from falling asleep by a rush of ideas and impressions you can't control or ignore or by the compulsion to perform fruitless acts like continually checking locked doors or reading over paperwork you needn't really deal with until the morning. The day's activities can build up a mass of unresolved conflicts and unanswered questions. In the moments before sleep you aren't going to be able to do anything about your relationship with your boss, the condition of your car, the fact that your backhand needs work, or the state of the world. You must turn off your mind and let your subconscious continue the struggle, if it must. You need your rest and you aren't going to get it unless you can block out the thoughts and impulses that are keeping you awake.

Thought-Stopping is certainly indicated if your floods of unwanted thoughts involve negative, self-defeating notions that undermine your confidence in your abilities and your worth. The technique can help those whose thoughts justify a failure to attempt some task or face some person or situation — those who say, "I could never learn to ski," "I'll make a fool of myself if I suggest those changes in the office routine," or "I never was any good at getting to know people, so why should I waste my time at that party." Such thinking is a way of setting things up to avoid risking failure — by never getting into the game. Such thinking can convince you that you have little worth and can keep you from engaging in many potentially rewarding activities that would in all likelihood disprove your lack of faith in yourself. And it can burden you with unnecessary anxiety.

The Thought-Stopping technique has the dual advantage of getting rid of the troublesome obsessions or compulsions and reducing the anxiety they generate.

Set a goal. Try the method in practice sessions of about half an hour twice a day for a week or two, at times when you aren't experiencing your problem. Your ultimate goal should be to make the technique work for you consistently in real-life situations, so a total of several weeks of formal practice and then real-life application of the method should be expected.

Practice on your own. Don't try to apply the technique in actual problem situations until you have mastered it under controlled practice conditions.

First, sit in a quiet, comfortable place. Close your eyes if that makes it easier. Intentionally force yourself to think about the sorts of things that usually flood your mind against your will. Make clear and specific thoughts, ideas, or images come and let them build, intensify, and interconnect until you are feeling burdened or even anxious.

Now shout aloud, "STOP!" Follow this command with a short interlude of relaxation using whatever method works best for you (see Relaxation and Autogenic Training). Part of your relaxation may include vocalizing a command like "relax" or "calm." Speak that relaxation-inducing word. Don't proceed until you are relaxed again.

Repeat the exercise, but this time say the stopping and relaxing command words softly. Then run through the routine a third time, saying "stop," then "relax" or "calm," to yourself, in your mind.

The idea is for you to associate a flood of unwanted thoughts (or compulsive urges) with a signal to end them and with relaxation rather than anxiety.

Practice the technique for up to thirty minutes at least twice a day for several days. After a day or so you should be able to confine yourself to the subvocal command to "stop" and should find that you relax almost at once after saying that word to yourself. At first you may require your full relaxation routine; later an abbreviated form or merely the subvocal command "relax" will work, depending on your skill at relaxation. So practice relaxing whenever you can.

Employ the technique in real-life situations. Once you have mastered the technique, once you can quickly and easily stop an unwanted train of thought and replace anxiety with relaxation, you are ready to employ the method in uncontrolled situations. Remember, up to this point you have induced the thoughts and made yourself anxious. From now on you will be responding to forces you have not unleashed, so be ready for the initial shock of doing real battle with real threats.

The first time you feel your mind filling with unwanted thoughts — perhaps as you are trying to get to sleep — shout "stop" to yourself and relax. One try should do it, but two or more applications are permissible. (If it continues to take more than one command, you may want to get in a few more practice days.) Even on the first try you should notice that your brooding is interrupted. It is being challenged by a new response. The very fact that you began to feel those thoughts and the first signs of anxiety they can bring should force you to respond with your Thought-Stopping technique, and that technique will automatically replace worry with relaxation. You will have conditioned yourself to respond to brooding with a command to stop and to relax, and Thought-Stopping will have become your natural reaction to the onset of obsessive thinking or an attack of compulsiveness.

I myself use Thought-Stopping regularly. For example, when I return home from my every-other-week poker game, usually quite late at night, my mind is filled with thoughts of the game. As I try to get to sleep images of all the hands played dance on my eyelids. Thoughts of plays I should have made and bets I should have covered run through my brain. Such a flood of thoughts is entirely without purpose. It would be more useful on the way to the next game, but now, when I want and need rest, it is an annoyance, a problem. I say, "stop" to myself and employ my relaxation routine. Without fail, the flow of unwanted images ends, I congratulate myself on my power to master my own mind, and I drop off to sleep in minutes.

I also use Thought-Stopping when extraneous thoughts keep me from concentrating on my work — when I find myself thinking not about what I am writing but about another project, household tasks, taxes, or social obligations. Thought-Stopping quickly makes possible the concentration required for me to make a living.

For the technique to do all of which it is capable, you must use it — without fail — every time you feel unwanted thoughts arising or discover that you are engaging compulsively in some habit. Let too many occasions slip by unchallenged and you will find it very hard to make the technique work at all because the automatic connection between your problem and the method's conditioning will have been weakened. Try to achieve as much relaxation as possible each time. Don't worry that you may be overusing this technique. You are trying to make its use habitual. Just as your old habits took time to develop, practice is required for your new habit to become established. The more you practice the sooner will your old problem of pointless rumination or fruitless compulsiveness be solved.

Try a variation on the method. If the method doesn't work as well or as rapidly as you would like, try a simple variation. In your original practice and learning sessions, and perhaps for a while in real problem situations (with the exception of periods when you are trying to get to sleep), pinch yourself every time you shout or subvocalize the command "stop." This will more deeply imprint the command in your mind and make the beneficial reaction to it more automatic later, when all you do is mentally repeat the command. Don't try to hurt yourself; a gentle pull on the wrist or forearm is sufficient, as long as you really feel it and you are pinching at the same time as you are saying "stop" — immediately after you become aware that your mind is under attack.

Monitor your behavior to detect changes. After learning Thought-Stopping and employing it in real-life situations over a few weeks, use the guidelines in the Introduction to determine if you have diminished your problem. You could find that your problem is virtually gone or at least that Thought-Stopping is now consistently effective whenever you use it.

Use the method for other problems. If you have success with one problem — say, floods of insomnia-inducing thought — try Thought-Stopping on something else, perhaps a habit like nail biting or a compulsion like rechecking locked doors at bedtime.

PRECAUTIONS

In the first few weeks of using Thought-Stopping you are likely to find that a target problem gets somewhat worse. Don't be alarmed. This is natural because our forced practice of the problem initially reinforces it, but continued practice soon overcomes this tendency and progress should be steady thereafter.

Thought-Stopping may not work at all, even after you have

made a number of conscientious attempts to employ it. Your problem may be too severe. If you are almost constantly caught up in aimless and anxious rumination, you could require professional assistance.

But for most people Thought-Stopping is amazingly easy to learn and really works. Just be sure you practice long enough before you test the technique on real problems and that you employ it faithfully every time your mind is assailed by uncontrollable thoughts or compulsive urges. If you only employ it now and then, it either won't work or may even reinforce and intensify your problems. You must use it unfailingly and immediately when needed. This doesn't mean giving your life over to practice. The technique works so well that in a short time you will have fewer and fewer occasions to apply it at all. But apply it you must, when needed, or it will lose its potency.

Finally, be aware that not all floods of thought are detrimental. It is possible to experience uncontrolled thinking that is welcome, as when you can't free your mind of images and ideas concerning someone with whom you may be falling in love. Let such thoughts come, let them take you as far as they will — enjoy them!

Sources of further information:

Bain, J. A. *Thought Control in Everyday Life.* New York: Funk & Wagnalls, 1928.

Campbell, L. M. "A variation of thought-stopping in a twelve-year-old boy: A case report." *Journal of Behavior Therapy and Experimental Psychiatry.* 1973, 4, 69-70.

Stern, R. S. "Treatment of a case of obsessional neurosis using thought-stopping technique." *British Journal of Psychiatry,* 1970, 117, 441-442.

Wolpe, J., and Lazarus, A. A. *Behavior Therapy Techniques.* New York: Pergamon, 1966.

Yamagami, T. "The treatment of an obsession by thought-stopping." *Journal of Behavior Therapy and Experimental Psychiatry,* 1972, 2, 133-135.

TECHNIQUE

Transcendental Meditation

May be useful in dealing with such problems as Anxiety, Fatigue and Lethargy, Insomnia, and a wide range of problems — such as overcoming addictions — that its supporters contend it can solve.

Supplementary or alternative techniques: Meditation, The Relaxation Response, Biofeedback, Relaxation, Autogenic Training, Prayer.

WHAT TRANSCENDENTAL MEDITATION IS

Known as TM, this form of Meditation is the most widely known and practiced in America. It is not, strictly speaking, a self-psyching technique. Proponents claim that one must go through training in TM with an instructor who provides a personal, secret *mantra* (the sound to be uttered during Meditation). One must also pay something like $125 for these attentions. While the goal of this book is to supply access to techniques that can be learned and practiced without expense or expert guidance, a discussion of TM is included because it has become so intimately associated with Meditation per se.

HISTORICAL DEVELOPMENT

The most visible proponent of TM, the man who was guru to the Beatles and who has regularly appeared on TV talk shows, is Maharishi Mahesh Yogi. American practitioners follow his precepts, and the TM craze has so vigorously swept the country in the last few years that somewhere between half a million and a million people are involved in TM, with several thousand joining the ranks each month. Its devotees include movie stars, members of Congress, students, scientists, and housewives.

Although based on ancient Indian practices, it seems to serve the needs of modern people in the Western world, and its destressing effects have been validated in several scientific studies.

HOW TO USE TRANSCENDENTAL MEDITATION

By definition, this technique requires the guidance of a TM instructor, so the authentic method cannot be outlined here. However, it is merely a form of *mantra* Meditation, using a sound, word, or phrase as a focus of attention. For details, see the article on Meditation.

PRECAUTIONS

There is good reason to believe that the positive benefits of TM can be obtained without actually paying for and becoming involved in the TM movement. In fact, it is advisable to try a self-regulated program of Meditation, such as one of those discussed in this book, before turning to TM (though you may want to do so after becoming a fairly accomplished meditator on your own). The important point is that there is evidence that Meditation can influence your physical and emotional well-being, as well as increase your awareness of both yourself and the world. According to testimonials from TMers, their way produces more profound and lasting results than other approaches.

There is considerable debate over TM's value. The greatest challenge to the claims of TM exponents has come from Herbert Benson, a professor at Harvard whose own research provided evidence that Meditation has measurable physiological benefits. Benson found that the same beneficial changes produced by TM can be achieved through a totally demystified, secular, self-regulated form of Relaxation training. (See The Relaxation Response.)

The debate between Benson and the TM followers is beyond the scope of this book. However, it would be prudent for you to try a form of self-regulated Meditation or The Relaxation Response before paying to join a TM group.

Whatever your final decision, if you know that TM, The Relaxation Response, and other Meditation methods have worked for many others, why not try to make them work for you. A little conscientious effort may go a long way.

Sources of further information:
Bloomfield, H. H.; Cain, M. P.; and Jaffe, D. T. *TM, Discovering Inner Energy and Overcoming Stress.* New York: Delacorte, 1975.

Ebon, Martin. *The Relaxation Controversy.* New York: Signet, 1976.

Forem, Jack. *Transcendental Meditation.* New York: Dutton, 1973.

Hemingway, Patricia Drake. *The Transcendental Meditation Primer.* New York: Dell, 1975.

Yogi, Maharishi Mahesh. *Transcendental Meditation.* New York: Penguin, 1967.

Work and Study Habits

The following techniques can help you become more efficient and make the most of the time you spend working, studying, or performing any task.

See the article on Desensitization for advice on breaking up a job into small and manageable parts. Also, by providing Rewards for the completion of various segments of the task, you can reinforce your resolve to continue and complete your work. The use of Stimulus Control and Changing the Sequence of Events can help you build sound work habits and avoid distracting or fruitless activities. And Assertiveness Training can build up your confidence so that you can approach any chore, while Thought-Stopping can make it easier to concentrate.

See also:
Procrastination

Techniques to try:
Desensitization
Rewards
Stimulus Control
Changing the Sequence of Events
Assertiveness Training
Thought-Stopping

Worrying

Worrying has its place. If you are driving along in your car and see the gas gauge on empty, you should worry about finding a gas station. If you experience clear physical symptoms of illness — dizziness, blood in your urine, blurred vision — you would be foolish to ignore them and wise to worry enough to consult a physician. Such worrying has a logical basis of palpable signs, not some vague dread.

Worry that is not triggered by specific situations or events is anxiety and should be treated as such. The article on Anxiety suggests numerous techniques for disposing of free-floating worry.

But even worries that are related to real and pressing demands may mushroom into problems worthy of attack through self-psyching. Chronic worry, which crowds out all other thoughts and impulses, preoccupies you, and interferes with your normal functioning, disrupts your life. It diminishes your powers of concentration, robs you of sleep, makes you ignore the work you have to do and the people who deserve your attention.

There are self-psyching techniques in this book for coping with many of the specific problems that you may be worrying about: facing disagreeable tasks and encounters, marital and sexual problems, overwork, inefficiency, and so on. But when worrying itself is the problem, when the process of worrying keeps you from handling other aspects of your life, Thought-Stopping is the technique to try. It is designed to free you of the tendency to worry uncontrollably, to end recurrent flights of thought that contribute nothing toward solving the problems that make you worry. Freed of such chronic and unproductive worrying, you should soon find yourself able to focus on and begin handling each of your problems in turn. You'll be able to step off the worry treadmill and onto solid ground.

See also:
Anxiety
Obsessions

Technique to try:
Thought-Stopping

PROBLEM

Worrying about Money

See:
Worrying
Anxiety
Obsessions